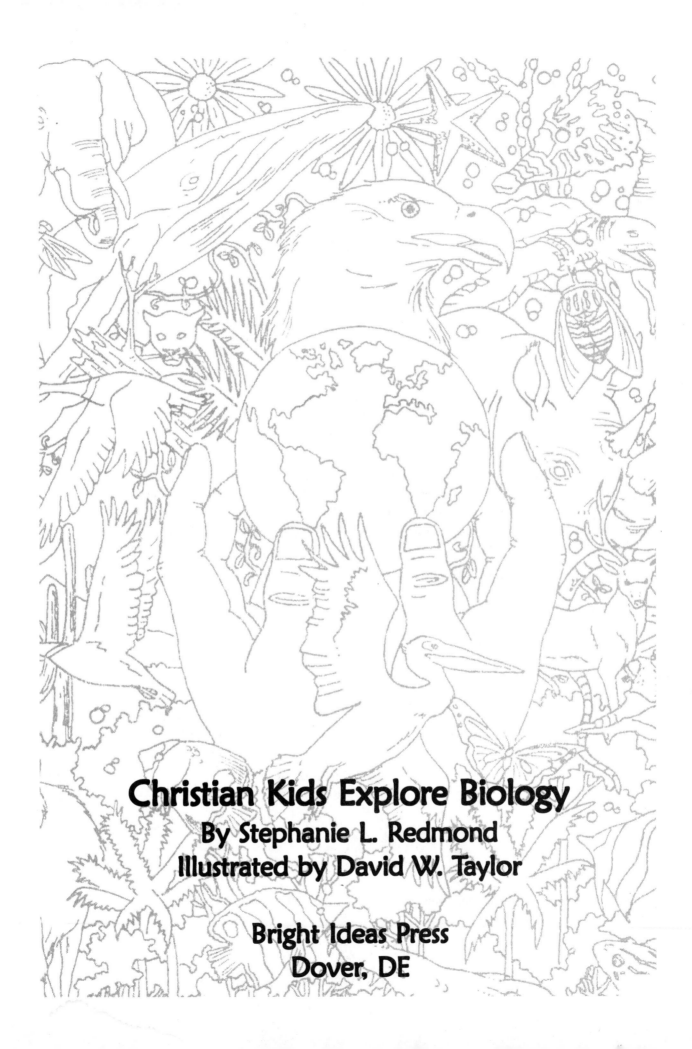

Christian Kids Explore Biology
By Stephanie L. Redmond
Illustrated by David W. Taylor

Bright Ideas Press
Dover, DE

Text, Copyright © 2003, Bright Ideas Press

Library of Congress Catalog Card Number: 2003109967
ISBN: 1-892427-05-2
First Edition

Printed in the United States of America

Bright Ideas Press
Dover, Delaware

www.BrightIdeasPress.com
info@BrightIdeasPress.com

10   9   8   7   6   5   4   3   2

To Andy…
I wouldn't trade anything for the past
twenty years with you.
Thank you for your incredible patience
and support during this project.
I love you.

ACKNOWLEDGMENTS

It is with the utmost gratitude that I thank the following. Without them, there is truly no way I could have written this book.

My Lord and Savior, Jesus Christ ~ That He could use me at all is amazing!

My precious children, Mike, Taylor, and Rachel ~ You were my guinea pigs, my pre-proofreaders, my encouragement. I love you all so very much.

My dear friend and publisher, Maggie Hogan ~ You believed in me all the way and kept me working, despite many interruptions.

My amazingly talented brother, David Taylor ~ Your artwork makes this book so special. Thank you, thank you! To his wife, Sherry ~ I know your support in this was necessary, and I thank you, too.

Elizabeth J. and Robert W. Ridlon ~ My science editors and friends, thank you. (www.JordanHallResearch.com)

Rebecca Delvaux ~ You prepared the most awesome resource list. Homeschooling parents everywhere will appreciate your dedication.

The CKEB test group ~ What can I say? You were my real guinea pigs. Thank you for trying us out and helping me find the many areas that could be improved on. I loved your letters and comments. Your work was invaluable.

Dr. Jay Wile ~ Your seminar encouraged me beyond words. You gave me the confidence to teach science and not give up.

David and Judy Taylor, my dad and mom ~ You taught me from a young age that I could do more than I thought myself capable of doing. Your love and encouragement mean more to me than you'll ever know.

Julie Gaubert ~ Thank you for jumping in and helping me with the recipes and supplemental activities. You're a great neighbor and friend!

Kathy Dix and Ivy Ulrich-Bonk, my editor and layout artist ~ I appreciate your professionalism and skill so much.

CONTENTS

CONTENTS

A NOTE FROM THE AUTHOR

I am like you. I am an average homeschool mom, working hard to ensure a sound education for my children and still maintain a respectable home. I have three precious children: Mike (16), Taylor (13), and Rachel (11). My husband, Andy, and I have been married for twenty wonderful years.

My main goal is to glorify God in all that I do. Part of fulfilling that goal is teaching my children to love the Lord their God with all their heart, soul, and might. If I am going to do that, I believe it is essential to teach them from a Christian worldview, using books that honor God.

In our years of homeschooling, I have used several types of study. Some I liked, others I didn't. However, a few years ago, I was introduced to classical education. Now, I'll admit we're not perfect examples of this, but I found it to be a wonderful way to set up our school. We follow the trivium, recognizing the grammar, logic, and rhetoric phases of our children's learning, and we teach history chronologically. We use Latin in our studies and read, read, read! However, for our elementary students, we've had a hard time finding just the right science book. I felt forced, at times, to use books that teach evolution as fact. While I was able to use this as an opportunity to teach my children God's truth, as presented in Scripture, I found that I longed for a *homeschool* book that would teach the same. From that, *Christian Kids Explore Biology* was born.

You must know that I am not a scientist. My credentials are that I homeschooled myself! Through much prayer and encouragement from friends, however, I found myself writing a homeschool science book. Therefore, I had this book reviewed and edited for science content by qualified people (see the Acknowledgments). During this process, I personally learned the joy of studying science and hope that I will be able to impart that excitement to you and your children. Most of all, I pray that your family is encouraged and God is glorified through the words of this text that seek to exalt God as Creator.

Because I am much like you, I understand the pressures that homeschooling mothers and fathers face. Time is critical and there is never enough of it. Therefore, this book has been designed taking that into consideration. First and foremost, *Christian Kids Explore Biology* **is written for multiple ages and grades.** While it is geared for 3rd to 6th graders, there are many ideas for younger ones, as well as for those who want to do more. The lessons are complete and concise, but there is room to bring in books from outside sources if you choose. Little advance preparation is needed. A list of the materials you will need is at the beginning of each unit so you can gather once per unit if you choose, instead of every week. Vocabulary lists are included, along with hands-on activities that reinforce learning. There is a gorgeous coloring page with each unit as well as a unit review. Also, there is an extensive book and resource list at the end of the book. This book seeks to offer you everything you need for a fruitful year of elementary biology, plus a little more.

Stephanie L. Redmond

"Be exalted, O God, above the heavens;
Let Your glory be above all the earth."
(Psalm 57:11)

HOW TO USE THIS BOOK

This book contains 35 lessons. Each lesson is designed to be completed in one week. If you teach science twice weekly, you'll need to allow for about 60 to 90 minutes each day. Of course, this will depend on the student and the number of outside resources used.

Each lesson consists of a **Teaching Time** and a **Hands-On Time.** I recommend doing each on a separate day.

Teaching Time

- As each new lesson is begun, the text is read. You may read it to your students or they may read it to themselves. In the case of very young students, you might read it on your own and then discuss the information at their level. They may enjoy completing a Coloring Page while listening to you.
- After this lesson is read, the student should complete a "Daily Reading Sheet."

To make the study complete, you will need to do a little more:

- First, review recent lessons, particularly as they apply to your newest lesson.
- Second, if you make flashcards as you go (with vocabulary words, lesson facts, Scripture verses, etc.), you will want to review these.
- Third, have your student list the vocabulary words (any in bold lettering in the lesson, plus any they listed on their Daily Reading Sheet) and define them in their science notebook.
- Last, you'll want to allow time for outside reading and picture perusing and researching topics of interest. I recommend having your students complete additional Daily Reading Sheets for their supplemental reading, even if they use just a few pages from a particular book. (It's quite acceptable to pick and choose pages and chapters to read rather than an entire book!) All completed forms and written work should be kept in their science notebook.

Hands-On Time

Most children love hands-on learning, and it helps keep science exciting for your children (and you!). Although Hands-On Time can be time consuming, try to also make time for a little review as you are working. The "Checking It Out" science experiment form will often be utilized on these days and should be completed and filed in the student's science notebook.

It can be tempting to eliminate these activities to save time; however, I strongly advise otherwise. Science can be so exciting, but it can also be dull. It all depends on how it is taught. Elementary science is about discovery and taking joy in the journey. Have fun with it!

Coloring Pages

There is one Coloring Page per unit and all of these, plus a few extra, are in the Appendix. These may be photocopied. Children of all ages will enjoy these beautiful drawings. Some will even benefit from keeping their hands busy with markers or pencils while having lessons read aloud to them.

Show What You Know!

The last event for each unit is a "Show What You Know" review. These can be used as tests or merely as unit wrap-ups; it's your choice. I've made the scoring fun, using thousands of points instead of one hundred. These, too, can be copied for each student and filed in his or her science notebook.

Reproducibles

There are several forms in the Appendix available for reproducing, according to your needs. The course is designed to be easily used with several children of differing ages, at the same time. If you do not have a home copier, make a trip to your favorite copy shop and reproduce several Daily Reading Sheets and Checking It Out forms (along with the Coloring Page and Show What You Know! page for each unit). The two forms are used frequently, so plan ahead. Is copying difficult for you? Make your own similar forms on the computer or simply use notebook paper. It's the content—not the form—that counts!

What a Daily Lesson Could Look Like

TUESDAYS

- **Memory Work**—Review flashcards and vocabulary. *5 minutes*
- **Discuss** last lesson. *5 minutes*
- **Teaching Time**—Read or have student read new lesson; ask comprehension questions as you go. *10 minutes*
- **Discuss** new information. *2–3 minutes*
- **Daily Reading Sheet**—Have student complete a Daily Reading Sheet. *10 minutes*
- **Vocabulary**—Have student fill out (or assist your student in filling out) a vocabulary sheet or make flashcards, if you prefer, of the key words in their lessons. *10 minutes*
- **Books**—Outside reading time. This is where they have the time to peruse other sources, perhaps from the library. *30 minutes or more, as necessary*

THURSDAYS

- **Memory Work**
- **Hands-On Time**—Complete a relevant experiment or activity. Student can also use part of this time for ABC Book activities (see Appendix D) and discovery (research) activities.

   Remember: Younger children do not need as much detail. Give them the facts and HAVE FUN! We are trying to include enough "work" for the older kids, but enough "fun" for the younger ones. If you have only young elementary (K–3) students, then even once a week is enough for science. If they are doing the memory work, though, bring out those flashcards two or three times per week. We like to go to the library and get lots of books on the subject at hand. (Not great for cells, but terrific for reptiles and nearly all else the course will go into.)

Instructions for Your Science Notebook

This section is addressed to your students; however, you may need to help them decide the best way to organize their science notebooks.

This year you will need to maintain a science notebook. The purpose of this notebook is to help you organize all your documents from your studies. An important part of good science is good record keeping. It is the only way to accurately track your findings.

I recommend a three-ring, loose-leaf notebook, about 1½ inches thick, with pockets on the inside of the covers. For tabs, I recommend tabs with labels. You have two options in this area:

- Option 1—Unit by Unit: For this method you will need eight tabs labeled "Unit 1", "Unit 2", and so on, through Unit 8. In each section you will file your Daily Reading Sheets, Checking It Out forms, and any other written work.
- Option 2—Type of Work: For this method you will need at least eight tabs, possibly more, and you will file your work chronologically, that is, in order by date. Your tabs should be labeled:

> Daily Reading
>
> Vocabulary
>
> Diagrams   (You might sketch some from your readings.)
>
> Checking It Out
>
> Reports
>
> Coloring Pages
>
> Field Trips
>
> Photos   (I highly recommend taking photos throughout the year of your Hands-On
> activities, field trips, and experiments.)

Your science notebook will provide an excellent record of your studies in biology!

UNIT ONE

BIOLOGY BASICS

UNIT ONE VOCABULARY

- big bang theory
- biology
- biomes
- biosphere
- carnivore
- cells
- cell wall
- consumers
- creationists
- cytoplasm
- decomposers
- ecology
- environment
- eukaryotic cells
- evolutionists
- food chains
- food web
- herbivore
- kingdom
- Kingdom Animalia
- Kingdom Plantae
- native
- nucleus
- omnivore
- organelles
- organisms
- plasma membrane
- producers
- prokaryotic cells
- stewards
- taxonomists
- taxonomy

MATERIALS NEEDED FOR THIS UNIT

- Science notebook
- A deck of cards OR craft sticks
- Modeling clay or play dough (See recipe in Appendix F.)
- Papier-mâché (See instructions for making papier-mâché in Appendix F.)
- 1 large package gelatin (light color recommended)
- Macaroni, jellybeans, squiggly noodles, beans, pickles, candy, licorice, hard-boiled egg
- 1 deep-dish pie plate or bowl, preferably clear
- Mixing bowl
- Copy of world map from Appendix A

Creation Coloring Page

LESSON 1

CREATION

TEACHING TIME:
Creation vs. Evolution

The dictionary defines **biology** as the "study of life and living organisms." In other words, it is the study of all the living things in our world.

When looking at our world, many of us want to know how it came into being. Did it get here by accident or was there a Creator? What a person believes about the beginning of the earth has a lot to do with how he interprets the things he reads and learns about biology.

Many people, called evolutionists, believe the world was formed by accident. They often claim that a big explosion took place in outer space, forming our Earth and solar system. This is commonly referred to as the **big bang theory.** **Evolutionists** also believe that life began with very simple cells that evolved, or changed, over billions of years, eventually becoming the plants and animals we see today. Many schools and books teach evolution as scientific fact. In truth, it is just a theory that cannot be proven.

While many scientists are evolutionists, you must know that all are not. There are thousands of scientists who believe that the theory of evolution has many problems. The Bible tells us God created the world and all the things in it. It does not mention evolution. People who believe that God created the world are called **creationists**. These people look at the world and see order and design and do not believe these things could have happened accidentally.

Not all creationists believe the world was formed exactly as the Bible says, but many do. Some creationists believe the world is billions of years old, yet others believe it may be only 5,000 to 10,000 years old. In the same way, not all evolutionists are in complete agreement. Then again, there are many people who are not sure what they believe.

When you read science books, it will help you to know whether the author is an evolutionist or creationist. Can you tell what I believe yet? Since the world cannot begin again or be recreated, neither side can truly prove its position. Technology is changing very rapidly. New discoveries are constantly being made. Often, new discoveries cause scientists and others to reconsider their positions. I believe that if you

"Be exalted, O God, above the heavens; Let Your glory be above all the earth." (Psalm 57:11)

look carefully and study diligently, you can see many reasons to believe that God created our world. Biology shows many examples of intricate design and balance. As you explore biology, you, too, can look for evidence of a divine Creator.

THE CREATION

Cecil Frances Alexander

All things bright and beautiful,
All creatures, great and small,
All things wise and wonderful,
The Lord God made them all.

Each little flower that opens,
Each little bird that sings,
He made their glowing colors,
He made their tiny wings;

The rich man in his castle,
The poor man at his gate,
God made them, high or lowly,
And ordered their estate.

The purple-headed mountain,
The river running by,
The sunset and the morning,
That brightens up the sky;

The cold wind in the winter,
The pleasant summer sun,
The ripe fruits in the garden—
He made them every one.

The tall trees in the greenwood,
The meadows where we play,
The rushes by the water
We gather every day—

He gave us eyes to see them,
And lips that we might tell
How great is God Almighty,
Who has made all things well!

Exploring God's Word

"In the beginning God created the heavens and the earth."
(Genesis 1:1)

CHECKING IT OUT

Materials: A deck of cards OR craft sticks.

- Throw your cards in the air. Look to see what was "created" with this event.

- Repeat this several times. Each time, consider if anything worthwhile was created.

- Now, use the cards and see if you can "create" something.

You should see that order does not automatically happen. It takes planning and a designer.

HANDS-ON TIME: Biblical Creation

Objective: To discover what the Bible says about creation and complete a hands-on project.

Discover!

1. Using a Bible, read Genesis, Chapter 1, and discover what it says about how God created the earth.

2. Then, choose one:

   - Make a drawing or chart that shows what happened each day of creation.
   - Using play dough or modeling clay, "create" an earth. You can also make some animals. See the recipe for play dough in Appendix F.
   - Make a papier-mâché earth. See instructions for making papier-mâché in Appendix F.

Quick Quiz

1. Biology is the study of _____ and of

   _____.

2. Do evolutionists believe our world is carefully designed? Yes No

3. How many days does the Bible say God used to create the world? _____

4. People who believe God created the world are called

   _____.

5. Briefly describe the main difference between evolutionists and creationists. _____

   _____

   _____

   _____

   _____

LESSON 2

CELLS

TEACHING TIME:
Cell-abration

Today we are going to learn about some very tiny forms of life. These forms of life are called **cells.** They are the building blocks of all living things, or **organisms**. Animals are made of cells. Plants are made of cells. Even your skin is made of cells. *All* living things are made of cells.

What Cells Do

Cells are basically like microscopic factories. They produce things that organisms need in order to live and reproduce. Not all cells are alike. For example, there are plant cells and there are animal cells. They differ from each other in appearance and function. (See the cell diagrams on the next page.)

Cell Structure

Let's discover a little more about cells. Most cells are so tiny they can be seen only with a microscope. (An egg, however, is actually a single cell.) It takes thousands upon thousands of cells to make up many of the organisms on Earth. Even though they are very tiny, cells are similar to a balloon that is filled with jelly. Animal cells have a **plasma membrane**, also called a cell membrane, that is similar to the balloon in our example. This plasma membrane separates one animal cell from another and surrounds the **cytoplasm**, which is like the jelly in our example. Plant cells have a **cell wall**, which does the same thing as the plasma membrane. Plant cells are filled with cytoplasm. Later in this lesson, you will actually create a cell model, using gelatin.

Now we're going to go even further. We're going to look inside the cytoplasm. Remember that I told you cells are like factories. They produce things that organisms need in order to live. Inside a factory are many jobs that work together to create a product. In many cases, the cytoplasm of a cell has special structures called **organelles**, which are membrane-covered sacs. These organelles carry out different tasks for the cell, like the jobs in a factory. In the diagram you will see many specific cell parts. These are the organelles, and each has a special task. **Eukaryotic cells** have a particular organelle inside called the **nucleus**, which stores necessary information for the cell.

"For the LORD Most High is awesome; He is a great King over all the earth." (Psalm 47:2)

8

Some cells do not have a nucleus. They are called **prokaryotic cells**. They are the simplest of cells.

Today we studied a lot of details about cells. Just think, this is only the beginning of all there is to know about cells! Cells are much more complex than most people realize. After all, they're the building blocks of life! This lesson should help to convince you that life is complicated and precious. It takes a lot of detail to create life. All life is a gift from God. What a reason to "cell"-abrate!

Discovery Zone

For great articles in creation science, especially for grades 2 through 6, go to www.discoverymagazine.com. Another fascinating and informative site is www.cellsalive.com.

ANIMAL CELL

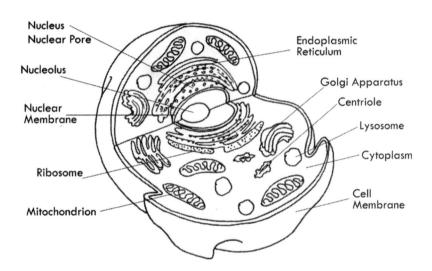

PLANT CELL

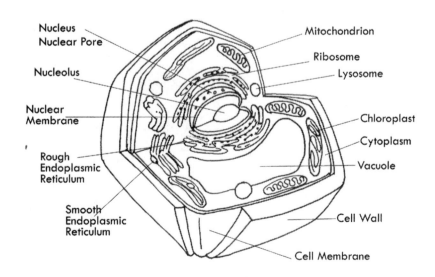

ONE STEP FURTHER

Using the diagram for the animal cell or the plant cell, research several organelles and discover their purposes. Add this information to your science notebook.

 ## HANDS-ON TIME: Make a 3-D Cell Model

Objective: To get an "oversized" view of a cell and its many parts.

Materials

- 1 large package gelatin, flavored or plain. (A light color is recommended, though not essential.)
- Any small foods that can resemble the parts of a cell: macaroni, jellybeans, squiggly noodles, beans, pickles, candy, licorice. A horizontal slice of a hard-boiled egg makes a good nucleus.
- 1 deep-dish pie plate or bowl, preferably clear
- Mixing bowl

Instructions

1. In mixing bowl, prepare gelatin according to package directions.
2. Put about one-third of gelatin into pie plate and place in the refrigerator until soft-set. Leave remainder of gelatin on counter to keep it soft.
3. Add various types of foods to the soft-set gelatin, using the diagram of the animal cell as a model, to create some organelles. Be sure to make a nucleus. Try to find similarly shaped foods.
4. Chill until set.
5. Layer with more gelatin and repeat the process.
6. Chill until fully set.
7. Take pictures!
8. Enjoy the gelatin!

Note: This could be done in one layer, but you won't get the 3-D effect.

 *Discovery Zone*

Balls made out of plastic foam that you find in craft stores make great model cells, too! A section can be sliced away to show the cell interior. Using dried beans, seashells, buttons, and yarn creatively, label and glue these cell pieces to the ball.

Discovery Zone

Another simple way to make a cell would be to form one on the floor with a jump rope. Use a variety of small toys to represent parts of the cell.

LESSON 3

TAXONOMY

TEACHING TIME:
Classified Information

Are you a fan of colorful plastic construction blocks? If so, you may have found that sorting your pieces by color, shape, or size is helpful when it comes to building your models. Humans sort all types of things. Have you ever tried to find something when it's in a jumbled pile of other things? Some people have drawers like this called "junk drawers." My kids call mine the "junky drawer" because it is so messy! Sorting or classifying things makes them easier to study, just like sorting the silverware at home makes it easier to find a fork or knife when you want one. A Swedish scientist named Carolus Linnaeus (1707–1778) developed one early method of sorting, or classifying, plants and animals. This method has been modified through the years but remains important in the classification system that scientists use today. This sorting process is called **taxonomy**. People who specialize in taxonomy are called **taxonomists.** Taxonomy is a good way to classify plants and animals for study. However, it doesn't mean that animals in the same classification are related. It means that they have some specific features in common and so are grouped accordingly.

How to Classify

The first layer of sorting is called **kingdom**. A kingdom is the largest group. Kingdoms are later broken down into smaller groups. There are five kingdoms: Monera, Protista, Plantae, Fungi, and Animalia. This year you will study Kingdom Plantae and Kingdom Animalia, so I'll explain them to you.

First of all, there is **Kingdom Plantae**. Can you make a reasonable guess what is in this category? If you said plants, you are correct. All flowers, trees, grasses, and plants belong to Kingdom Plantae.

The second kingdom you will learn about this year is **Kingdom Animalia**. You probably realize that this is the kingdom for all animals.

Once the kingdom is determined, organisms are sorted into a phylum. The sorting process continues with class, order, family, genus, and species. Each category is smaller and more specific than the last. Organisms are grouped according to their individual features and matched up with other similar organisms.

Who named all the animals?

"Out of the ground the LORD God formed every beast of the field and every bird of the air, and brought them to Adam to see what he would call them. And whatever Adam called each living creature, that was its name."(Genesis 2:19)

How can we remember the order for these categories? It's simple. Take the first letter of each category and make up a saying using each one in order. A popular saying for the classification system is: **K**ing **P**hillip **c**ried **o**ut, "**F**or **g**oodness **s**ake!"

K _____

P _____

C _____

O _____

F _____

G _____

S _____

King	=	Kingdom
Phillip	=	Phylum
Cried	=	Class
Out	=	Order
For	=	Family
Goodness	=	Genus
Sake	=	Species

In the space provided on the side, try to write your own memory phrase.

HANDS-ON TIME: Make Flashcards

Objective: To memorize the primary phyla for Kingdom Animalia.

Memory Work!

1. Using the list below, make flashcards for these phyla. (Phyla is the plural word for phylum.)
2. Work a few minutes a day until you have the phyla and their characteristics memorized.

 *Discovery Zone*

Try this! Use the sorting process of taxonomy to organize all the things you've collected. How many different ways could you sort your cars, dolls or action figures, building blocks, and other collections?

PRIMARY PHYLA FOR KINGDOM ANIMALIA

Annelida (true worms): Wormlike creatures that are segmented. *Ex.:* Earthworms, leeches.

Arthropoda: Invertebrates (having no spine), with segmented bodies and jointed legs in pairs. *Ex.:* Insects, spiders.

Chordata: Vertebrates (having a spine). *Ex.:* Humans, birds, fish, reptiles.

Echinodermata: Symmetrical marine vertebrates that have a water vascular system. *Ex.:* Starfish, sea urchins, sea cucumbers.

Mollusca: Invertebrate marine animals that have soft bodies, usually with shells. *Ex.:* Octopuses, clams, snails.

Nematoda (roundworms): Unsegmented, cylindrical bodies. *Ex.:* Hookworms, pinworms.

Cnidaria: Invertebrates; simple tissues with a mouth surrounded by tentacles; have stinging cells. *Ex.:* Jellyfish, corals.

Porifera: Simplest of all animals; have no tissue or organs. *Ex.:* Sponges.

Mollusca

Invertebrate marine animals that have soft bodies, usually with shells. Ex.: Octopi (plural of octopus), clams, snails.

Chordata

Vertebrates (having a spine). Ex.: Humans, birds, fish, reptiles.

Annelida
(true worms)

Wormlike creatures that are segmented. Ex.: Earthworms, leeches.

Arthropoda

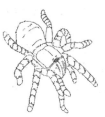

Invertebrates (having no spine), with segmented bodies and jointed legs in pairs. Ex.: Insects, spiders.

LESSON 4

THE BIOSPHERE

TEACHING TIME:
How Scientists Study the Earth

You have already learned that all the plants and animals in our world can be put into groups, making them easier to study. This is important because there are so many plants and animals. As you know, they are grouped by what they have in common. Well, it is not so different with the earth itself. Scientists have divided the earth, or **biosphere,** into smaller groups for study. The study of the organisms in the biosphere and their environment is called **ecology.** An organism's **environment** refers to the climate, air, vegetation (or plant life) and water in the area where the organism lives. In other words, the environment is the organism's surroundings.

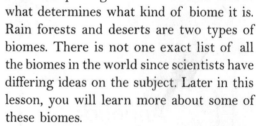

Who put mankind in charge of the earth?

"Then God said, 'Let Us make man in Our image, according to Our likeness; let them have dominion over the fish of the sea, over the birds of the air, and over the cattle, over all the earth and over every creeping thing that creeps on the earth.'"
(Genesis 1:26)

Break It Down

The whole biosphere would be too much to study at one time so it is divided into smaller groups. As with other things, there is more than one way to do this. One way is to divide it according to the large regions distinctly visible from space called **biomes**. There are several types of biomes in our world. The climate and plant growth of a certain area is what determines what kind of biome it is. Rain forests and deserts are two types of biomes. There is not one exact list of all the biomes in the world since scientists have differing ideas on the subject. Later in this lesson, you will learn more about some of these biomes.

Biomes can also be divided into smaller groups for study. Some examples of these smaller groups are ecosystems, habitats, and communities.

Why Does It Matter?

The plants and animals that are **native** to, or exist naturally in, different biomes today exist because ecological conditions are favorable for them. If an animal is taken into a different biome, it can dramatically upset the ecological balance. For instance, no one is allowed to bring snakes of any kind into Hawaii. Why? Because snakes are not native to Hawaii and have no natural enemies there. What do you think would happen if snakes began to multiply in Hawaii?

The snake population would grow out of control. This could cause serious problems. Such situations have happened before, and humans have had to learn some costly lessons about altering a biome.

Christians and Ecology

Every plant and animal in any biome is important for the growth or control of another plant or animal. As humans, we must consider what our role should be in protecting the balance that exists. You may notice that there are many people today who tell us we need to "save water," "save the trees," "save the baby whales." As Christians, we must be careful when we listen to such groups. Why? Many of these groups imply that we are in control of our world and we must make our resources last or else we will all be in extreme danger. The truth is that God is in control of how long this earth exists. However, he has made humans the managers, or **stewards**, of the earth. We are not to worship the creation, but rather the Creator. The reason that we care for the earth and our environment is that God made it and He is a perfect designer. When we tamper with the balances God has created, we interfere with His perfect plan. When we waste, we are not being good managers of the resources God has given us. Be careful when others try to make you feel like you must do this or that to keep the earth going. God is in control, not us. This earth will be here as long as He decides, not us.

Some Verses to Consider

• According to these verses, who owns the earth?

_____

• Will the earth last forever?   _____

• Did God give authority of the animals over to anyone?

_____   If so, whom? _____

God promises that He will take care of everyone who believes in Him when the time comes for the earth to end. We do not need to be afraid or worry about that day. God's Word promises that He will have a new heaven and a new earth for us one day (Rev. 21:1). For now, we should care for this earth because God made it and put us here on it. We will enjoy it more if it is clean and orderly.

 *Discovery Zone*

Longest Snakes

Here is a list of the longest snakes in the world:

Royal python	*35 feet*
Anaconda	*28 feet*
Indian python	*25 feet*
Diamond python	*21 feet*
King cobra	*19 feet*
Boa constrictor	*16 feet*
Bushmaster	*12 feet*

Exploring God's Word

Psalm 24:1

Isaiah 51:6

Genesis 2:19, 20

ONE STEP FURTHER

Antarctica is called a desert. Can you discover why? When you make your discovery, please write a paragraph that explains what you learned and add it to your science notebook.

 *Discovery Zone*

World's Driest Inhabited Places

Here is a list of the world's driest inhabited places. Numbers given are average annual inches of rainfall!

Aswan, Egypt	.02
Luxor, Egypt	.03
Arica, Chile	.04
Ica, Peru	.09
Antofagasta, Chile	.19

REVIEW IT!

1. What is the name of the study of the organisms and their environment that make up the earth? _____

2. What is another name for the earth, in terms of ecology? _____

3. The biosphere is divided into smaller groups visible from outer space called _____.

4. Why do scientists divide the earth into these smaller groups? _____

5. Name at least three things that make up an organism's environment.

_____

_____

_____

HANDS-ON TIME: Biome Project

Objective: To discover characteristics of the biomes in our world. *(This activity is geared for able fourth to sixth graders. Another option is to have your child learn about just a few of these.)*

Inquiring Minds Want to Know

What are some major biomes? I've included a list here. Using a science encyclopedia or a dictionary, find out what each of these biomes is like. Your reference may include some biomes that are not on this list. Please include these on your list,

also. Write a simple definition for each biome.

- Chaparral
- Coniferous forest
- Desert
- Estuary
- Grassland
- Rain forest
- Savanna
- Tundra

Map It!

Use the world map in Appendix A to note where these biomes are located. Remember to make a key!

GRADES 1–3 OPTION: Picture the Desert

You have learned there are different types of biomes. One type of biome is the desert. Your job is to find out what a desert looks like and draw a picture of one on the next page. Can you find out what kinds of animals live in deserts? List below your picture any that you discover.

WHAT A DESERT LOOKS LIKE

SOME ANIMALS THAT MAY LIVE IN THE DESERT

_____   _____   _____

_____   _____   _____

_____   _____   _____

LESSON 5

FOOD WEBS

TEACHING TIME:
What's for Dinner?

In the last lesson, you learned that biomes are divided into ecosystems. An important factor in any ecosystem is the **food chains** that are present there. A food chain is the list of who eats whom. Each ecosystem consists of many food chains. These chains often intertwine with one another and together make up a **food web**, as shown in the diagram on the next page.

What Makes Up a Web?

Plants and animals make up food webs. We can group animals according to the type of food they eat. There are three categories: herbivores, carnivores, and omnivores. If you have studied Latin, you may be able to figure out what each one means. Let's go over them, to be sure you know.

Herbivore comes from the Latin word *herba*, meaning "vegetation" or "plant." Therefore, herbivores are the plant eaters.

Carnivore is from the Latin word *carn*, meaning "flesh" or "meat." Where does meat come from? Meat comes from animals. You probably know by now that carnivores are the meat eaters.

Well, then, what is an **omnivore**? Let's go back to Latin one more time. The word *omni* in Latin means "all." So, then, omnivores eat it ALL, plants and animals alike.

So, now you know another way to classify animals.

The Rest of the Story

Organisms can also be classified according to their role in the food web. Again, we have three main categories.

The first category is **decomposers**. Decomposers are things like fungi and molds, which feed on the dead remains of other organisms. As they feed, they break down, or decompose, the organism. Eventually, these decomposed organisms end up back in the soil and are nutrition for plants.

Second, there are **producers**. As their name suggests, they produce something. What do you think it is? Producers make their own food. Plants are producers. Using a process called photosynthesis (which you'll learn about later), plants produce the food they need to grow.

Last, there are **consumers**. Do you know what consumers do? I'll guess that you said consume, but what do they consume?

What did John the Baptist eat?

"Now John himself was clothed in camel's hair, with a leather belt around his waist; and his food was locusts and wild honey."
(Matthew 3:4)

FOOD WEB

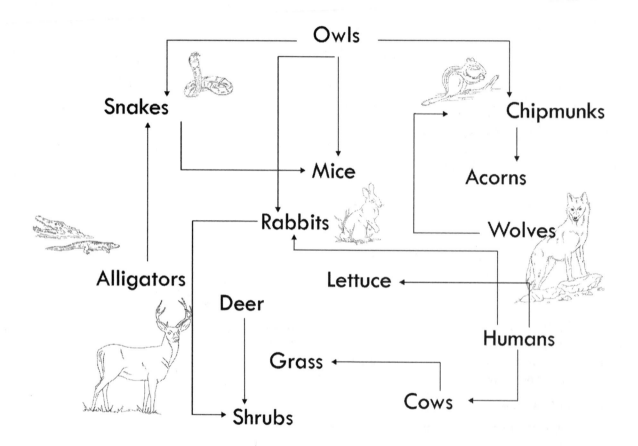

Herbivores, carnivores, and omnivores are all consumers. They eat other consumers or producers. There are primary consumers and secondary consumers. Primary consumers eat producers. They are the herbivores. Secondary consumers eat other consumers and producers. They are omnivores and carnivores. They are at the top of any food chain and can eat whatever they want!

REVIEW IT!

1. What are the three categories of organisms according to the type of food they eat?

a. _____

b. _____

c. _____

2. What are the three categories of organisms according to their role in a food web?

a. _____

b. _____

c. _____

3. Make a list of the many different types of food that you eat. Can you decide which categories you would be listed in?

_____

_____

_____

_____

_____

 *Discovery Zone*

Go to www.answersingenesis.org for a bonanza of information, including free weekly and monthly e-mails for teachers, home educators, and students.

 *Discovery Zone*

The Institute for Creation Research has a stockpile of great articles about creation science, fascinating radio broadcasts, and much more for parents and teachers at www.icr.org.

HANDS-ON TIME: UNIT ONE WRAP-UP

Show What You Know!

Answer as many questions as you can without using your book or notes. You get **10,000** points for each correct response. After going through the review once with your book closed, open your book and try again. You get **5,000** points for each additional correct answer. So, **show what you know!**

1. According to the Bible, how did the earth come into existence?

   _____

   _____

   _____

   _____

2. The study of life and living organisms is known as

   _____.

3. An organism is _____.

4. The building blocks of all organisms are _____.

5. Structures within cells with specific jobs are called

   _____.

6. Cells with a nucleus are called

   _____.

7. The simplest cells, having no nucleus, are called

   _____.

8. Name the seven main divisions in the classification system from largest to smallest.

   a. _____

   b. _____

   c. _____

   d. _____

   e. _____

   f. _____

   g. _____

9. Match the animal to its proper phylum by writing the phylum next to the animal.

Birds _____   Annelida

Starfish _____   Arthropoda

Jellyfish _____   Chordata

Earthworms _____   Echinodermata

Insects _____   Mollusca

Clams _____   Nematoda

Sponges _____   Cnidaria

Roundworms _____   Porifera

10. The study of all living organisms and their environments is called _____.

11. The earth is also referred to as the _____ in ecological terms.

12. What are biomes? _____

13. Plant-eating animals are called _____.

14. Meat-eating animals are called _____.

15. Animals that eat plants *and* animals are called _____

16. Organisms that feed on the dead remains of plants and animals are called _____

_____.

17. Producers are special because they can _____.

18. Animals that eat producers are called _____.

FIRST ATTEMPT _____

(number of correct responses x 10,000)

SECOND ATTEMPT + _____

(number of correct responses x 5,000)

TOTAL NUMBER OF POINTS _____

 WRITING ASSIGNMENT

In your science notebook, complete the creative writing assignment below. If you don't recognize a type of biome, you can look it up in the dictionary. Have fun with it!

As a real estate tycoon, you know the importance of producing effective brochures to advertise the properties you are selling. Persuade your client to purchase land in the biome of your choice by describing the property and explaining the advantages of living in that biome. Tell everyone about the beautiful evergreens and snow in the taiga, or point out how successful your client could be as a farmer in the grasslands. Maybe you want to advertise a tropical rain forest or even suggest an experimental community in an underwater biome.

UNIT TWO

PLANTS IN GOD'S WORLD

UNIT TWO VOCABULARY

- anthers
- broad-leaved trees
- carbon dioxide
- catalyst
- chlorophyll
- CO_2
- coniferous trees
- cross-pollination
- deciduous trees
- drupes
- dry fruits
- erosion
- evaporated
- false fruit
- flowers
- glucose
- H_2O
- hydrogen
- juicy fruits
- leaves
- ovaries
- ovules
- oxygen
- photosynthesis
- pollen
- pollination
- pomes
- reproduce
- roots
- self-pollination
- stems
- true fruit

MATERIALS NEEDED FOR THIS UNIT

- Science notebook or sheet of paper
- 1 or more small bedding plants
- Colored pencils or crayons
- Clear container such as a goldfish bowl, 2-liter bottle with narrow top cut off, or a small aquarium
- Cover for container (can be plastic wrap and rubber band)
- Potting soil
- Small plants and moss
- Fork
- Small stones for decoration
- Tiny rocks or gravel
- Variety of flowers, including some buds
- Sharp knife, scissors, scalpel
- Cutting board
- Magnifying glass
- Variety of fruits and vegetables

Flower Coloring Page

LESSON 6

INTRODUCTION

TEACHING TIME:
Digging Into Plants

Plants are a very important part of life on Earth. They provide nourishment for many animals, as well as oxygen for them to breathe. They help prevent **erosion**. (Do you know what erosion is? Look it up and add the definition to your vocabulary list.) Plants are also part of the beauty of our world.

Plants are created with several key features. First of all, plants have **roots**. Roots are vital for absorbing moisture from the soil, and they help hold the plant in place. Can you imagine a plant without roots enduring a storm? Even mighty trees with highly developed root systems can have trouble in a storm.

Stems are another main feature of plants. Stems are the support system for the leaves and flowers, as well as a storehouse for water and nutrients. If you were to break the stem of a plant, you would very likely see the moisture ooze out of the plant. The water in the plant keeps the plant sturdy and upright. A wilted plant is a signal to water it.

Leaves are the next main part of plants. Leaves store an important ingredient called chlorophyll. Chlorophyll is important for feeding the plant and also produces the green color in the plant. You will learn more about this process later. For now, it is enough to remember that chlorophyll is stored in the leaves.

Last, there are the **flowers**. I can almost guarantee that you know what flowers are, but do you know what their purpose is? They do more than make the plant pretty. Flowers are where the reproductive parts of the plant are located. That means they are important in making new "baby" plants.

Do you remember the name of the kingdom for plants? It is Kingdom Plantae, or the Plant Kingdom.

"Then God said, 'Let the earth bring forth grass, the herb that yields seed, and the fruit tree . . .'" (Genesis 1:11)

Putting It All Together

Please complete the plant diagram on the next page, labeling the main parts of the plant. *Older students* should note the purpose of each part, as well.

BASIC PLANT DIAGRAM

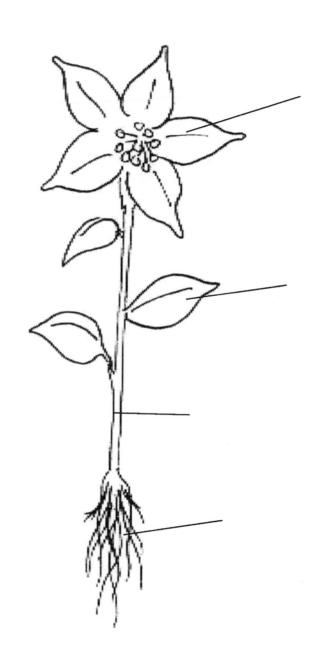

HANDS-ON TIME: Examine Plant Design

Objective: To examine plant specimens for basic plant parts.

Today we will make use of the "Checking It Out" form found in Appendix A in the back of this book to record your work. Scientists always record their work and evaluate it. Please add the completed page to your science notebook.

Materials

- 1 or more plant specimens. (You need to be able to examine the plant, roots and all, so a small bedding plant is recommended.)
- Colored pencils or crayons
- Sheet of paper or your science notebook

Instructions

1. Gently remove the plant from its container.
2. Examine the plant.
3. Draw a diagram of the plant.
4. Label its roots, stem, leaves, and flower.
5. Repeat for each type of plant you study.
6. Complete a "Checking It Out" form.

 *Discovery Zone*

Place the freshly cut stem of a Queen Anne's lace or a white carnation into a vase of water dyed with your choice of food coloring. What happens? Why?

PHOTOSYNTHESIS

TEACHING TIME:
How Do Plants Grow?

Did you know that there was not always rain on the earth?

" before any plant of the field was in the earth and before any herb of the field had grown. For the Lord God had not caused it to rain on the earth . . ." (Genesis 2:5)

Just as He did with humans and other animals, God created plants with the ability to grow. You know that for growth to occur, an organism must be fed. Well, an obvious question is, "Who feeds the plants?" Sometimes we feed the plants in our gardens with products we buy to help them grow. But that does not explain how the millions of other plants in our world get fed. God has created plants with an ability to make their own food. The process is called **photosynthesis**.

The Greek root *photo* means "light." You now have the first ingredient for God's plant food. It is light. Where does the light come from? We will need a very large source of light in order to take care of all the plants on the earth. I'm sure you have figured out by now that the light source needed for photosynthesis is the sun. The sun provides most of the energy needed for the earth.

What do you think is the next ingredient for photosynthesis? If you said water, you are correct. All plants need water. You probably remember that a key feature in plants is their root system and that the roots' purpose is to absorb water from the ground. Water is made up of two parts **hydrogen** and one part **oxygen**. Hydrogen and oxygen are elements that God placed in our world, and each has a special function. For example, many animals, including humans, need oxygen to breathe. Since two parts hydrogen and one part oxygen equal water, scientists call water H_2O.

The third ingredient for plant food may surprise you. It is a gas called **carbon dioxide**. *Di* means "two" and *oxide* means "oxygen." How many parts of oxygen do you think there are for each part carbon? Did you say two? You are correct. Scientists call carbon dioxide CO_2. You can call it that, too. CO_2 is the gas we breathe out.

All right, we have determined three ingredients necessary for photosynthesis. However, I'm sure you remember that **chlorophyll** is important for this process as well. What is chlorophyll and what does it do? Chlorophyll is found in leaves. It is what makes the leaves green. Chlorophyll is also a **catalyst**. In this case, a catalyst is *something that forces something else into motion*. So, the chlorophyll's job is to force the energy from the sun, the H_2O, and the CO_2 into motion.

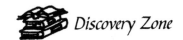
Two things happen when chlorophyll puts everything else into motion. First of all, oxygen is produced. As humans, we should be very interested in this since we need oxygen to breathe. Second, a type of sugar called **glucose** is produced. Glucose becomes the plant food, and it helps the plant grow.

Summing it all up, there are four ingredients for photosynthesis. They are light, water, carbon dioxide, and chlorophyll. When put all together, they make glucose for the plants and oxygen for animals. Have you figured out that many of God's creatures, including you, need the oxygen put out by plants and that plants need the carbon dioxide put out by animals? Here we have another example of God's great design.

Photosynthesis Components

- Complete the "recipe" card on the following page, showing all elements needed for photosynthesis.
- Memorize the "Mary, Mary" verse that follows the recipe page. Color it in and keep it in your science notebook.

ONE STEP FURTHER

Look up two Bible verses about plants. Choose one to add to your science notebook.

 ## HANDS-ON TIME: Build a Terrarium

Objective: To observe how water is **evaporated**—or drawn into the air from the soil, forming "rain"—and to prove that your plants are able to grow without constant tending.

Now that you have made your recipe card for plant food, it is time to get busy! Today you are going to make something called a terrarium. A terrarium is a small, contained garden that basically takes care of itself.

Materials

- A clear container, such as a goldfish bowl, a 2-liter bottle with its narrow top cut off, or a small aquarium
- A covering for your container—can be plastic wrap and a rubber band, clear plastic cut to fit, even a plate or saucer
- Potting soil
- Small plants and moss from the garden center
- A fork
- Tiny rocks or gravel
- Small stones, and the like, for decoration

(Hands-On Time continues on page 36.)

Discovery Zone

For more plant coloring pages and diagrams, go to www.enchantedlearning.com!

 *From God's Kitchen*

RECIPE FOR:

SERVES:

INGREDIENTS:

INSTRUCTIONS:

MAKES:

(1)

(2)

Mary, Mary

Mary, Mary, Quite contrary,
How does your garden grow?
With sunshine and water,
To name just two,
Add in chlorophyll and CO_2!

Method

1. Make sure your container is clean and dry. Do not leave soap in it.

2. Place gravel in your container, about ¼ to ½ inch deep. This is to provide good drainage for your plants.

3. Add potting soil, 2 to 4 inches deep, depending on the size of your container. (You may need more, depending on the size of the roots of your plants.)

4. Now you will plant your plants. Using the fork to scoot the soil around, make a hole deep enough to plant your plants, covering the entire root system of each. Be gentle as you place the plants in the container, or you may damage them.

5. Add a little more soil.

6. Cover the soil with a thin layer of moss.

7. Carefully water the plants. Do not overwater. This will harm the plants.

8. Place your decorative stones in the container.

9. Put on the lid.

10. You will need to place your container in a well-lit area. Be sure to ask the garden center if your plants need full sun or just good lighting. This does make a difference. Not all plants have the same needs. Some even prefer shade.

11. You should observe your terrarium on a daily basis in the beginning to make sure your plants are doing well. If they continue to look healthy, you can check on them weekly. If your lid does not fit well, your terrarium could dry out. You need to make sure the terrarium stays moist. Add water occasionally, if necessary.

12. Complete a "Checking It Out" form.

 *Discovery Zone*

Looking for exciting, educational garden ideas? Then go to www.kidsgardening.com.

 *Discovery Zone*

While you are online, see what you can discover about the famous botanist George Washington Carver.

LESSON 8

PLANT REPRODUCTION

TEACHING TIME:
Blooming Babies

Flowering plants are a fascinating way to see God's wonderful design up close. Flowers have special parts that help them **reproduce**, or make more plants. Plants multiply through a process called **pollination**. God uses things other than flowers in this process, however. He also uses bees, birds, and the wind. Let's see how.

Reproductive Parts of Flowers

First you need to learn about the reproductive parts of the flower. Almost all flowers have both male and female parts. The main female parts are the **ovules** and the **ovaries.** They are located deep inside the flower blossom. The **anthers** are the main male parts. The anthers are located in the center of the flower and are usually easily seen and reached. (See the flower anatomy diagram on the next page.)

There are more male and female parts than what I have mentioned here, but this is a good start.

Pollination

As I stated earlier, pollination is the process used to make, or reproduce, more plants. Birds, as well as bees and other insects, can be part of this process. Wind, water, and mammals can play a part as well. For reproduction to happen, **pollen,** a substance produced by the anthers, must be moved to another flower.

There are two types of pollination: self-pollination and cross-pollination. **Self-pollination** means that a plant can get pollen from its own anthers down to its own ovules. Although some flowers can do this, most cannot.

Flowers that cannot self-pollinate must get pollen from other flowers. Since plants can't move around, how does the pollen get from one plant to another? The bees, birds, and others move it. This process is called **cross-pollination.**

Bees' Knees

Let's concentrate on the involvement of bees. First of all, God has designed flowers to produce nectar. Second, bees feed on nectar and need it. Third, God designed plants with very bright flowers, which attract the bees. When the bees buzz into the flower blossoms to collect nectar, they also collect pollen. The pollen sticks to the bees' legs, and when the bees travel to the next flowers to collect more nectar, the pollen is

Exploring God's Word

How do we grow and blossom in the Lord?

See Psalm 1:1-3.

FLOWER ANATOMY

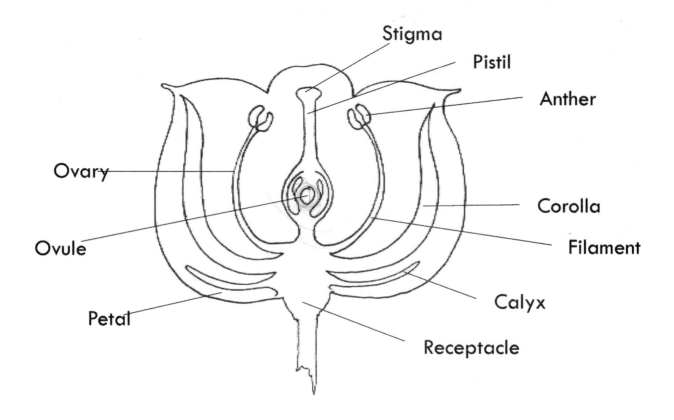

deposited on the new flowers. (See the bee diagram on the next page.) Cross-pollination has occurred. Since the nectar is deep in the flower, the bee must move in deep to get it. This helps the pollen get to the female parts, and the ovules are fertilized. This produces new seeds that are spread in a variety of ways, giving us new plants.

As I said at the beginning of today's lesson, flowers are a wonderful way to get a glimpse of God's design. Are you amazed at how He created bees to desire the nectar produced by flowers, so that pollen could be carried to other flowers? He even gave them a way to find the nectar by making the flowers so bright and attractive. You may notice that when you wear shirts with bright flowers on them, bees are often attracted to you!

Did You Learn It?

Let's see how much you learned from the reading. See if you can answer the following questions without looking back at the lesson! If not, then use the lesson for assistance.

1. Name the female reproductive parts of flowers.

_____

_____

2. Name the main male reproductive parts of a flower.

_____

3. Name three things involved in carrying pollen from one flower to another. (There are actually more than three.)

_____

_____

_____

4. How does God attract bees to flowers?

_____

_____

_____

5. What are the bees actually looking for?

_____

6. In your science notebook, draw a simple diagram showing the pollination process, or list the steps.

 *Discovery Zone*

The best way to study plants is to observe them closely. Look for details of the flower, fruit, stem, and leaves. Where is it growing, and what other plants grow nearby?

Bee Diagram

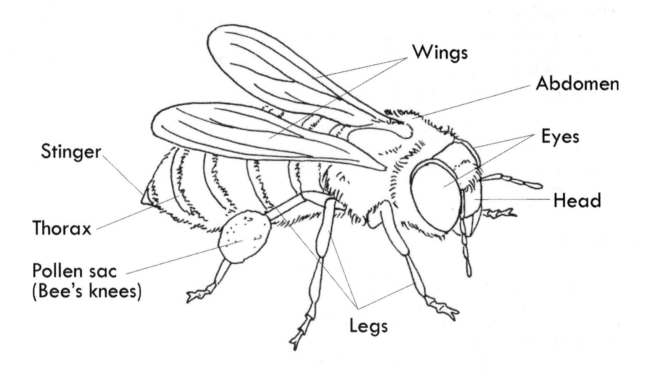

Wings

Abdomen

Eyes

Stinger

Head

Thorax

Pollen sac
(Bee's knees)

Legs

HANDS-ON TIME: Dissect a Flower

Objective: To personally look inside a flower and see all the parts we have talked about and maybe even some we have not.

Materials

- A few varieties of flowers, including some buds
- Sharp knife, scissors, scalpel
- Cutting board
- Magnifying glass

Instructions

Adult supervision required.

1. Slice through a bud and look for all the parts shown on the diagram.

2. Using a scalpel, preferably, slice off the petals. Count the petals. Different families of flowers have different numbers of petals. Does this prove to be true in your dissection?

3. Remove the stamens. Using your magnifying glass, examine the tips of the stamens to see the anthers.

4. Examine the more mature flowers, looking for seeds. You may find some.

5. Complete a "Checking It Out" form.

ONE STEP FURTHER

There are many different variations of demonstrations of how plants grow. Often, these simple activities require just bean, pea, or radish seeds; clear plastic cups; and potting soil. Look for one in a book or on the Internet and begin it today. (Lima bean seeds work well, but they do best if soaked in water overnight.) Some methods have you plant several identical seeds and then grow them under different conditions (with light, without light, with water, without water, and so forth). This is a great activity for all ages. Older students should keep a record of their findings.

You might choose to use the "Plant Observation Form" in Appendix A for each seed planted. Or simply record observations in your science notebook.

LESSON 9

FRUITS AND VEGETABLES

TEACHING TIME:
Fruit Facts

*"Then God said, 'Let the earth bring forth grass, the herb that yields seed, and the fruit tree that yields fruit according to its kind, whose seed is in itself . . . ' "
(Genesis 1:11)*

What is a fruit? Do you know? Most people think fruits are juicy, edible parts of plants. While this is true, the actual definition of a fruit is more complicated. You may be surprised to learn that nuts are fruits, as well as many vegetables that you eat.

Fruits are formed from the ovaries of flowers. The ovaries mature and swell and contain the seeds for new plants. Fruits come in many different shapes, sizes, colors, and textures. Some are sweet. Some are not. Some are very juicy throughout. Some are not juicy at all. Some fruits have very hard skins or shells, while some fruits have soft skins. Let's discover how God designed fruits and what their purpose is.

True or False

When you studied the reproductive parts of flowers, you learned that ovaries and ovules were important in the process. And, as I said above, a flower's ovaries grow into fruits. What about the ovules? Well, the ovules are basically the "eggs." When pollen is carried from one plant to another, it works its way deep into the ovaries of the plant. This is where the ovules are located. Through contact with the pollen, the ovules are fertilized. They then develop a hard exterior coating, which protects them. At this point they are called seeds. The ovary then grows around the seed. This is the fruit, and it is there to protect the seeds. Sometimes a **false fruit** also grows, as in the case of apples and pears. The false fruit is the part you eat. The **true fruit** is the core. If you find this confusing, don't worry. When you study biology in high school, you will learn more about it.

Name That Fruit

Fruits can be broken down into four basic groups. There are **dry fruits**, **juicy fruits**, **pomes,** and **drupes**. (There are other ways to classify fruits. This is just one.)

Examples:

- Dry fruits: Nuts, pods, grains
- Juicy fruits: Berries, tomatoes, cucumbers, oranges—contain many seeds
- Pomes: Apples, pears—have a core
- Drupes, or stone fruits: Peaches, avocados, olives—contain a pit that holds a seed

How Seeds "Travel"

The main reason all fruits exist is to deliver new seeds far enough away from the parent plant for them to grow. How does this happen? First of all, animals carry off some seeds. A seed can take root either when an animal opens the fruit, as in the case of an acorn, and the seed drops to the ground or when an animal eats the fruit and the seed spills onto the ground. It may even take root because an animal ate the fruit, seed and all, and the seed is delivered back to the ground through the animal's waste. There are other seeds that are dispersed through the wind. Are you familiar with "helicopters," the little seeds that look like they have wings, which are often seen zooming from trees? These are dry fruits that are looking for a place to land, far enough away from the parent tree to grow. Acorns are another example of dry fruits. How do you think they get to a new "home"?

Though understanding all the different types of fruit may be difficult, there are a couple of main points you can remember. First of all, keep in mind that if the seeds are contained *inside* the specimen, it is called a fruit. Even God's Word teaches this. Genesis 1:11 says, "Then God said, 'Let the earth bring forth grass, the herb that yields seed, and the fruit tree that yields fruit according to its kind, **whose seed is in itself,** on the earth.'" [emphasis mine] That makes tomatoes, squash, watermelons and pumpkins, peas and strawberries, all fruits. Second, remember that a fruit's main purpose is to help the seed get to a place where it can take root and grow. If it happens to feed you, too, all the better!

Let's Explore

- Go on a dry-seed hunt.
- Collect as many different types as you can. Do not be discouraged if you don't find any or many. Some areas will have more than others.
- Look over what you find and compare their similarities and differences.
- Write several sentences that explain what you did and what you found.
- Younger students: You can discuss this with your teacher and make a drawing instead of writing about it.

ONE STEP FURTHER

Dry seeds can be turned into beautiful arrangements or collages. If you have extra time today, use your dry seeds to create something artistic.

Discovery Zone

Although many kinds of seeds, nuts, and berries are delicious, there are dozens of poisonous plants, too. Do you know which plants in or around your home might be poisonous?

HANDS-ON TIME: Dissect Fruits and Vegetables

Objective: To examine the insides of foods to observe the differences in fruits and vegetables.

Materials

- Sharp knife
- Cutting board
- Variety of fruits and vegetables: apples, oranges, nuts, blackberries, strawberries, cucumbers, squash, broccoli, carrots, and more
- Sheet of paper or your science notebook

Instructions

Adult supervision required.

1. Using a knife, slice the specimen in half.
2. Look for seeds.
3. Determine which are fruits.
4. Locate the ovary of the plants.
5. Diagram your findings.
6. Label each drawing as the type of fruit it represents: dry, pome, drupe, juicy.
7. Taste each specimen and note its characteristics (sweet, juicy, sour, spongy, wet, dry, and so forth).
8. Complete a "Checking It Out" form.
9. Eat your leftovers!

 *Discovery Zone*

Fruit Dip

4 ounces cream cheese
1-1/8 cups marshmallow fluff
½ cup vanilla yogurt
dash of cherry juice for color

Mix all ingredients until smooth and enjoy!

 *Discovery Zone*

Spinach Veggie Dip

1 pint sour cream
1 can drained, chopped water chestnuts
1 red onion, grated
1 package dry vegetable-soup mix
1 box frozen spinach, thawed

Mix all ingredients. Great for dipping veggies or crackers.

LESSON 10

TREES

TEACHING TIME:
Conifers and Broadleaves

Have you ever noticed all the different kinds of trees in our world? There are tall trees and short trees, fat trees and skinny trees. In the autumn, there are some trees whose leaves have bold colors. In the winter, some trees have no leaves at all.

Even though our world has many varieties, or species, of trees in it, there are only five main categories. Three of those categories are fairly rare. They are the gingkoes, cycads, and tree ferns. The rest of our trees fall into two basic categories: broad-leaved and coniferous.

Broad-leaved trees are not too difficult to spot. Their leaves are broad, as the name tells us, as well as thin. They are often rather flat like paper. These trees produce flowers at certain times of the year. They are often **deciduous trees**. This means they lose their leaves in the autumn. Some examples of broadleaved trees are oaks, elms, maples, and dogwoods. Broad-leaved trees are very common in many parts of the world.

Coniferous trees are also quite common. Coniferous trees are known by their leaves as well. Their leaves are actually more like needles. They are tough and often sharp. These trees are called coniferous because they produce cones of some sort. Sometimes the cones are cone-shaped with distinct sharp points, like pinecones. Other times the cones are small "berries." The cones can be male or female. The female cones contain the ovules. The male cones contain the pollen. Conifers are often evergreen. This does not mean they never lose their leaves. They simply lose them a little at a time, rather than all at once. This way they are never bare and always have their green color. This is why we say they are *ever*greens. They usually have a fragrant, pine scent. Two examples of conifers are spruce and junipers. They can be very tall trees or more shrub-like.

Autumn Colors

Have you ever wondered why leaves change colors in the autumn? In preparing for winter, trees must conserve, or hold back, some of their nutrients. In order to do this, certain trees are designed by God to lose their leaves. If the tree does not have to feed all those leaves, it can have enough nutrients to survive the cold months. So, some trees are designed to stop

We can be like a tree of life if we are righteous.

"The fruit of the righteous is a tree of life, And he who wins souls is wise." (Proverbs 11:30)

feeding their leaves and sending water to them. Because of this, the leaves can no longer produce chlorophyll. Do you remember that chlorophyll is what causes the green coloring in plants and leaves? This lack of chlorophyll creates changes in the leaves, and those changes can result in colored leaves. In other words, colored leaves are the result of a lack of chlorophyll that comes from the tree's preparing to lose its leaves for winter.

Not all deciduous trees can change colors in the fall, but the ones that can are a sight to see! When I see beautiful autumn colors, I am reminded that God is preparing the trees to lose their leaves so they can stay healthy during the cold months. I'm so glad He chose such a beautiful way to do it!

Discovery Zone

Trees are often easiest to identify by their leaves. The shape of the tree and its bark also provide useful clues.

REVIEW IT!
Trees, Trees, Trees

1. There are *five main* groups of trees. The *two most common* types are:

   _____

   _____

2. The *three rarest* types are:

   _____

   _____

   _____

Conifers

3. Name at least three traits that conifers possess. You can list more here, if you know them.

   _____

   _____

   _____

4. Name some examples of conifers.

   _____

   _____

   _____

Discovery Zone

Using a camera, notebook, and reference materials, make your own "Field Guide to Trees."

Idea!

Do you have any conifers in your yard or surrounding area? Why don't you check it out and take a photograph of one, or draw a picture of one. Be creative and have fun. See how many different types of conifers you can locate next time you go to a park. Do the same thing with the broad-leaved trees.

Broad-leaved Trees

5. Name two traits that broad-leaved trees possess.

_____

_____

 *Discovery Zone*

Do you have any "famous" trees in your community? Many cities or regions boast of trees known for their age, size, or historic value. Find out if there are any near your home.

HANDS-ON TIME: UNIT TWO WRAP-UP

Show What You Know!

Answer as many questions as you can without using your book or notes. You get **10,000** points for each correct response. After going through the review once with your book closed, open your book and try again. You get **5,000** points for each additional correct answer. So, **show what you know!**

1. All plants are in Kingdom _____ .

2. Name the four main structures all plants have.

   _____   _____

   _____   _____

3. Which part of a plant contains the reproductive parts? _____

4. Name the part of a plant that contains the chlorophyll. _____

5. What is the name of the process that helps plants make their own food? _____

   _____

6. Chlorophyll makes leaves look _____

   and is a _____ for photosynthesis, meaning it forces the other

   ingredients into action.

7. Photosynthesis produces two primary results: _____

   and _____ .

8. Name all four components for photosynthesis.

   _____   _____

   _____   _____

9. Which part of a flower becomes a seed when fertilized? _____

10. Which part of a flower produces pollen? _____

11. Describe a way that pollen can be transferred from one plant to another. _____

    _____

12. Which part of a flower contains the ovules? _____

13. Is this part considered male or female? _____

14. Name four basic types of fruits.

_____   _____

_____   _____

15. _____ trees have long, sharp needles for leaves.

16. _____ trees lose their leaves in autumn.

17. What causes leaves to change color in the autumn? _____

_____

_____

_____

_____

FIRST ATTEMPT _____
(number of correct responses x 10,000)

SECOND ATTEMPT + _____
(number of correct responses x 5,000)

TOTAL NUMBER OF POINTS _____

WRITING ASSIGNMENT

In your science notebook, complete the creative writing assignment below. Have fun with it!

What would happen if photosynthesis stopped working on Earth? Write a story about the problems this would cause and how people might try to solve them. Especially consider what to do about food and oxygen.

UNIT THREE

BIRDS OF THE EARTH

UNIT THREE VOCABULARY

- aquatic birds
- birds of prey
- birds that don't fly
- cambered
- Class Aves
- diving birds
- game birds
- hummingbirds
- nocturnal
- pellet
- Phylum Chordata
- songbirds
- swimming birds
- wading birds
- warm-blooded

MATERIALS NEEDED FOR THIS UNIT

- Science notebook
- Sketchbook or notebook paper
- Pencil
- Colored pencils or crayons
- Gallon-size plastic milk carton
- Hay, straw, twigs, pine needles, or grass
- Twine
- Scissors
- Owl pellet (for purchase information, see Hands-On Time, Lesson 12)
- Old newspapers
- Small jar
- Dishwashing liquid (hand, not dishwasher)
- Strainer, coffee filter, or paper towels
- Dissection kit or tweezers and toothpicks
- Black paper, poster board (if desired)
- Camera
- Pinecones
- Peanut butter
- Birdseed
- String or yarn

Songbirds Coloring Page

LESSON 11

TAXONOMY

TEACHING TIME:
How Birds Are Classified

Have you ever heard of birds of prey? Birds of prey are the hunters. They are large birds. They have talons and hooked beaks to help them eat mice, snakes, and other small creatures. Birds of prey constitute just one type, or class, of bird. Today, you are going to discover other ways to group birds.

Since you have already studied the classification system, you know that all birds are in Kingdom Animalia. Now, if I tell you that birds have backbones, can you figure out which phylum they are in? You would be correct in putting them in **Phylum Chordata**. I have another question. Do you remember what comes after kingdom and phylum? If you do not, think of King Phillip. The next division in the classification system is *class*. All birds are in **Class Aves**. To belong in Class Aves, a creature must be warm-blooded (meaning its body maintains a constant temperature, relatively independent of its surroundings) with a four-chambered heart. It must have feathers, lightweight bones, and lay eggs. Does this sound like a bird? Of course it does.

There is more to classifying birds than this, though. Class Aves, like all classes, is then divided into orders. There are actually 27 orders of birds, and the order names are very difficult to spell and pronounce. Going through all of these would be quite a challenge. Instead we will learn about some other ways to group birds.

First of all, did you know that not all birds fly? These birds can be grouped together and include ostriches and penguins. Can you imagine what a penguin would look like flying? We'll call this group **birds that don't fly**.

Next there are the **birds of prey** that we mentioned before. They include eagles, hawks, and vultures. You can recognize birds of prey by their hooked beaks and long, sharp talons.

Next we have the **game birds.** These are the ones many people hunt. Quail, doves, and pheasants are in this group. Many people also like to eat these birds.

Swimming birds are another division. They have webbed feet and include ducks and geese. **Diving birds** are the ones that catch prey with their bills—unlike birds of prey, which

"So God created . . . every winged bird according to its kind. And God saw that it was good." *(Genesis 1:21)*

use their talons. Pelicans are an example of diving birds. There are also **wading birds,** such as herons and flamingos. Sometimes you will find swimming, diving, and wading birds all grouped together and called **aquatic birds,** or waterbirds.

Last, there are **songbirds** and **hummingbirds.** The songbirds are birds such as robins, nightingales, and mockingbirds. Hummingbirds belong in their own group because they are the only birds that can fly backward. They fly backward to get out of flowers.

This is definitely a simplified version of bird orders. As you read other books on birds, you may find other categories. You may hear of perching birds and running birds, for example. The orders can be grouped in a variety of ways since there are 27 of them. This is just a start.

Birds are wonderful fun to observe. The best way to observe them is to sit very still. Once they get used to your presence, they will go on about their routine. By being very still and quiet, you can watch them build their nests, gather food, and feed their young. You may also notice how they communicate with one another. Sitting quietly in my yard one night, I even had the joy of watching an owl silently, but very quickly, fly through on some great hunt.

Discovery Zone

What's the official bird of your state? Check out www.50states.com/bird/ to find out.

REVIEW IT!

List the key traits required for Class Aves.

_____

_____

_____

Discovery Zone

An Amazing Story!
Read about God's remarkable design of the emperor penguin. The way these penguins lay eggs and tend their chicks will surprise you!

HANDS-ON TIME: Bird Watch

Objective: To observe birds in their normal routine.

Materials

- Sketchbook or notebook paper
- Pencil
- Colored pencils, crayons

Instructions

1. Go on a bird watch. Be prepared to sit still and watch. Talking will discourage birds from behaving routinely. Morning and early evening seem to be good times to see birds in action.

2. Observe the bird activity around you. What are the birds doing? Are they making noises? Can you detect bird "families"?

3. In your sketchbook, make a page for each bird.

   • Sketch the bird, as best you can. You may even want to color it in. *Note:* Sketches are quickly made and are not intended to be perfect. Do not try to make your sketch perfect.

   • On the page, write the type of bird, if you know it.

   • On the same page, list the types of activities you notice the bird doing.

   • If you find the bird's nest, you might want to write down facts you notice about the nest. Suggestions: Is it high or low? What is it made of? What kind of tree is it in?

4. You can continue this project, adding a little each day. You may discover a new hobby!

GRADES 1–3 OPTION: Make a Birdhouse

Materials

   • Gallon-size plastic milk carton
   • Hay, straw, pine needles, or grass
   • Twine
   • Scissors

Instructions

Adult supervision required.

1. Cut two large holes in the side of the milk jug.

2. Line the bottom of the jug with pine needles or other materials from the list.

3. Securely tie the twine onto the handle of the jug.

4. Hang the jug in a tree, high enough to be safe from dogs, cats, and kids! Make sure it is not in an area with too much activity.

5. Wait and see! Carefully check it out on a regular basis and see if a bird has adopted it as a home. Is a nest being built? You may want to keep a small pile of straw nearby, as well as twigs for the bird to use.

6. Complete a "Checking It Out" form (found in Appendix A).

 *Discovery Zone*

What's a scientist who studies birds called?

Answer

Ornithologist

 *Discovery Zone*

Take part in the "Great Backyard Bird Count," where your input matters. Go to www.birdsource.org for more information.

LESSON 12

Bird Diets

TEACHING TIME:
Eating Like a Bird

The Bible uses many kinds of birds to teach us things about ourselves.

"But those who wait on the Lord
Shall renew their strength;
They shall mount up with
wings like eagles,
They shall run and not be weary,
They shall walk and not faint."
(Isaiah 40:31)

Has anyone ever said that you eat like a bird? Did you wonder what they really meant? When people use that phrase, they usually mean that someone does not eat very much. In truth, eating like a bird would depend on the type of bird. Just as bird feathers, wing design, and size vary from bird to bird, so does diet.

Birdseed and a Lot More!

Have you ever fed birds from your yard? Did you put out birdseed? If you did, you may have noticed that birds such as robins, blue jays, and mockingbirds turned up. They are songbirds or perching birds, and they eat seeds. These are not the only seed lovers. Certainly, these are some of them, though. (Squirrels are seed lovers, too!) These birds do not eat only seeds, however—insects are also a favorite part of their diet. I'm sure you've also noticed that many of these birds feed worms to their babies. With a diet of seeds, worms, and insects, would you classify them as herbivores, carnivores, or omnivores?

There are many birds that feed primarily on fish. Eagles are one of them. Wading birds, also, are often fish eaters, and it should not surprise you that diving birds, such as pelicans, are, too. Some wading birds also eat frogs and shrimp.

Other Diet Favorites

Birds of prey often eat mice and other rodents. They also eat fish and insects. You can see they are basically carnivores. Most birds of prey hunt during the daylight hours.

Owls differ from other birds of prey in that they are primarily active at night. This is called **nocturnal**. Owls feed on living animals, from insects to rodents. The size of the owl determines the size of prey that can be handled. Bigger owls eat bigger prey. Owls usually eat their food whole. The parts that cannot be digested, like bones and feathers, are formed into a ball called a **pellet**. These pellets are then coughed up, basically. By dissecting a pellet, you can see exactly what the bird ate.

Plants are a favorite of some of the birds that don't fly, such as ostriches and emus. Birds such as pigeons and doves enjoy fruits and seeds. Hummingbirds feed on nectar and insects.

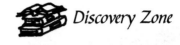

As you can see, eating like a bird can mean many things. Fortunately for the birds, God designed each of them with the bills and claws that they need for finding, catching, and eating food. Birds of prey have their hooked beaks, specially made for tearing meat from bones, while flamingos have a strainer of sorts in their mouths that lets the water out and leaves the food in. Hummingbirds were created with long, narrow bills that can reach deep into flowers for nectar. Flying backward helps them get out again. Having read all of this, I'm sure you'll think twice when someone says that you eat like a bird!

 Discovery Zone

There are 17 species of barn owls world-wide, but only 1 species lives in North America. See if you can learn more about our native barn owl.

HANDS-ON TIME: Dissect an Owl Pellet

Objective: To learn more about owl diets and digestion.

(First to third graders may have difficulty with this experiment, therefore an alternate activity is provided for them below.)

Note: Owl pellets can be ordered from many different companies. I ordered mine from www.sciencestuff.com.

Materials

- Owl pellet
- Old newspapers
- Small jar
- Dishwashing liquid (hand, not dishwasher)
- Strainer, coffee filter, or paper towels
- Dissection kit or tweezers and toothpicks
- Black paper, poster board (if desired)
- Camera!

Method

1. Read the booklet that accompanies your owl pellet.

2. Gather all necessary materials and prepare your work area. Cover your work surface with newspapers before beginning

3. Fill a small jar with water and add a few drops of hand dishwashing liquid. Soaking your pellet is not necessary, but it does make the dissection easier.

4. Add your pellet to the jar, gently shaking it. This will help break your pellet apart.

5. Using a strainer lined with a coffee filter or a couple of paper towels, carefully pour the contents of your jar into the sink or yard. BEWARE: You will basically have a lot of wet animal fur or bird feathers. Be prepared!

6. Use tools found in a dissection kit or a tweezers and toothpicks to carefully sort out the contents of the pellet.

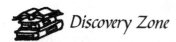 *Discovery Zone*

The study done of one barn owl revealed over the course of a year the following diet:

1,407 mice
143 rats
7 bats
5 young rabbits
375 house sparrows
23 starlings
54 other birds
4 lizards
174 frogs
25 moths
52 crickets

7. Sort all the bones onto a piece of black paper and discard the fur.

8. According to your booklet, try to determine what your animal remains are. You can then glue your bones down on paper or poster board.

9. Don't forget to take pictures!

Evaluation

1. What is the purpose of this experiment?

_____

_____

2. What size owl pellet did you receive?
   Small   Medium   Large

3. Explain below what you knew about owl pellets before the dissection, especially about what they are and how they are formed.

_____

_____

_____

4. What do these pellets contain? _____

_____

5. When removed from its packaging, the pellet looked:

   (Circle your answers.)

Color	Red	Brown	Black
Shape	Flat	Round	Oval
Texture	Smooth	Rough	

6. Did you soak the pellet?

   YES   NO

7. If so, describe your reaction when you strained it.

_____

_____

_____

_____

8. What did your pellet contain?

    (Check all that apply.)

    ❑ Grass

    ❑ Straw

    ❑ Bones

    ❑ Animal Skull

    ❑ Fur

    ❑ Feathers

    ❑ Animal Tail

    ❑ Claws

    ❑ Nails

    ❑ Dirt

    ❑ Other

    _____

9. How many bones did your pellet contain?

    ❑ Zero

    ❑ 1–10

    ❑ 11–20

    ❑ 21–50

    ❑ More than 50

10. What type of animal did your pellet appear to contain?

    ❑ Vole/mouse

    ❑ Bird

    ❑ Shrew

11. I enjoyed/did not enjoy this experiment. In my opinion,
    this experiment was successful/unsuccessful because

    _____

    _____

    _____

    _____

 *Discovery Zone*

Bird Bath

Birds love baths! Place a shallow pan (an old pie plate or garbage can lid) under a low tree branch. Hang a garden hose over the branch and turn it on so that a trickle of water makes a little splash in the pan. You'll have lots of visitors for a bath!

GRADES 1–3 OPTION: Feed-the-Birds Activity

Materials

- Pinecone (or several, if you wish)
- Peanut butter
- Birdseed
- String or yarn

Instructions

1. Tie a piece of yarn around the pinecone. Leave a long tail extending.
2. Spread peanut butter all over the pinecone, heavily.
3. Roll the pinecone in birdseed, getting as much birdseed as you can on it.
4. Hang the pinecone from a bush or tree. Try to hang it where it will be somewhat protected from the rain (or snow).
5. Observe what happens over the next few days. Do birds begin to come to it? Do they eat from it? How long does it take for the birdseed and peanut butter to disappear? How much food is still on the pinecone each day?

Evaluation

1. In your science notebook, write "Day 1," "Day 2," and so on. Record what you see each day, especially if you actually see birds eating from your pinecone.
2. Fill out a "Checking It Out" form. Put the form in your science notebook.

LESSON 13

Bird Structure

TEACHING TIME:
Bird Bones and More

Birds are fascinating creatures. They range in size from 7/100 of an ounce, as in the case of certain hummingbirds, up to 275 pounds for the larger ostriches. Most birds can fly and, as you have already learned, some can dive into water. Some can even glide in the air for hours at a time. There are more than 8,500 species of birds.

Specialized Equipment

God made sure when he created birds that they had all the equipment they would need. One special piece of equipment He gave birds is hollow bones. All their bones are not hollow, but many are. Can you think of a reason birds would need hollow bones? Well, the biggest reason is that these hollow bones help them stay light enough to fly. Even though hollow bones are beneficial, they could make the skeleton weak and too easily broken. For added strength, God designed birds with tiny, crisscrossing, tube-like structures throughout their skeleton. These "tubes" add great support to the skeletal system. As a result, a bird's frame is both lightweight and very sturdy.

Also in the area of flight, God designed birds with a variety of feather types. The differing shapes of the feathers, as well as of the wings, are very important for flight. Some birds even have silent wings. By that, I mean that when these birds flap their wings, virtually no sound is heard. What kinds of birds would need silent wings? Predatory birds, of course, would need this feature because it allows them to swoop in on their prey and catch it unaware. Noisy wings would not help an owl catch a mouse, would they?

Different types of birds have different numbers of toes. Did you know that? Some birds have two toes, some have three, and some even have four. Before we end our study of birds, we should discuss the primary features of birds. Birds have:

1. Beaks instead of teeth

2. Hooked beaks, in the case of birds of prey

3. Keen eyesight (which means very good eyesight)

4. Slender, light legs and feet

5. **Cambered**, or curved, wings for lift

Have you ever dreamed of flying? The psalmist wished he could at a time when many were against him.

"So I said, 'Oh, that I had wings like a dove! I would fly away and be at rest.' " (Psalm 55:6)

 *Discovery Zone*

1. What's the largest flightless bird?
2. What's the fastest flying bird?

Answers

1. Ostrich. 2. Spine-tailed swift

Birds and Airplanes

Do you know that birds and airplanes can be similar in design? The largest airplane in America's fleet is the C-5. It weighs 769,000 pounds when it is full of cargo and fuel. Do you remember the little crisscrossing bones we discussed? Well, the C-5 has a similar feature. Like birds, the C-5 uses smaller pieces inside the wing to strengthen it. Airplanes also have cambered, or curved, wings like birds. The camber causes the air to move across the wing in such a way that there is a pressure change. This change in air pressure creates lift. While modern science has enhanced flight in unbelievable ways, the basics are still very similar to God's original designs.

Birds and the Bible

The Bible refers to birds many times. God even uses birds to encourage us about His love for us. Jesus tells us that we don't have to worry about what we will eat, drink, or wear. He then gives an example saying, "Look at the birds of the air, for they neither sow nor reap nor gather into barns; yet your heavenly Father feeds them. Are you not of more value than they?" (Matthew 6:26) This reminds us that God takes care of the birds and He will also take care of us.

ONE STEP FURTHER

There is much more to learn about all that airplanes and birds have in common. If you are interested in knowing more about this, you should find books on airplanes and books on birds and compare their features.

HANDS-ON TIME: UNIT THREE WRAP-UP

Show What You Know!

Answer as many questions as you can without using your book or notes. You get **10,000** points for each correct response. After going through the review once with your book closed, open your book and try again. You get **5,000** points for each additional correct answer. So, **show what you know!**

1. How many different species of birds are there? Circle the correct group.

    - 1–100
    - 100–1,000
    - 5,000–10,000

2. Unscramble this word to name the curve of a bird's wing: R M C A E B

   _____

3. Are birds warm-blooded or cold-blooded? (Circle the correct answer.)

4. List as many categories of birds as you can.

   _____

   _____

   _____

   _____

5. What is the only type of bird that can fly backward? _____

6. Please describe what a bird pellet is.

   _____

   _____

7. What special features do birds of prey have that help them catch and eat their prey?

   _____

   _____

   _____

   _____

8. Birds are classified in:

    • Kingdom _____

    • Phylum _____

    • Class _____

9. Name at least three traits required for Class Aves.

    _____

    _____

    _____

    _____

FIRST ATTEMPT

_____
(number of correct responses x 10,000)

SECOND ATTEMPT   +

_____
(number of correct responses x 5,000)

TOTAL NUMBER OF POINTS _____

WRITING ASSIGNMENT

In your science notebook, complete the creative writing assignment below. Have fun with it!

Happy birthday to you! You just successfully pecked and poked your way out of that pesky egg. Creatively describe one year of your life as a migratory bird. Include details about the terrain you fly over, the food you eat, the predators you escape from, and so forth.

UNIT FOUR

Mammals in the Wild

UNIT FOUR VOCABULARY

- aquatic mammals
- baleen whales
- bears
- bipedal
- canids
- Class Mammalia
- duck-billed platypus
- felines
- marsupials
- monotremes
- nocturnal
- non-placental
- opposable thumbs
- placenta
- placental
- primates
- toothed whales
- uterus

MATERIALS NEEDED FOR THIS UNIT

- Science notebook
- Atlas or globe
- Encyclopedia
- Copy of world map from Appendix A
- Crayons or colored pencils
- Twine or chalk
- Boxed cake mix
- Licorice
- Variety of cookies (vanilla and chocolate)
- Jelly beans, small candies
- Cake-decorating icing, in tubes
- Frosting (vanilla and chocolate)

Mammals Coloring Page

LESSON 14

INTRODUCTION

TEACHING TIME:
A Hairy Story

We have been very busy this year studying all types of animals, along with learning about plants and cells. I hope you are having fun and learning many facts, too. Today we begin our study of one of the smallest but most popular classes of animals. We are going to explore **Class Mammalia**, or mammals, as most of us refer to them. Class Mammalia is still in Kingdom Animalia, Phylum Chordata.

Mammals include many different types of animals. Some live on the land, some in the water, and some inhabit the skies. With all these different types of habitats, you may be wondering what in the world all these mammals have in common. Let's find out.

First, and foremost, all mammals have hair. Some have thicker types of hair that we call fur, and others have hair that is hardly noticeable at all, but all mammals have it somewhere. (Now you know why I called this "A Hairy Story.") Second, all mammals feed milk to their young. God designed female mammals with an ability to produce milk for their babies. This is good because He also created baby mammals to need milk! Third, all mammals are warm-blooded. Do you remember what that means? It means that their bodies maintain a constant temperature, unless something is wrong. Can you name some animals that have these traits? In your science notebook, make a list of as many mammals as you can.

Humans are mammals, too! God cares so much about you that He knows the number of hairs on your head.

Jesus says in Matthew 10:30, "But the very hairs of your head are all numbered."

Two Major Categories

There are two major categories of mammals. They are called **placental** and **non-placental.** That probably doesn't help you too much, so let's figure out what a **placenta** is. A placenta is something that develops in the area of a female's body where babies grow. Its function is to nourish the growing baby until it is time for the baby to be born. Most mammals are placental mammals. Their babies grow inside a **uterus** in the female's body and are fed by the placenta until they are born. Placental mammals give birth to live, fully developed babies. Non-placental mammals, as you might figure, do not have placentas. They do not deliver fully developed young. We will learn more about non-placental mammals in another lesson.

 *Discovery Zone*

1. What's the heaviest land animal?

2. What's the fastest land animal?

Answers

1. The African elephant weighs a whopping 14,432 pounds! (An American bison weighs a mere 2,205 pounds.)

2. A cheetah zips along at 70 miles per hour while a squirrel can only manage 12 miles per hour.

Here's a note about mammal classification. There are 15 orders of mammals. Out of these 15, only 2 are non-placental. They are the monotremes and marsupials. You will study these in your next lesson. The other 13 are all placental mammals.

REVIEW IT!

1.   Name the three major points for distinguishing mammals from other animals. (Remember, these are the major traits. There are others.)

_____

_____

_____

2. What are the two types of non-placental mammals?

_____

_____

3. What is the main job of a placenta?

_____

_____

_____

HANDS-ON TIME: Research a Mammal

Objective: To learn more about a specific type of mammal.

Discover!

Today your job is to research a mammal. The choice of which mammal to research is up to you.

First of all, you will need to find some reading material on this mammal. Encyclopedias, the Internet, and books from the library are all good possibilities. After you read about this mammal, you are to write a report in your science notebook. Your report could include the following information:

1. The name of your mammal (both the common name and the scientific name)

2. The type of mammal it is (marsupial? monotreme? feline?)

3. Where your mammal is found in the world

4. The term for its offspring (cub? kitten? puppy?)

5. Its feeding habits

6. Its full-grown size

7. A drawing of your mammal

8. Whether or not this mammal would make a good pet

I'm sure you'll have many other ideas of things to include in your report. Hopefully, these suggestions will get you started.

 *Discovery Zone*

Some of the most common names of our pets:

Female Dogs

Princess
Lady
Sandy
Sheba
Ginger

Male Dogs

Max
Rock
Lucky
Duke
King

Female Cats

Samantha
Misty
Patches
Calico
Muffin

Male Cats

Tiger/Tigger
Smokey
Pepper
Max
Simon

LESSON 15

MONOTREMES AND MARSUPIALS

TEACHING TIME:
Pocket Pals

Were monotremes and marsupials on the ark?

"You shall take with you seven each of every clean animal, a male and his female; two each of animals that are unclean, a male and his female."
(Genesis 7:2)

Do you remember what you learned about monotremes and marsupials in our last lesson? You learned that they are the only two orders of non-placental mammals. You also learned that they do not give birth to fully developed young. I promised you would learn more about that, and today is the day.

Would you believe me if I told you that some mammals lay eggs? That might surprise you, but it is true. Often, books say that mammals give birth to live young. The truth is some mammals do, but some don't. Some actually lay eggs. These are the **monotremes**. Now remember, monotreme is an *order* of mammals, *not* a specific animal. The most famous monotreme is the **duck-billed platypus**. This creature is probably the most unusual in all of God's creation. It has a bill like a duck, fur like a beaver, webbed feet, and it lays eggs! It looks even stranger than it sounds. This animal is found in Australia, New Guinea, and Tasmania. Another type of monotreme is the spiny anteater. It is also called an echidna. The spiny anteater is an egg-laying, insect-eating mammal.

Both the platypus and the spiny anteater cause the evolutionists difficulty. They are such odd combinations of animals that evolutionists cannot determine how they evolved or from what! God is so creative!

The other type of non-placental mammal is a **marsupial.** Marsupials nourish their young in the uterus for a few weeks from an egg yolk. After this stage, the underdeveloped baby is born. It is far from ready to survive apart from the mother, so God designed the mother with a pouch to carry this new creature. The baby attaches itself to the mother where it is constantly nourished by her milk. Eventually, it is developed enough to leave the pouch. Kangaroos, koalas, and opossums are three types of marsupials. Most marsupials are **nocturnal**, meaning they are primarily active at night.

HANDS-ON TIME: Mapping Marsupials and More

Objective: To locate the native homes of marsupials and monotremes.

Materials

- Atlas or globe
- Encyclopedia
- Copy of world map from Appendix A
- Crayons or colored pencils

Instructions

We learned today that the duck-billed platypus is found in Australia, Tasmania, and New Guinea.

1. Using the world map in Appendix A and a globe or atlas, find these three locations.
2. Put a "P" on each of these areas.
3. Next, find out in which part(s) of the world kangaroos live and put a "K" on this/these location(s).
4. Now, find out where opossums live.
5. Put an "O" on this/these area(s).
6. Last, you can do this with any other marsupials you come across in additional reading.
7. Be sure to make a map key which shows what each letter stands for.
8. Label your map "Non-Placental Mammals."

GRADES 1–3 OPTION: Discover the Land of Marsupials

1. Find out where Australia is on a map or globe.
2. Discover what other types of animals live there. Point out any that are marsupials or monotremes.
3. Using the world map in Appendix A, color in Australia.

LESSON 16

CANIDS, FELINES, AND BEARS

TEACHING TIME:
Lions, Tigers, and Bears, Oh My!

Exploring God's Word

The Bible tells of David's encounters with both lions and bears.

See 1 Samuel 17:34-37.

Let's talk today about the largest and fiercest group of mammals. They are found in Order Carnivora. From this name, can you figure out what the main item is on their menus? Did you say meat? In case you didn't, let me remind you that carnivores are meat eaters. We learned this in our first unit.

Order Carnivora includes animals such as lions and tigers, but that is not all. This order is also made up of **canids**, such as dogs and wolves; **felines**, such as cats, tigers, and lions; and **bears**.

Canids

First of all, let's look at the canid family. You know that dogs and wolves are part of this family. What other animals would belong in this family? Foxes, coyotes, and jackals are also canids. These animals usually have thick fur and bushy tails. Like all carnivores, they have sharp teeth for tearing apart their prey. These animals often live in packs and hunt together.

Felines

Members of the cat family are also known as felines. They range in size from small housecats up to very large lions. Cats are especially known for their claws. They are very sharp and can usually be retracted, or drawn away, into the feet. Cheetahs, however, do not have retractable claws. Other members of this family are leopards, jaguars, and ocelots (**oss** eh lots). Some type of cat is found on nearly every continent.

Bears

Last, let's take a brief look at bears. Bears have heavy, round bodies, claws on their feet, and round heads with round ears. They are classified as carnivores but are really omnivorous. You remember, I'm sure, that omnivores eat both plants and meat. Do you think bears would be at the bottom or top of a food chain? Even though we haven't talked about food chains in a long time, you probably recognize that bears would be at

the top. Bears are very large and strong. Not many animals could overpower them. However, one of their favorite meals is caught not because bears are so big but rather because they have claws. These claws help them catch fish. Bears are able to sweep their paws through streams and catch fish quite easily. Another favorite food of many bears is berries. Bears live on all continents except Australia, Antarctica and Africa.

 REVIEW IT!

1. What is the name of the order with lions, tigers, and bears? _____

_____

2. Name at least three members of the dog family.

_____

_____

_____

3. Name at least three members of the cat family.

_____

_____

_____

4. What can most cats do with their claws?

_____

_____

5. Do you think these animals are warm-blooded or cold-blooded? Why? _____

_____

_____

_____

_____

 *Discovery Zone*

Animal Collective Names

> *Leap of leopards*
> *Pride of lions*
> *Sloth of bears*
> *Troop of kangaroos*
> *. . . for more names, see Appendix B*

 *Discovery Zone*

Tigers are the world's largest cats. They weigh over 600 pounds and can grow up to 11 feet (head to tail) long! Their life span ranges from 12 to 20 years.

HANDS-ON TIME: Decorate Carnivora Cupcakes

Objective: To review the differences between canids, felines, and bears, and to make a tasty treat!

Materials

- Boxed cake mix
- Licorice
- Variety of cookies (vanilla and chocolate)
- Jelly beans and other small candies, as desired
- Cake-decorating icing, in tubes
- Frosting (vanilla and chocolate)

Instructions

1. Bake cupcakes according to package directions.
2. Frost with your choice of vanilla or chocolate frosting, depending on the color of your "animal's" fur.
3. Using the assorted toppings, decorate your cupcakes to resemble dogs, cats, and bears. For example: for a panda bear use white frosting, chocolate-sandwich cookies for ears, a black jelly bean for a nose, black frosting for circles around eyes, and white jelly beans for eyes.
4. Have lots of fun and remember all the things you learned this week!

Discovery Zone

For animal facts A-Z, visit the Oregon Zoo online: www.zooregon.org. Click on kidszone and then on Animal Facts.

LESSON 17

MONKEYS AND APES

TEACHING TIME:
Monkeying Around

Have you ever wondered what the difference is between monkeys and apes? Did you even know there is a difference? Many people think they are the same thing, but they are not. Did you know that humans are in the same order as these animals? If you didn't know these things, then you have something to learn today. Let's get started.

As we begin, let's review a little first. We are studying mammals. You know from all of your hard work that mammals are a class. When we first began this unit, we learned about two orders of mammals that are different from all the others. These are the non-placental animals, which are monotremes and marsupials. Next, we learned about the Order Carnivoras, like dogs, cats, and bears. These are mostly meat eating, and often, large animals with sharp teeth. You will also recall that all mammals are warm-blooded and produce milk for their young.

Similarities and Differences

Now we are ready to move on to the order called **primates**. Monkeys, apes, and humans are all in Order Primates. What would make an animal qualify for this category? First of all, primates are **bipedal**. That's a big word; what does it mean? Well, *bi* means two and *pedal* refers to feet. In other words, primates can walk on two feet. Most primates, however, also use their arms to help them get around, making humans the only *truly* bipedal primates. Primates are very social animals. There are some exceptions, but for the most part they live in large societies. Primates are able to see in a way that other mammals cannot. They can perceive depth, which is the difference between looking at a picture (two-dimensional) and looking at something in real life (three-dimensional). The major feature of most primates is something called **opposable thumbs**. This feature means that one of the fingers (the thumb) can meet with each of the other fingers to form a circle. (Try it out!) This is special to primates. It enables us to pick things up and handle them in ways other animals cannot.

Now that you know these similarities, let's find out about some differences. Many people mistake monkeys and apes, thinking they are the same thing, but you know they are not.

What mammals were among the treasures brought in by King Solomon's ships?

"For the king had merchant ships at sea with the fleet of Hiram. Once every three years the merchant ships came bringing gold, silver, ivory, apes, and monkeys." (1 Kings 10:22)

79

The easiest way to know a monkey from an ape is that a monkey has a tail and an ape does not. Another difference is that apes are usually larger than monkeys. Last, but not least, an ape's arms are usually longer than its legs; this is not true of monkeys.

Based on the above information, can you tell whether each of the following animals is an ape or a monkey? (If you cannot, find a picture of each in a book or using the computer.)

- Gorilla   ape or monkey?

- Chimpanzee   ape or monkey?

Hopefully, you were able to determine that each of these animals is an ape, not a monkey. Next time you go to the zoo, see if you can correctly identify the apes and the monkeys!

Humans Are Special

I told you before that humans are also primates. Please do not think that makes us like apes and monkeys. We have some things in common, but we also have many differences. Just by looking at humans and other primates, you can see differences. God created us with special features that separate us from the other primates. In your next unit, you will learn much more about humans.

More Collective Animal Names

Band of gorillas
Troop of monkeys

Discovery Zone

The koala's name comes from an aboriginal word meaning "no drink" because the koala rarely drinks, obtaining most of its moisture from food.

HANDS-ON TIME: Research Detective

Objective: To put your knowledge of classification and research to use and to experience life without opposable thumbs.

Your Research Assignments

1. Your first assignment is to complete the classification of monkeys and apes from Kingdom down through Order. You have been given a list of the classification names, but you must find out which is the Kingdom, which is the Order, and everything in between. In addition, not all the divisions are listed and you must find out what they are. Here is what you have:

Divisions	Classification Names
Kingdom	Primates
_ _ _ _ _ _	Animalia
_ _ _ _ _ _	Mammalia
Order	Chordata

80

In your science notebook, write the list of the divisions, in order from largest to smallest, filling in the blanks. (Hint: King Phillip . . .) Using the list provided, write the proper classification name beside the division name.

Example: Kingdom—Animalia

2. The remaining task you have as a researcher is to figure out why opposable thumbs are so important. You decide the best way to conduct this research by personal experience, or you can try the following activities.

   a. Tape your thumbs up against your remaining fingers. Your fingers should be free to move around, but not your thumbs.

   b. Try doing ordinary tasks like writing. True, monkeys and apes don't need to write, but humans do, so you can experience the difference thumbs make. Throughout your experiment (which should last as long as your teacher deems necessary), try picking up different items. If you have a tree that you climb, try to pull up on a low branch.

   c. Try to eat your meal without your thumbs. Your research would benefit greatly by trying to peel a banana and an orange without using your thumbs. (You might want to use a plastic cup with a lid for your beverage!)

   d. Last, as any good researcher should, record your findings. Create a chart showing the things you attempted to do without using thumbs. You should note whether each task was simple or difficult, and you should record any difficulty you encountered.

   e. It is time for you to draw a conclusion from your research. Do you think opposable thumbs make a difference in the lives of monkeys, apes, and primates like you? Why or why not?

   f. Complete a "Checking It Out" form (found in Appendix A) and add this form, plus your conclusions, to your science notebook.

 *Discovery Zone*

What sounds do different primates make? Check out a chimpanzee scream and a gorilla belch at www.indiana.edu/ ~primate/primates.html.

LESSON 18

AQUATIC MAMMALS

TEACHING TIME:
Splish, Splash

Did God create whales and porpoises, or did they evolve slowly over time?

"So God created great sea creatures and every living thing that moves, with which the waters abounded . . . "
(Genesis 1:21)

We have learned much about mammals so far. We have learned that they have hair, feed milk to their young, and usually have a placenta. In most cases they give birth to live creatures, although some lay eggs. There are many different types of mammals including lions, tigers, monkeys, gorillas, and even the duck-billed platypus. Even with all these varieties, there is a type of mammal we have not yet covered. These are the **aquatic mammals**, or water mammals. Perhaps you're wondering what kind of mammal lives in the water. Let's find out.

The types of animals I'm talking about live in the oceans. They are often mistakenly called fish. They are not fish, however. To begin with, they do not lay eggs as fish do. They actually give birth to live animals. Second, the mothers feed their babies milk that their bodies produce. They even have hair, though you may never see it. Last, fish get their oxygen from the water through gills. These creatures actually have lungs and must come to the surface for air. What are these animals? They are whales, porpoises, and dolphins. Are you surprised? Did you think these animals were fish? Now you know—they're mammals.

Whales

First of all, let's look at whales. Their incredible size alone makes them interesting. Whales are the largest creatures on

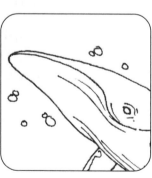

earth. The smallest whales are about 7 feet long, but the largest are almost 100 feet long. Although there are several different species of whales, there are two main types. These are **toothed whales** and **baleen whales.** Toothed whales, as you might guess, have actual teeth and are able to eat large fish. Baleen whales, on the other hand, have whalebone plates instead of teeth. They open their mouths and take in large amounts of water, fish, and tiny organisms. Next, they close their mouths and the water strains out, leaving the food behind. So, you see, just because whales are very large doesn't necessarily mean they eat large animals.

Porpoises and Dolphins

Porpoises and dolphins are two aquatic mammals that people often confuse. Dolphins can be recognized most easily by their long, sleek bodies and pointed beaks. Porpoises, on the other hand, have beaks that are more rounded, and their bodies tend to be a little more rounded as well. Marine biologists can get close enough to see another type of difference . . . their teeth. Dolphins and porpoises do not have the same types of teeth. God created these animals with differences even though, to most of us, they look the same.

Aquatic mammals are so cool! They fascinate people all over the world. In many coastal areas, people pay money to go out on boats just to look at whales, dolphins, and porpoises. And to think, they are mammals!

Discover!

- Learn more about an aquatic animal of your choice. Read books about this animal and fill out a "Daily Reading Sheet" (found in Appendix A) for each. Keep these in your science notebook.

- What's the largest species of whale? Find out.

- After reading about its size, measure out its dimensions in your yard or a parking lot, using twine or chalk to mark its head and its tail.

 *Discovery Zone*

Have you ever seen dolphin on a menu in a restaurant? Don't worry—that kind of dolphin (often called mahi-mahi) is actually a type of fish, not the mammal dolphin.

 *Discovery Zone*

Did you know that dolphins have no sense of smell but do have the best hearing of any animal?

HANDS-ON TIME: UNIT FOUR WRAP-UP

Show What You Know!

Answer as many questions as you can without using your book or notes. You get **10,000** points for each correct response. After going through the review once with your book closed, open your book and try again. You get **5,000** points for each additional correct answer. So, **show what you know!**

1. Name three traits that are common to mammals.

2. Name the two orders of mammals that are non-placental.

3. Where do the babies of placental mammals grow before they are born?

4. What is the main job of the placenta?

5. List a type of monotreme.

6. Is a kangaroo a marsupial or a monotreme?

7. Where do marsupials continue to develop after they are born?

8. Name the order that contains lions and tigers and bears.

9. Are animals in this order primarily meat eaters or plant eaters?

10. Name some animals that are felines.

11. What special features do bears have to help them catch fish?

12. Define *bipedal.*

13. To which order do monkeys and apes both belong? _____

14. Do you think opposable thumbs are important? Why or why not? _____

_____

_____

_____

15. What kind of whale strains its food through its teeth, enabling it to live on very small types of food?

_____

16. Are dolphins mammals or fish? _____

FIRST ATTEMPT _____

(number of correct responses x 10,000)

SECOND ATTEMPT + _____

(number of correct responses x 5,000)

TOTAL NUMBER OF POINTS _____

 ## WRITING ASSIGNMENT

In your science notebook, complete the creative writing assignment below. Have fun with it!

You are the host for the game show, "Name That Mammal." Make a set of clue cards for a series of mammals of your choice. Each card should include three clues on one side and the mammal's name on the other. Try to have a few from each category of mammals you studied, and try to choose clues that narrow the choices without giving too much away. You may devise your own rules if you wish. Otherwise, just gather a group of friends or family members together, give them each several turns, and see who has the most points at the end.

Award 15 points if someone guesses the correct answer after one clue, 10 points after two clues, 5 points after all three, and 0 points if the guesser misses completely.

UNIT FIVE

THE HUMAN FACTOR

UNIT FIVE VOCABULARY

- arteries
- auditory nerve
- belly button
- bitter, salty, sour, sweet
- capillaries
- cardiac muscle
- circulatory system
- cochlea
- cornea
- eardrum
- epidermis
- five senses
- fraternal twins
- Homo sapiens
- identical twins
- inner ear
- integumentary system
- involuntary muscles
- iris
- joints
- lens
- lungs
- middle ear
- muscular system
- nerve endings
- olfactory receptors
- optic nerve
- outer ear
- ova
- placenta
- reproduction
- respiratory system
- retina
- skeletal muscles
- skeletal system
- skull
- smooth muscles
- sperm
- taste buds
- umbilical cord
- uterus
- veins
- vessels
- voluntary muscles
- womb

MATERIALS NEEDED FOR THIS UNIT

- Science notebook
- Notebook paper and sketchbook, if desired
- Potato slices
- Apple slices
- Salt
- Sugar
- Lemon slices
- Orange slices
- Vanilla extract
- Almond extract
- Canned tuna
- Canned chicken
- Vinegar
- Water
- Flour
- Powdered sugar
- Blindfold

88

LESSON 19

INTRODUCTION

TEACHING TIME:
Created in Love

Today we are going to begin a study God's most important creation . . . mankind. We'll look at what the *Bible* says, and then we'll look at the body and some of its special components.

As we begin our study about humans, or mankind, let's find out what the *Bible* says about you. The Bible tells us in Psalm 139 that you were "fearfully and wonderfully" made (Psalm 139:14). In Genesis, we learn that "God created man in His own image; in the image of God He created him; male and female He created them" (Genesis 1:27). This is terrific news! So many of us do not like the way we look. We may think we are too tall, too short, too skinny, or too fat. Sometimes we look in the mirror and wish our hair was red or blonde. Apparently some teenagers think they would look better with blue hair! Well, if you have ever been unhappy with how you look, let me reassure you. You are "fearfully and wonderfully" made. God planned it all out before you were even born. Relax, God is not shocked by your looks.

While scientists classify humans as animals, we are not the same as all other animals. We are unique. First of all, humans can think and reason. Animals can only respond by instinct. Another way humans are different from animals is that humans have emotions. Emotions are feelings such as love, sadness, and anger. Animals do not feel these emotions like we do. Humans also have the ability to love God. Not only can humans love God, they also can sin against God. Sin means we didn't live up to God's standard. God knows that we sin, and He provided a way for us to be forgiven through Jesus. You can learn more about this by reading your Bible. God loves all humans in a very special way.

"So God created man in His own image; in the image of God He created him; male and female He created them." (Genesis 1:27)

Think About It!

Let's think about ways in which humans are different from animals.

1. **First of all, we'll look at eating habits.**

    • What kinds of foods do animals eat?

    _____

    _____

- Where do animals get their food?

  _____

  _____

- Do animals cook their food?

  _____

- Can animals make a recipe?

  _____

 *Discovery Zone*

Do you know that it takes 17 muscles to smile?

2. **What about humans? You're a human, so I'll ask about you!**

   - What kinds of foods do you eat?

     _____

     _____

   - Where do you get your food?

     _____

     _____

   - Do you eat cooked or raw food?

     _____

   - Can you make a recipe?

     _____

3. **All right, now let's talk about housing.**

   - Name some of the different types of homes that animals have.

     _____

     _____

     _____

     _____

     _____

• Now list some of the types of homes that people live in.

_____

_____

_____

• Do you notice any differences? If so, what kind?

_____

_____

_____

There are many other differences between humans and animals. Hopefully, you can see that you are a very special part of God's creation and all human life is important to God. In the next section of this lesson, you will get to look at the Bible and find out more about how much God loves you and how He created you!

 ## HANDS-ON TIME: Mini Bible Study

Objective: To explore God's Word, the Bible, and find out about how He created humans (or mankind).

Note to Parents

1. I recommend that you sit down with your children and read the Scriptures listed below. Then, using the format shown, help them make a list (on a separate piece of paper or in their science notebooks), verse by verse, of everything they learn about God. Please try to keep the wording as close to Scripture as possible and list each fact separately. The first verses have been completed as examples.

2. Next, go through the Scriptures given and help them make a similar list of all they learn about man, again keeping the wording as close to Scripture as possible.

3. Discuss your findings. Help your children, even the very young, to see that God is in control of life and that we are all created with love. This is a wonderful time to teach how well God knows us, even our thoughts.

 *Discovery Zone*

Note to Teacher: This type of Bible study is known as inductive. Precept Ministries, among others, produces many inductive studies for all ages.

Exploring the Bible

WHAT I LEARN ABOUT GOD

God . . .

✝ Genesis 1:1   *was in the beginning.*
                       created the heavens and the earth.

✝ Genesis 1:26   _____

✝ Genesis 1:27   _____

✝ Genesis 1:28   _____

✝ Genesis 1:29   _____

✝ Genesis 1:30   _____

✝ Genesis 1:31   _____

✝ Genesis 2:7   _____

✝ Genesis 2:18   _____

✝ Genesis 2:21   _____

✝ Genesis 2:22   _____

✝ Psalm 139:1   _____

✝ Psalm 139:2   _____

✝ Psalm 139:3   _____

✝ Psalm 139:4   _____

✝ Psalm 139:5   _____

✝ Psalm 139:8   _____

✝ Psalm 139:9   _____

✝ Psalm 139:10   _____

✝ Psalm 139:13   _____

✝ Psalm 139:14   _____

WHAT I LEARN ABOUT MAN

Man . . .

✝ Genesis 1:27   *was created in the image of God.*
                                      was created male and female.

✝ Genesis 2:18   _____

✝ Genesis 2:20   _____

✝ Psalm 139:6   _____

✝ Psalm 139:7   _____

✝ Psalm 139:13   _____

✝ Psalm 139:14   _____

✝ Psalm 139:14   _____

✝ Psalm 139:16   _____

THE HUMAN BODY

TEACHING TIME:
From the Outside In

The first man is created!

"And the Lord God formed man of the dust of the ground, and breathed into his nostrils the breath of life; and man became a living being."
(Genesis 2:7)

Humans are classified as Kingdom Animalia, Phylum Chordata, Class Mammalia. So far, this is the same as all other mammals. Do you remember what traits are common to mammals? See how much you can remember without referring to your notes. Write out a list in your science notebook.

Hopefully, you noted that they have hair or fur, feed milk to their young, and give birth to live babies instead of laying eggs that will hatch later. These are some of the basic traits of all mammals. Let's continue looking at the classification of humans. Humans are of the Order Primates (like apes), Family Hominidae, Genus Homo, Species Sapiens. You may hear humans referred to as **Homo sapiens**, which is a combination of the genus and species. Earlier you learned some very special things that make humans different from other animals. Today we will begin to explore the human body.

Integumentary System

First of all, your body is very complicated. It is designed with many special parts that make it work in the best way possible. Let's start with what you see on the outside. When you look in the mirror, you can see the largest organ of the human body. Do you know what it is? It is your skin! It is also known as the **integumentary system**. Your skin's main job is to protect all the rest of your body. The outermost layer of the skin is called the **epidermis**. This is the part you can see. New cells are constantly replenishing it as older cells die and are shed. The accompanying skin diagram gives you a good look at the skin and its components.

Under your skin are several more systems. Each system has a specific job to do. The systems all work together to make one great body. Let's look at a few of these systems.

Skeletal System

One that you are probably familiar with is your **skeletal system**. Can you guess or do you already know what makes up a skeletal system? If you said bones, you are absolutely correct. Your skeletal system consists of 206 bones. Your major bones are shown in the accompanying human skeleton diagram. Would you believe that your **skull**, or head, has 20 bones? It may be hard to believe, but it is true.

SKIN DIAGRAM

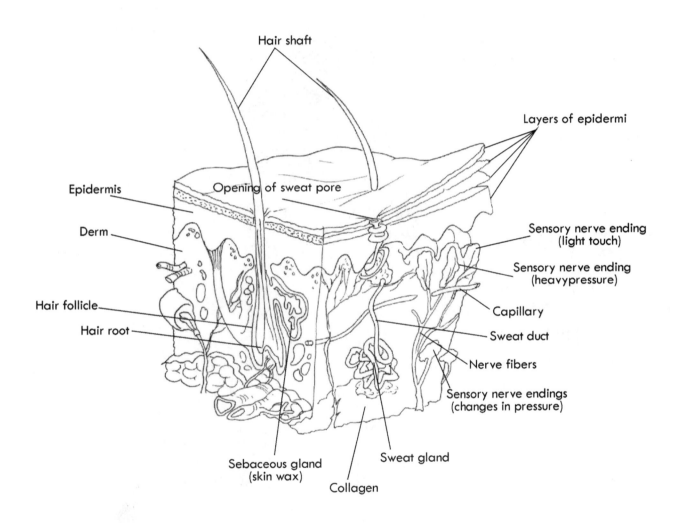

Hair shaft

Layers of epidermi

Epidermis

Opening of sweat pore

Derm

Sensory nerve ending
(light touch)

Sensory nerve ending
(heavypressure)

Capillary

Hair follicle

Sweat duct

Hair root

Nerve fibers

Sensory nerve endings
(changes in pressure)

Sebaceous gland
(skin wax)

Sweat gland

Collagen

SKELETON DIAGRAM

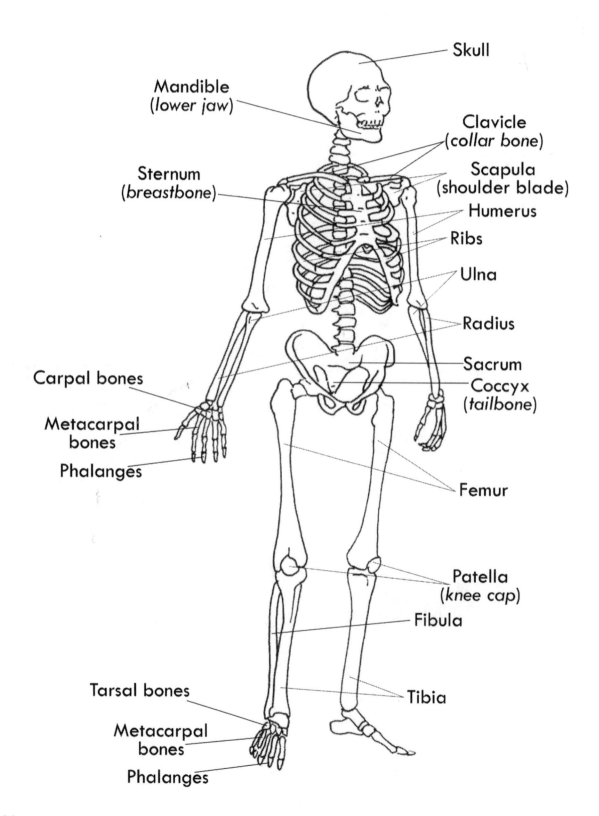

Skull

Mandible
(*lower jaw*)

Clavicle
(*collar bone*)

Scapula
(*shoulder blade*)

Humerus

Sternum
(*breastbone*)

Ribs

Ulna

Radius

Sacrum

Coccyx
(*tailbone*)

Carpal bones

Metacarpal
bones

Phalanges

Femur

Patella
(*knee cap*)

Fibula

Tarsal bones

Tibia

Metacarpal
bones

Phalanges

Joints are the places where bones meet. There are two different types of joints: "ball-and-socket" joints and "finger" (or "hinge") joints. See the diagram of a knee joint on the next page. It is an example of a "finger" (hinge) joint.

Using a science reference book or a computer, look these up and compare the differences. Can you discover which type of joint a hip is? What about an elbow? Look at yourself and find as many joints as you can. Imagine what it would be like to *not* have these joints!

Muscular System

Another major system in our bodies is the **muscular system**. As you can tell by its name, this system is made up of all the muscles in your body. The muscles are necessary for moving the bones. Strong muscles make moving and lifting easier. The best way to strengthen muscles is to use them. There are **voluntary muscles,** which you move whenever you want to, and **involuntary muscles,** which are controlled by the brain, without your thinking about it. Voluntary muscles are also known as **skeletal muscles** because they are attached to your bones. Involuntary muscles are also called the **smooth muscles**. One last type of muscle is the **cardiac muscle**, which is found in your heart.

Circulatory System

When I say "circulatory system," do you have any idea what I am talking about? **Circulatory system** refers to all your blood and to the special "tubes," or **vessels**, that carry that blood around. There are three main types of vessels. First of all, there are **veins**, which carry your blood to your heart. Second, there are **arteries**, which carry your blood away from your heart. Last, there are tiny vessels called **capillaries**. The flow of blood to and away from the heart is illustrated in the accompanying diagram.

There is much more to your circulatory system, including other types of blood vessels. These are just three.

Respiratory System

The **respiratory system** is what makes breathing possible for you. Your **lungs** are the main feature of this system. The lungs draw air in and "blow" it out. You can control your breathing to some degree, but your body regulates this activity for the most part.

These are some of your body's major systems and certainly enough to think about for one day. Other systems include the central nervous system and the digestive system. In the next section of this lesson, you will learn more about one of the systems of your body and how it works.

 *Discovery Zone*

A 154-pound man has about 5½ quarts of blood circulating in his body.

KNEE JOINT (HINGE) DIAGRAM

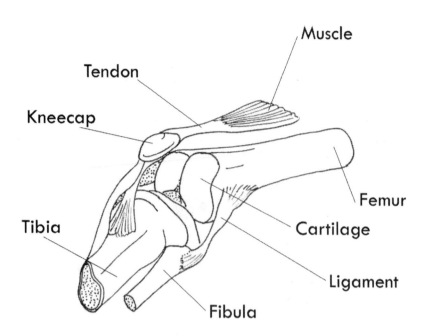

Muscle

Tendon

Kneecap

Femur

Tibia

Cartilage

Ligament

Fibula

HEART DIAGRAM

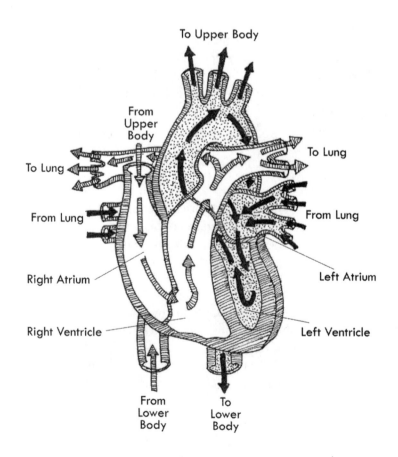

To Upper Body

From Upper Body

To Lung

To Lung

From Lung

From Lung

Right Atrium

Left Atrium

Right Ventricle

Left Ventricle

From Lower Body

To Lower Body

HANDS-ON TIME: Research a System

Objective: To study a system of the human body in greater detail.

In the first section of this lesson, you learned about several important systems at work in your body. Today I want you to learn about one of these systems.

Instructions

1. Using a book from the library or a science encyclopedia, look up one of the systems we discussed in our last lesson.

2. As you read, write down in your science notebook some of the most significant facts you discover about this system.

3. Carefully study any diagrams given. Try to sketch one of them in your science notebook or sketchbook. Remember, sketches are not intended to be perfect.

4. Write a summary paragraph about what you read. Be sure to include the name of the system, the purpose or main function of the system, and the main components of the system. Add a sentence or two that explains the possible consequences of *not* having this system.

5. Title your page "The _____ System of the Human Body."

GRADES 1–3 OPTION: Learn More About Your Body

Note to Parents

Help your child decide which of the systems discussed to study further, then help your child select appropriate reference books for more information.

Student's Instructions

1. Using one or more of the books your parent helped you choose, look up the system you decided to study.

2. There are probably drawings of the system in your book. Look at those drawings and see what you can learn from them.

3. Discuss with your parent what would happen if you didn't have this body system.

4. Have your parent read the information to you from the book.

5. In your science notebook, complete the following sentences. Put a heading at the top of your page called "The _____ System of the Human Body." You may add more sentences if you want to (or if your teacher says to!).

Discovery Zone

In the United States, the most common blood types are O+ (O positive) and A+ (A positive).

• Today I learned about the _____

  system of the human body.

• The main purpose of this system is _____

  _____

  _____

  _____

  _____

  _____

• It is important because _____

  _____

  _____

  _____

  _____

  _____

6. Draw a picture of yourself on the page.

LESSON 21

OUR FIVE SENSES

TEACHING TIME:
Touchy, Touchy

Our last two lessons dealt with some of the systems of the human body. There is so much more to learn than we will discuss here. You can always take the time and study further. Don't worry; you will get many more opportunities in your life to delve deeper into the systems of the body. Today, however, we're going to study the **five senses** of the body. Do you know what I mean by the "five senses"? I am talking about your ability to taste, smell, touch, see, and hear. There are some people who cannot do all of these things. For instance, not everyone can see. The body is designed for sight, however, as well as for the other four senses I mentioned.

Taste

First of all, let's look at the sense of taste. I'm tempted to say it's my favorite of the senses because I love great-tasting things. However, I'm not sure I have a real favorite. I like all of my senses! Your tongue is the organ used for tasting. It is covered with parts called **taste buds** that allow you to know one taste from another. As shown in the tongue diagram, these taste buds are grouped in zones on your tongue. Each zone is responsible for a different taste. The different tastes your tongue can pick up are **bitter**, **salty**, **sour**, and, my favorite, **sweet**.

Smell

Our sense of smell is closely related to our sense of taste. Of course, you already know the organ responsible for smelling. It is your nose. You may be able to think of a time when you had a really stuffy nose. You may have lost your ability to taste. Whether you know it or not, you use your nose to help you taste your food, so when you can't smell, it is hard to taste. Your nose is filled with special receptors called **olfactory receptors**. These are your "smellers," and they override your taste buds. Because of this, cooks often add special "flavors" that smell really good. A good example is vanilla. These smells tell our brain the food tastes yummy. It may sound crazy, but I told you that taste and smell are closely related! Humans can sense over 10,000 smells. I guess that is good news—as long as the smells are good ones!

How many of the five senses can you find in this verse?

"My voice You shall hear in the morning, O Lord;
In the morning I will direct it to You,
And I will look up." (Psalm 5:3)

TONGUE DIAGRAM

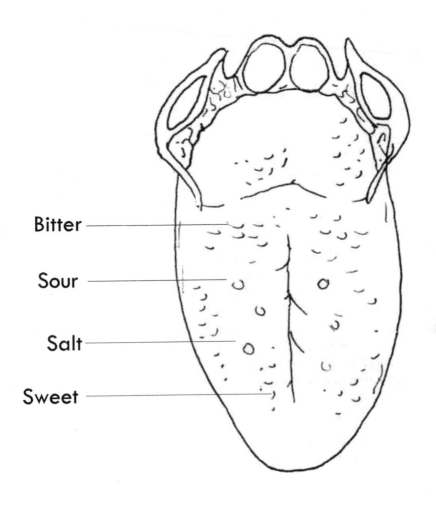

Bitter

Sour

Salt

Sweet

Touch

The sense of touch is another one of our senses. We have already learned some things about our skin, which is the touch organ. Let's learn some more. Your skin is filled with millions of nerve endings. These **nerve endings** tell you if something is hot or cold, smooth or rough. They even let you know when your clothes are too scratchy. The sense of touch is so important, as scientists have discovered, that babies who are not held enough will not thrive, or grow well. Certain parts of your body, like the lips, tongue, and hands, have more nerve endings than others and therefore are much more sensitive. For instance, if you touched a hot pepper to your leg, you might not care at all. However, if you touched it to your lip, you might even want to cry.

Sight

The fourth sense we will explore is sight. Now, I know you can live without being able to see, but it would make life more difficult. As humans, we rely heavily on our ability to see. Our eyes, which are our sight organs, absorb large amounts of information, which are then processed by our brain. The part of the eye called the **retina** contains sensors, which are able to detect light. The **lens** and **cornea** help to focus the light. The **iris** controls the amount of light that enters the eye. The **optic nerve** sends the messages to the brain. (See the eye diagram for a better understanding of the structure of the eye.) Humans, unlike many other animals, are able to see color. I am so glad! That tells me God put all this beautiful color in the world especially for us!

Hearing

Last, let's look at our sense of hearing. This process is really quite amazing. There are three main sections of the ear. They are the **outer ear**, the **middle ear**, and the **inner ear**. When we hear a sound, what we are actually hearing is a series of pulses or vibrations. The ear is designed to receive these vibrations through the opening in your outer ear, pass them through a canal, and then vibrate the **eardrum**, which is between the outer ear and the middle ear. The eardrum then causes three small bones to vibrate, which in turn vibrates a fluid located in the inner ear. The **cochlea**, a small, spiral-shaped part of the inner ear, detects these movements and sends the information to the brain, through the **auditory nerve**, and the brain interprets the sound and "tells" you what you heard. (Study the accompanying ear diagram to get a better idea of how this process works.) Considering how fast this all happens, I'd say it is amazing and is more evidence of a Master Designer!

 *Discovery Zone*

The three bones of the ear are commonly known as the hammer, anvil, and stirrup. These bones are shown in the ear diagram in this chapter.

EYE DIAGRAM

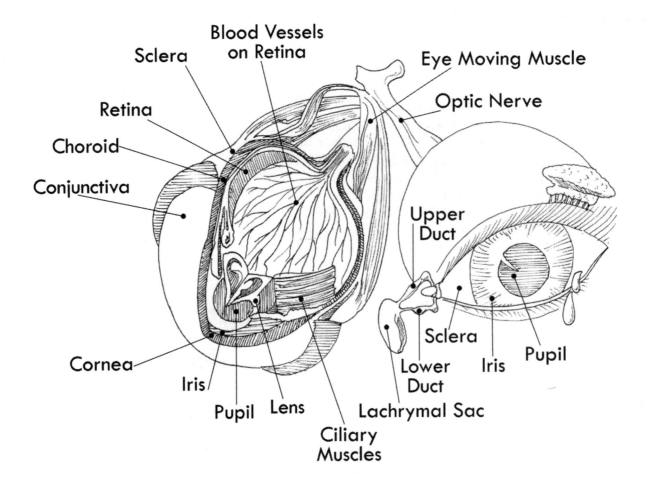

Sclera

Blood Vessels
on Retina

Eye Moving Muscle

Retina

Optic Nerve

Choroid

Conjunctiva

Upper
Duct

Cornea

Sclera

Iris

Pupil

Pupil

Lens

Iris

Lower
Duct

Ciliary
Muscles

Lachrymal Sac

EAR DIAGRAM

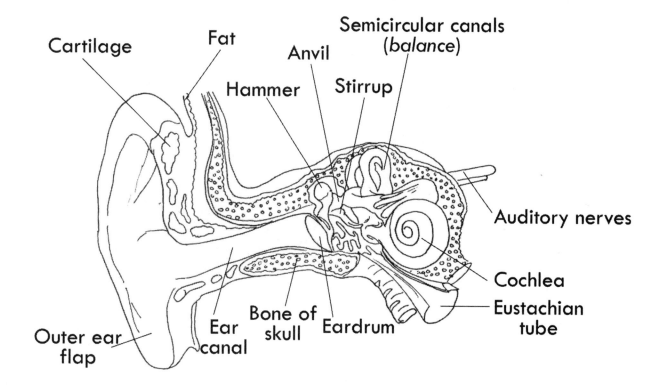

Cartilage

Fat

Anvil

Hammer

Semicircular canals
(*balance*)

Stirrup

Auditory nerves

Cochlea

Eustachian
tube

Outer ear
flap

Ear
canal

Bone of
skull

Eardrum

The five senses are all part of protecting us, but they also add a great deal of pleasure, and sometimes pain, to our lives. They help us understand all that is going on around us. It is so important that we take care of our senses. Protect your eyes when you're doing yard work or building things. Protect your ears from very loud or close noises. God gave you these senses for your pleasure and protection.

REVIEW IT!

1. The four taste zones of the tongue are

   _____ , _____ ,

   _____ , and _____ .

2. The nose is filled with _____

   _____ , which make me able to smell.

3. My skin is filled with millions of _____ ,

   which help me feel things.

4. The _____

   in the eye sends messages to the brain.

5. The three main sections of the ear are the

   _____ ,

   _____ ,

   and _____ .

HANDS-ON TIME: Sense-ational Experiment

Objective: To see how the five senses help us in everyday life.

Materials

Potato / Apple slices (peeled)

Salt / Sugar

Lemon / Orange slices (not peeled)

Vanilla / Almond extracts

Canned tuna / Canned chicken (a few chunks of each, drained)

Vinegar / Water

Flour / Powdered sugar

Blindfold

Helper

Instructions

1. LISTEN as your helper reads these instructions to you.

2. Gather the pairs of foods listed above. Place each pair in separate, unmarked bowls, side by side.

3. Have a helper mix up the placement of each pair of bowls. Now LOOK at each pair. Can you see the difference? Notice the sense you are using.

4. Have your helper blindfold you for the following experiments.

5. TOUCH each pair. Can you feel the difference?

6. Pinch your nose. TASTE each pair. Can you taste the difference?

7. Let go of your nose. SMELL each pair. Can you smell the difference?

8. Now, TASTE each pair again. Isn't it amazing how God made all our senses to work together?

Make a chart listing each pair and each test. Mark an "X" on the chart if you could tell the pair apart. How many X's do you have? How many blank spaces do you have? Are there more X's or more blank spaces?

HUMAN REPRODUCTION

(Parental Discretion Is Advised)

TEACHING TIME:
Baby Talk

It is God who makes all babies grow.

"For You formed my inward parts; You covered me in my mother's womb." (Psalm 139:13)

Many children want to know about where babies come from. We have learned that God designs all life. He created our world and all that is in it. We also know from our plant studies that God designed a special way for new plants to grow. We called this **reproduction**. In a similar way, God designed a special way for new babies to be made. Let's learn more.

Like flowers, females have ovaries. These ovaries hold eggs, or **ova**, that are released once a month into a woman's body. This process usually begins around 11 or 12 years of age. In order for the egg to become a baby, though, it must be fertilized, just like flower ovules must also be fertilized. Once the egg is released into the woman's body it must be fertilized within about 24 hours for it to become a baby. Sometimes a woman's body will release two eggs instead of one. If they are both fertilized, twins will be born. Twins that come from two separate eggs are **fraternal twins**. **Identical twins,** on the other hand, are the result of one fertilized egg that splits.

A major difference between flower reproduction and human reproduction is that flowers usually have both the male and female parts. Humans, on the other hand, are either male or female. Men are males and women are females. Whereas women have the ova, men have the ingredient needed to fertilize the ova. It is called **sperm.** God designed a special process, intended for married people, to get the sperm to the egg.

When the egg is fertilized, it travels to a place in the woman's body called the **uterus**, sometimes also called the **womb**. This is the place where the baby will grow until it is ready to be born. A woman's body is designed to nourish, or feed, the growing baby. A **placenta**, which is also in the womb, does this. The baby is connected to the placenta by an **umbilical cord**. This cord is cut when the baby is born. Within a few weeks after birth, the small portion of cord still attached to the baby dries up and falls off, leaving behind the **belly button** where it was attached. It takes about 40 weeks, or nine months, for the baby to develop enough to be born. God designed a woman's body with a special place for the baby to come out.

Once the baby is born, the mother's body produces milk, which can be fed to the baby. However, some mothers choose to feed their babies formula that they buy at the store.

Many people call this whole process the "miracle of life." So many things must happen at just the right time for a baby to develop and grow, that it is a miracle!

ℝ REVIEW IT!

1. What body part do women have in common with flowers?

   _____

2. Another name for human eggs, which are in a woman's

   body, is _____ .

3. Sperm is needed to _____

   the egg.

4. Babies grow in the part of a woman's body known as the

   _____ .

5. Unscramble the letters to see the name of the organ that

   nourishes the baby while it is in the uterus. APTLANEC

   _____

6. Babies are connected to this organ by the

   _____ , which is cut at birth,

   leaving the belly button behind.

HANDS-ON TIME: UNIT FIVE WRAP-UP

Show What You Know!

Answer as many questions as you can without using your book or notes. You get **10,000** points for each correct response. After going through the review once with your book closed, open your book and try again. You get **5,000** points for each additional correct answer. So, **show what you know!**

1. What class and order are humans in? _____

2. What part of the body is called the epidermis? _____

3. Name the two different types of joints in the skeletal system. _____

    _____

4. How many bones are in the human body? _____

5. Name the system containing your blood and all the vessels that carry your blood throughout your body.

    _____

    _____

6. Which vessels carry blood to your heart? _____

7. Which vessels carry blood away from your heart? _____

8. Which system makes breathing possible? _____

9. Name the five senses of the human body. _____

    _____

10. Name at least two tastes your tongue can detect. _____

    _____

11. How many smells can humans sense? Check one.

    ☐ 10–100

    ☐ 100–1,000

    ☐ 1,000–10,000

    ☐ Over 10,000

12. The nose is filled with _____ , which make you able

to smell.

13. Your skin has millions of _____ , which help you
feel

_____

things.

FIRST ATTEMPT _____

(number of correct responses x 10,000)

SECOND ATTEMPT + _____

(number of correct responses x 5,000)

TOTAL NUMBER OF POINTS _____

WRITING ASSIGNMENT

In your science notebook, complete the creative writing assignment below. Have fun with it!

Did you eat a peanut butter cup lately? See a giraffe? Get tickled by an ant running across your toes? Hear a concert? Smell brownies baking?

Pick a recent experience that used one of your senses and describe how the sensation was relayed from your taste buds, eyes, skin, ears, or nose to your brain.

UNIT SIX

REPTILES ALL AROUND

UNIT SIX VOCABULARY

- alligators
- camouflage
- cold-blooded
- crocodiles
- Gila monster
- lizards
- Mexican beaded lizard
- pit viper
- scutes
- snakes
- terrapins
- tortoises
- turtles
- venomous
- warm-blooded

MATERIALS NEEDED FOR THIS UNIT

- Science notebook
- Sketchbook, if desired
- Old T-shirts
- Face paints
- Hats
- Index cards
- Alligator and crocodile stickers

Reptile Coloring Page

LESSON 23

INTRODUCTION

TEACHING TIME:
The Cold-Blooded Facts

Today we begin our unit on reptiles. Some people think they don't like reptiles, but still, there are many fascinating things to learn about them. Reptiles are in Kingdom Animalia, Phylum Chordata, and Class Reptilia. From this classification, you know immediately that reptiles have backbones. How can you know? You know because I told you they are in Phylum Chordata and animals in this phylum have backbones.

What features are special to Class Reptilia, however? Some of the main features are:

- Tough, dry scales (NOT slimy!)
- Cold-blooded
- Three-chambered heart (not four, like birds)
- Egg-layers
- Egg shell usually leathery (not brittle, like birds)
- Legs in pairs, if they have legs at all

(*Note*: There are some exceptions to these basic features. For instance, not all snakes lay eggs. Some give birth to live snakes instead.)

Now, can you name some animals with these features? If you said snakes, alligators, lizards, and turtles, you are correct. These are all reptiles.

Most of the characteristics of reptiles can be easily understood. However, you may be confused about the term *cold-blooded*. All animals are either warm-blooded or cold-blooded. What is the difference? **Cold-blooded** animals have no way to automatically warm themselves. Their body temperature changes according to their surroundings. This is not the case with **warm-blooded** creatures like humans. Unless a human's body is exposed to very extreme temperatures or unless he is sick, the body temperature stays at about the same temperature all the time. All humans have a body temperature of about 98.6 degrees. By contrast, however, the bodies of cold-blooded creatures are only warmed by warm surroundings, like sunny rocks and warm days. When they get very cool, they slow down or even go into hibernation. They must be warm to be active. This is why you don't usually see reptiles in cold weather.

When Jesus sent out the early disciples, He mentioned four types of animals. Which one was a reptile?

"Behold, I send you out as sheep in the midst of wolves. Therefore be wise as serpents and harmless as doves."
(Matthew 10:16)

Reptiles and the Food Chain

Like many other animals, reptiles can be dangerous. However, they can also be very helpful. For example, snakes help control rat populations. Snakes, crocodiles, and alligators all help to control rabbits, as well. This is something to be thankful for. Remember, all animals are important in the food chain and in the biomes. Rabbits and mice reproduce at alarmingly fast rates. Can you imagine what would happen if we didn't have these reptiles to help control the population? Why, it would get OUT of control really fast! Believe it or not, even rabbits can be less than cute when they are eating your plants and vegetables.

Throughout this unit you will learn about different types of reptiles. Snakes, crocodiles, alligators, lizards, turtles, and tortoises are all reptiles. By the end of this unit, you will know what makes one reptile different from another.

 HANDS-ON TIME: Research a Reptile

Objective: To learn about a specific type of reptile.

Discover!

1. Today you need to choose one type of reptile and learn as much as you can about it.

2. You should read about your animal for 30 minutes or more.

3. In your science notebook, write at least one paragraph about your animal. Some information you might include:

   • Name of the animal
   • Where it is found
   • Its primary features—length, weight, color/patterns
   • Number of eggs it lays at a time
   • Whether it is poisonous
   • Whether it is endangered

5. You might also draw a picture of your animal in your notebook or a sketchbook.

LESSON 24

SNAKES AND LIZARDS

TEACHING TIME:
Scutes and Scales

Snakes and lizards form one group of reptiles. They are very similar to each other. Like all reptiles, they are covered in dry scales. Both snakes and lizards are cold-blooded, as you learned before. Do you remember the difference between warm-blooded and cold-blooded animals? We learned that cold-blooded animals' bodies can't regulate their temperature. Because of this, they must warm themselves by other methods, like sitting in the sun. Another feature common to both snakes and lizards is their long, slender bodies. A major difference, however, is that lizards have legs, but snakes don't. Let's learn more about both snakes and lizards.

Snakes

As mentioned before, **snakes** do not have legs. How, then, are they able to move? God created snakes with special scales on their underbellies called **scutes**. These scutes enable snakes to *scoot* around.

Snakes are basically deaf. Can you imagine a snake with ears? Of course, not all ears stick out like those on humans— some are flat. But this is not the case with snakes. They have no external ears.

They also generally have poor eyesight. You may wonder how they manage to find their food and protect themselves when they are deaf and can't see well. The answer is, snakes are created with a very keen sense of smell. Some snakes, such as rattlesnakes, have pits on the sides of their heads that can detect the heat in warm-blooded prey. This type of snake is called a **pit viper.** Pit vipers are **venomous**, or poisonous. Snakes are also very sensitive to movement. In most cases, if you were to happen upon a snake, you would be better off to stand absolutely still and call for help, rather than move.

You may be wondering about the eating habits of snakes. Snakes are predators. For the most part, snakes eat mice, rabbits, and other small mammals. They also eat eggs. Whether they kill their prey before eating it or not depends on the type of snake. For instance, boa constrictors squeeze their prey to death first, then eat it. Venomous snakes inject their poison by biting the animal first, thus killing it before eating it. In all cases, snakes cannot chew

> ☙ *Exploring God's Word*
> *God knows better than we how to show love.*
>
> *See Matthew 7:7-12.*

their food but must swallow it instead. Therefore, God designed snakes with jaws that can swing open very widely. Because of this feature, some snakes can even manage to eat something as large as a deer!

Lizards

As you'll learn, **lizards** are different from snakes in several key ways. First of all, lizards usually have two pairs of legs. There are some lizards with no legs, but this is the exception. Second, lizards have ears and can hear. As far as size goes, most lizards are quite small. There are only a few lizards that are large. While snakes eat mammals and eggs, most lizards eat only insects.

There are only two types of venomous lizards. The first is the **Mexican beaded lizard**, and the other is the **Gila** (**hee la**) **monster**. Many other lizards rely on tails that snap off easily and **camouflage** (the ability to blend in with their environment) to protect them in the wild. God created some lizards with the ability to change their skin color to match their surroundings.

 *Discovery Zone*

The smallest reptile is the gecko, which is a type of lizard.

HANDS-ON TIME: Camouflage Yourself!

Objective: To appreciate God's miracle of camouflage and see how it helps animals in the wild.

Materials

- Old T-shirts
- Face paints
- Hats

Camouflaged Humans

We are not like the many animals in the world created with the ability to automatically change to blend in with their surroundings. However, we can still camouflage ourselves. For instance, when my children play at a place in our neighborhood called "sandhill," they often like to go in camouflage. Since sandhill is very sandy, they often wear brown T-shirts and hats. If they are playing tag in the dark, they wear jungle camouflage army jackets and dark hats, so that they can move around the yard and blend in with the bushes easily.

This technique can also be used for observing animals in their habitats. When animals can't see or hear you, they are more likely to linger out in the open.

1. Decide on the background you are going to try to blend in with.

2. Choose clothing that will match the background as much as possible.

3. You can smear face paints on your face and arms to help you "hide."

4. Using limbs and leaves, you can create a more thorough covering.

5. Be sure to write this up in your science notebook, including any animals you are able to observe.

LESSON 25

ALLIGATORS AND CROCODILES

TEACHING TIME: My, What Sharp Teeth You Have!

Crocodiles and alligators are both of the Order Crocodilian. They are carnivores with sharp teeth and long snouts. Hard, square scales cover their bodies. They live on land and in water. They are known for their strong legs and very powerful tails. I am sure you have noticed their eyes. Their eyes, as well as their nostrils, are set high on their heads. Can you figure out why God created them this way? It allows them to see and breathe, while keeping their bodies mostly underwater. This is important in surprising their prey. Crocodiles and alligators are among the largest living reptiles. Because they are reptiles, you can know that they lay eggs and are cold-blooded. Being cold-blooded, they primarily live in warm climates.

God even made crocodiles and alligators.

"And God made . . . everything that creeps on the earth according to its kind. And God saw that it was good." (Genesis 1:25)

Alligators

With all these similarities, you may be wondering what makes them different. To begin with, **alligators** are freshwater reptiles. You have not studied water life yet, but freshwater is found in lakes, streams and rivers. Freshwater is not salty. The ocean is salty and is called saltwater. So, alligators are found in and around lakes and rivers, primarily. Alligators have broad, flat snouts that are rounded in front. Alligators and crocodiles both have 2 teeth on the lower jaw that are bigger than the rest. In alligators, these teeth are hidden when the jaw is closed. There are only two species of alligators, the American alligator and the Chinese alligator. The American alligator has webbed feet; the Chinese alligator does not. Alligators can grow up to 20 feet long and weigh up to 550 pounds. They can live to be up to 50 years old. They lay their eggs in clutches with about 30-60 eggs in a clutch.

Crocodiles

Crocodiles vary from alligators in a few ways. Instead of broad, flat snouts, crocodiles have long, narrow, snouts that are rather pointed in front. When a crocodile closes his jaw, the two large teeth on the bottom can be seen. Unlike alligators, crocodiles can be found in both freshwater and saltwater. The largest crocodiles can be up to 23 feet long and weigh over 2000 pounds. They can live up to 65 years and can lay up to 90 eggs in a clutch.

While alligators and crocodiles are big and bulky looking, do not be fooled. They can run very fast, though only for short distances. In the water they are especially dangerous due to their speed and power. They normally feed on mammals, fish, frogs, and snakes.

 REVIEW IT!

Use the following chart to list the differences between alligators and crocodiles.

DIFFERENCES BETWEEN ALLIGATORS AND CROCODILES

Trait	Alligators	Crocodiles
Snout Shape		
Lower Teeth: Hidden or Visible?		
# of Eggs in Clutch		
Life Span		
Freshwater or Saltwater?		

 HANDS-ON TIME: Gator Mix-Up Game

Objective: To review facts about the Order Crocodilian.

Materials

- Index cards
- "Gator" and "croc" stickers for decoration

Preparation

This game is for one or more players.

1. Make one card for each fact below:

- Order Crocodilian
- Carnivores with sharp teeth & long snouts
- Hard, square scales over body
- Powerful tails
- Live on land & in water
- High-set eyes
- Reptiles

- Lay eggs
- Cold-blooded
- Largest living reptiles
- Live in warm climates

2. Make 11 cards that say "Both." The facts above match "Both" alligators and crocodiles.

3. Make one card for each alligator fact below:

  - Freshwater only
  - Broad, flat snouts, rounded in front
  - All lower teeth hidden when jaw is closed
  - Only two species
  - Grows up to 20 feet long
  - Weighs up to 550 pounds
  - Lives up to 50 years old
  - Lays 30–60 eggs in a clutch

4. Make 8 cards that say "Alligator."

5. Make one card for each crocodile fact below:

  - Long, narrow, pointed snouts
  - Two teeth visible on lower jaw when mouth closed
  - Freshwater & saltwater
  - Grows up to 23 feet long
  - Can weigh over 2,000 pounds
  - Lives up to 65 years old
  - Lays up to 90 eggs in a clutch

6. Make 7 cards that say "Crocodile."

 *Discovery Zone*

Note to Teacher: This game can be used to memorize facts for other types of animals.

How to Play

1. Once all cards are made, mix them thoroughly.
2. Lay cards out, face down, in neat rows.
3. Turn two cards face up.
4. See if you have a match. A match is made when you turn up a card with a fact and a card with the correct matching animal. If the fact applies to both "crocs" and "gators," it only matches a "Both" card.
5. If you have a match, you get to keep the set and take another turn.
6. If you do not get a match, it is the next player's turn.
7. Play until all cards are gone. The player with the most cards wins.
8. You can play this game alone easily.

LESSON 26

TURTLES, TORTOISES, AND TERRAPINS

TEACHING TIME: What's the Difference?

Do you know the difference between a turtle and a tortoise? How about a turtle and a terrapin? We tend to think they are all the same thing, but that is not correct. Although they are often all grouped together as turtles, there are differences, as well as common traits.

Turtles, tortoises, and terrapins all have short, broad bodies. They have bony shells and an outer horny covering. Their heads, legs, and tails can be drawn into their shells for protection. Instead of teeth, they have horny beaks.

Turtles

When it comes to differences, unlike tortoises, **turtles** live on land and in water. There are two types of turtles, marine (saltwater) and freshwater. Both types breathe through lungs and must come to the surface periodically for oxygen, although some can stay submerged for up to several days. They can stay underwater for many months during hibernation. They are usually omnivorous. The largest marine turtle is the leatherback sea turtle. Its shell length can be up to 8 feet long, and it can weigh over 2,000 pounds! Turtles have somewhat flat, streamlined shells that make them better at swimming and diving. They have long toes with webbing, also useful for swimming. The most specialized swimmers are sea turtles. Their front "legs" are actually more like flippers. Their rear legs work as rudders for steering.

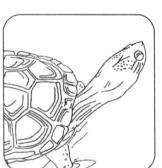

Freshwater Turtles

Terrapins are a special type of turtle. They are the freshwater turtles. The largest terrapin is the alligator snapping turtle. It can be up to 31½ inches long. It has a particularly long tail and a very spiky shell. Soft-shelled turtles are also terrapins and are the fastest swimmers of all turtles. They can swim faster than most fish.

Tortoises

Unlike turtles, **tortoises** are land dwellers. That is their home. They are known for long life spans. Some live over 150 years! There are 41 different species of tortoises. They are

When did God create sea turtles?

"So God created great sea creatures and every living thing that moves, with which the waters abounded, according to their kind . . ." (Genesis 1:21)
"So the evening and the morning were the fifth day." (Genesis 1:23)

MARINE TURTLE

found all over the world except in Australia and Antarctica. The smallest tortoise is only about 4 inches long. It is the Madagascan spider tortoise. The Aldabra giant tortoise is the largest, measuring up to 4½ feet long and weighing in at over 560 pounds. Tortoises typically have a dome shape to their shells, making it difficult for predators to get hold of them! Most tortoises are herbivores. Living on land and being very slow movers makes it very difficult for them to catch their prey.

 REVIEW IT!

Fill in the blanks with turtle, terrapin, or tortoise.

1. Land dweller _____

2. Somewhat flat, streamlined shell _____

3. Can stay submerged for several days _____

4. Dome-shaped, horny shell _____

5. Largely herbivores _____

6. Found in saltwater and freshwater

   _____

7. Lives in freshwater _____

8. Omnivores _____

9. Alligator snapping turtle _____

10. Leatherback sea turtle _____

11. Long, webbed toes _____

12. Can live up to 150 years _____

13. Largest specimen can weigh over 2,000 pounds

    _____

14. Largest specimen weighs about 560 pounds

    _____

 *Discovery Zone*

A group of turtles is a bale or a dole.

HANDS-ON TIME: UNIT SIX WRAP-UP

Show What You Know!

Answer as many questions as you can without using your book or notes. You get **10,000** points for each correct response. After going through the review once with your book closed, open your book and try again. You get **5,000** points for each additional correct answer. So, **show what you know!**

1. Name the order that both crocodiles and alligators are categorized in.

_____

2. Are crocodiles found in freshwater or saltwater?

_____

3. I have a long, slender body; am basically deaf; and have very poor eyesight. What am I?

_____

4. Describe the feature that helps protect lizards from predators.

_____

_____

5. What special ability did God give many animals to help them "hide" in the wild?

_____

6. I live in freshwater; have a broad, flat snout; and there are only two species of me. What am I?

_____

7. Explain the difference between cold-blooded and warm-blooded animals.

_____

_____

_____

8. Are reptiles cold-blooded or warm-blooded?

_____

9. If I live in freshwater and carry my house on my back, am I a marine turtle or am I a terrapin?

_____

10. What feature do marine turtles have to help them in the water?

_____

11. I have a long, narrow snout and have two lower teeth that stick out when I close my jaw.

Am I a crocodile or an alligator? _____

12. Name two differences between turtles and tortoises.

_____

_____

13. Describe the feature that enables snakes to eat even very large animals.

_____

_____

14. What does _venomous_ mean?

_____

_____

15. What trait is common to pit vipers, and what does it do?

_____

_____

FIRST ATTEMPT _____

(number of correct responses x 10,000)

SECOND ATTEMPT + _____

(number of correct responses x 5,000)

TOTAL NUMBER OF POINTS _____

 WRITING ASSIGNMENT

In your science notebook, complete the creative writing assignment below. Have fun with it!

Imagine that you are an explorer and you have just discovered a new species of reptile. Write a press release to tell the media of your new discovery, or send a field report home to your grant committee. Include information such as the new reptile's habitat, eating habits, physical features, and so forth. If you wish, draw an illustration. Make sure you use lively details that will convince the media to cover the story or persuade your grant committee to continue your funding.

UNIT SEVEN

INSECTS HIGH AND LOW

UNIT SEVEN VOCABULARY

- abdomen
- chrysalis
- Class Insecta
- complete metamorphosis
- drones
- head
- honeybees
- incomplete metamorphosis
- Karl von Frisch
- metamorphosis
- Order Lepidoptera
- Phylum Arthropoda
- pupa
- queen bee
- round dance
- thorax
- waggle dance
- wasps
- worker bees

MATERIALS NEEDED FOR THIS UNIT

- Science notebook
- Pencil
- Magnifying glass
- Old clothes
- Shovel
- Metal coat hanger
- Construction paper
- String or yarn
- Brown pipe cleaner
- Glue stick
- Hole punch
- Scissors

Insect Coloring Page

LESSON 27

INTRODUCTION

TEACHING TIME:
Insectamania

Do you know that spiders are not insects? Have you ever wondered why they are not considered insects? Let's go back to what you learned about the classification system. You learned that scientists put animals into groups according to their common features. Do you also remember that as you work your way through the classification system the groups get smaller and more specific?

Let's review the main categories in the classification system. In your science notebook, list these classification categories from largest to smallest, beginning with Kingdom.

K _____

P _____

C _____

O _____

F _____

G _____

S _____

Where do we learn that it is wise to follow the example of ants?

Proverbs 6:6-8 tells us: "Go to the ant, you sluggard! Consider her ways and be wise."

Insect Taxonomy

You know that insects and spiders are both in the Kingdom Animalia. I'll tell you that both insects and spiders are in **Phylum Arthropoda**. You should remember this from your flashcards. The next category is class. Let's look at **Class Insecta**. For a creature to belong to Class Insecta or to be called an insect, it must:

- Have three pairs of jointed legs
  (Spiders have four.)
- Nearly always have wings in at least one stage of its life
  (Spiders never have wings.)
- Have antennae
  (Spiders don't have these either.)
- Have three different body segments—**head, thorax,** and **abdomen**
  (You guessed it! Spiders are not created this way.)

In addition to the above, insects do not have lungs. Air is passed through their skeletons instead. Also, nearly all insects go through some type of metamorphosis.

See the ant diagram on the next page that illustrates the three body segments—head, thorax, and abdomen—of an insect.

Metamorphosis

You have very likely heard the word **metamorphosis** before. You may know that this is the process caterpillars go through to become butterflies. If you think this, then you are exactly right. It means changing from one thing into another. It is important to learn about because, as I already mentioned, nearly all insects go through some type of metamorphosis.

There are two main types of metamorphosis. There is **complete metamorphosis** and **incomplete metamorphosis.**

Complete metamorphosis has four stages.

1. Stage 1—egg
2. Stage 2—larva   (This is a wormlike stage.)
3. Stage 3—pupa   (The insect has a case over itself.)
4. Stage 4—adult.

Butterflies and moths are two animals that go through complete metamorphosis.

Incomplete metamorphosis has only three stages.

1. Stage 1—egg
2. Stage 2—nymph (This is a smaller version of the adult.)
3. Stage 3—adult

Grasshoppers and locusts, among many others, go through incomplete metamorphosis.

Now that you see the list of requirements for insects, can you understand why it is a mistake to call a spider an insect? Spiders simply do not meet the criteria. They belong to their own class called arachnids. We will not be studying spiders this year. However, for your enjoyment, there is a spider coloring page in the back of this book. If you want to know more about them, you'll need to go to the library!

Discovery Zone

Insects are beneficial for pollination of fruits and vegetables, as well as being important members of the food chain.

ANT DIAGRAM

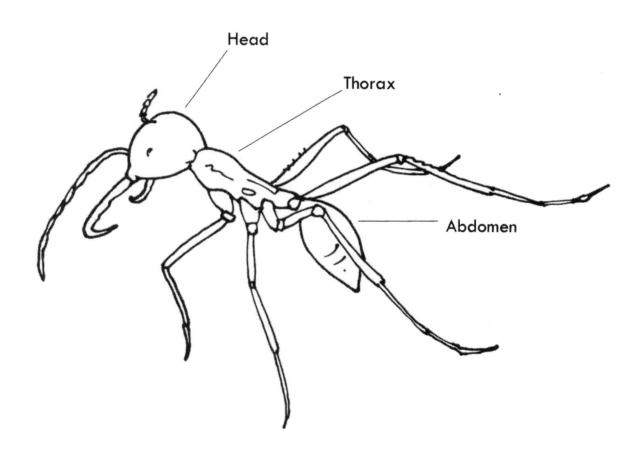

Head

Thorax

Abdomen

HANDS-ON TIME: Inspect for Insects

Objective: To find insects in the wild, observe their behavior, and notice their design

Today I want you to go outside and look for insects. Doesn't that sound like fun? You need to be careful because some insects, such as bees and wasps, can be dangerous.

Materials

- Pencil
- Science notebook
- Magnifying glass   (Suggestion: We like clear plastic boxes that have a magnifying glass on the top. These allow you to put a bug inside and look at it closely.)
- Old clothes
- Shovel

Instructions

1. Either at a park or in your own yard, you are going to inspect for insects.
2. You can use the shovel to dig in areas that your parents have okayed and look for insects.
3. Notice the air around you. Do you see flying insects?
4. When you find an insect or group of insects, write it down in your science notebook and sketch the insect.
5. Using your magnifying glass, look a little closer. Can you see wings? Can you see the head, thorax, and abdomen?
6. Remember that some insects may not have completed their metamorphosis yet. Look on trees for cocoons.
7. Try to identify the insects you've found today.

 *Discovery Zone*

Some insects, such as mantises and ladybugs, are predators, feeding on harmful insects.

LESSON 28

BUTTERFLIES AND MOTHS

TEACHING TIME:
Different As Night and Day

I think you would agree that butterflies are some of God's most beautiful creatures. Their presence delights us. We want to chase and catch them just so we can get a closer look at them. Their wings fascinate us. Today you are going to learn about butterflies, as well as moths. These two are very similar, yet they have many differences.

Let's look at their similarities first. First of all, they are both insects. You know that this means they have six legs, wings in at least one stage, antennae, and three segments to their bodies. Can you recall the names of the three segments, or parts? They are the head, thorax, and abdomen. Both insects have four wings, whose patterns are symmetrical, or the same, on both sides. Their wings are quite large in comparison to their bodies. Both are of the **Order Lepidoptera**, which means they have scaled wings.

We have already mentioned that butterflies and moths both go through complete metamorphosis. Specifically, they begin life as eggs. The eggs hatch into caterpillars. The caterpillars spin a cocoon, sometimes called a **chrysalis**. This is the **pupa**, or resting, stage. During this stage the actual metamorphosis takes place. When the change is complete, the caterpillar is no more, but is instead a butterfly or a moth. The adult insect wriggles its way out of the cocoon and hangs until its wings are dry. It is then able to fly away.

Butterflies

With so much in common, how can we tell butterflies and moths apart? To begin with, the bodies of butterflies are slender and their wings are bright and colorful. When resting, or perching, they usually fold their wings up over their bodies. They have knobs on the ends of their antennae and are active mostly during the daylight hours. There are about 18,500 known species of butterflies. They can often be found in open, sunny areas such as hillsides, meadows, and streams.

Moths can destroy things as they eat. They eat the leaves on trees and destroy them. I've even had sweaters destroyed by moths.

Jesus taught us to "lay up for yourselves treasures in heaven, where neither moth nor rust destroys . . . "
See Matthew 6:20.

Moths

Moths are different from butterflies in several ways. First of all, their bodies are relatively thick and hairy. Their wings are most often a dull gray or brown with little color on them, though there are exceptions. At rest, their wings usually lie flat. The antennae on a moth can be very thin or somewhat feathery. There are no knobs on their antennae. Most moths are nocturnal, meaning active in the nighttime hours. There are over 200,000 species of moths, far more than butterflies. Moths can usually be found in wooded areas.

Discovery Zone

Callaway Gardens, in Pine Mountain, Georgia, has a very large butterfly garden that is open to the public. There you can see many species of butterflies and even watch them emerge from their cocoons.

HANDS-ON TIME: Make a Butterfly Life-Cycle Mobile

Objective: To reinforce understanding of the complete metamorphosis process.

Today you are going to create a mobile that shows the complete metamorphosis of a butterfly. As you work, remember how detailed God is in His design.

Materials

- Metal coat hanger
- Construction paper
- String or yarn
- Brown pipe cleaner
- Glue stick
- Hole punch
- Scissors

Instructions

1. Draw a leaf on green construction paper. Cut it out, then glue tiny white or yellow circles (made with the hole punch) to the bottom of the leaf. *Eggs* are usually laid in a cluster on the underside of the leaf.

2. Cut five strips of green construction paper, 1½ inches long by ¼ inch wide. Link them together with glue to make your *caterpillar*. Don't forget to draw eyes and a mouth (for eating all those leaves).

3. Fold a brown pipe cleaner in half, three times. Twist the folded pipe cleaner into a tight cocoon. This is your *chrysalis*, where metamorphosis will take place.

4. Fold half of a piece of colorful paper in half. Draw and cut out one set of wings along the fold line. Use black construction paper to make the butterfly's body (remember that there are three parts). Decorate your *adult butterfly* symmetrically.

5. Attach string or yarn to all four stages, then hang them from a coat hanger. Now you can hang your mobile in your room or school area and be reminded of this incredible process.

LESSON 29

BEES AND WASPS

TEACHING TIME:
What's All the Buzz?

Bees and wasps are neat, but sometimes scary, insects. As insects, they both have six legs. They also have wings. They are considered social insects, living in groups called colonies. However, some are solitary, meaning they live on their own. Honeybees form some of the largest colonies of all bees and wasps. Bees and wasps normally feed on plants, though some wasps eat insects.

Bees

In each colony there are three types of bees. First of all, there is a **queen bee**. The queen bee lays the eggs in the hive and has no stinger. Then there are other female bees called **worker bees**. Worker bees gather all the food for the colony and do all the work to build and support the hive. They also protect the hive. **Drones** are the male bees. Their only purpose is to mate with the queen bee so that more bees can be born.

Have you ever had a bee appear when you were eating or drinking outside? Did that bee leave, only to have several more return? This happens for a reason. A scientist named **Karl von Frisch** (1886–1982) discovered that bees have a way of telling other bees in their colony where food can be found. When a bee returns to its colony after discovering food, it does something called a dance. Of course, it is not dancing, as we know it. It is a special way the bee moves around the hive, and it tells the other bees where they can find food. It is like when you give a friend directions to a party! There is a dance called the **"round dance"** that a bee does when food is nearby. The **"waggle dance"** is done when food is farther away. The way the bee moves shows the other bees the direction in which to fly. This does not sound like something that could have happened by accident. This sounds like God specifically created bees to do this.

You are probably familiar with **honeybees**. By their name, you can correctly guess that these are the bees that make honey. Honeybees live in very large colonies, sometimes up to 80,000 strong. Their hives are made of wax produced by the workers and are very strong and durable. These hives are able to hold much more honey than the bees need.

How did bees contribute to John the Baptist's diet?

Matthew 3:4 tells us: " . . . and his food was locusts and wild honey."

Wasps

Wasps have slender bodies with very constricted, or drawn-in, abdomens. They have two pairs of wings. Wasp stings are especially painful because of their long stingers. They build their nests out of a mixture of deadwood and their own saliva. These nests are not strong like those of honeybees.

Hornets are a type of wasp. They build very large, papery nests. They often lay their eggs in other wasps' nests and sometimes have no workers. Another type of wasp is the yellow jacket. Yellow jackets are known by their extensive yellow markings.

Bees are dependent on flowers for their food. They are very important in pollinating flowers and crops. Even though bees can sting, they usually will not bother you unless they feel threatened. It is wise to avoid all bees' nests.

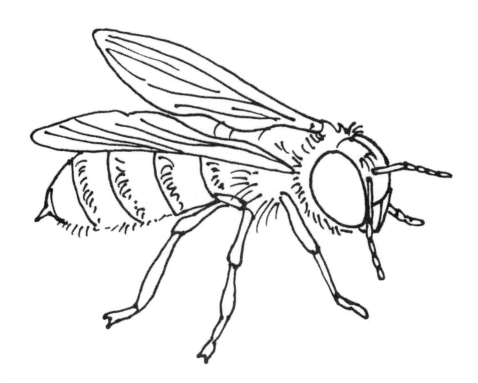

 **HANDS-ON TIME: UNIT SEVEN WRAP-UP**

Show What You Know!

Answer as many questions as you can without using your book or notes. You get **10,000** points for each correct response. After going through the review once with your book closed, open your book and try again. You get **5,000** points for each additional correct answer. So, **show what you know!**

1. Between moths and butterflies, which has the more slender body and knobs on their antennae?

   _____

2. Do moths and butterflies go through complete or incomplete metamorphosis? How do you know?

   _____

   _____

   _____

3. Name the three main body parts of insects. _____

   _____

   _____

4. Where is an insect's skeleton located? _____

5. What is this type of skeleton called? _____

6. Name the three types of bees in each colony. _____

   _____

   _____

7. How do bees notify each other when food is found? _____

   _____

8. How do bees help flowers grow? _____

   _____

   _____

FIRST ATTEMPT _____

   (number of correct responses x *10,000)*

SECOND ATTEMPT + _____

   (number of correct responses x *5,000)*

TOTAL NUMBER OF POINTS _____

146

WRITING ASSIGNMENT

In your science notebook, complete the creative writing assignment below. Have fun with it!

"What's the Buzz?" is your new talk show. The first segment will be taped next week. Research the background of your insect guests and prepare a set of questions to ask. Use this information to write the script of your first show. It should include at least four different insect families that you will interview about their habitats, favorite foods, unique features, pet peeves, life cycles, most humorous moments, and so forth.

If you have access to a video camera and a few siblings or friends, act out the script while someone videotapes it. You could even create some insect costumes. You may want to invent an extra insect and see if your audience can guess which one you made up.

UNIT EIGHT

WATER CREATURES

UNIT EIGHT VOCABULARY

- amphibian
- bivalves
- buoyant
- cephalopods
- chambered nautilus
- chitons
- Class Chondrichthyes
- crustaceans
- dorsal fin
- dual life
- dwarf dogfish
- erosion
- exoskeleton
- freshwater
- gastropods
- gills
- great white sharks
- Phylum Mollusca
- placoid scales
- rain cycle
- saltwater
- submerged
- tadpoles
- tooth shells
- tropical waters
- whale sharks

MATERIALS NEEDED FOR THIS UNIT

- Science notebook
- Copy of world map from Appendix A
- Copy of United States map from Appendix A
- Atlas or labeled world map
- Index cards
- Scissors
- Copy of Shell Identification page (Lesson 31)
- Yardstick or measuring tape
- 1–2 pounds of raw shrimp, preferably unpeeled (Lesson 33)
- Crab-boil spices
- Oil for frying
- 2 eggs
- 1 cup of flour
- Salt and pepper
- Ketchup, cocktail sauce
- Water
- Ice
- A zippered plastic sandwich bag
- Cooking utensils
- Potholders

Saltwater Coloring Page

LESSON 30

INTRODUCTION

TEACHING TIME:
Let's Go Swimming!

Throughout most of the year, we have been studying different types of animals. We have looked at birds, reptiles, and mammals. We have even studied humans. Today, we are going to shift directions and study a biome. Early in the year, we learned about how scientists study our world. We learned that the earth is the biosphere and that it is divided into areas called biomes for study. Some scientists consider the waters of our earth a biome. We are going to begin a study of life in water.

Do you know how to swim? If so, you more than likely swim in a pool. However, some of you may also go to the ocean or a lake to swim. Have you ever noticed the living things in the water? Have you ever noticed the taste of the water? There is much to learn about life in water. We will study the two different types of water, as well as some of the animals that live there.

First of all, not all bodies of water are the same. The earth has two main types of water—**saltwater** and **freshwater**. The oceans and seas are all saltwater. Oceans cover about 70 percent of the surface of the earth. Obviously, they have salt in them. It comes from the **erosion** of the continental rock. (More on that next year!) Salty is how God created them. There is also freshwater on earth. Freshwater is found in lakes, streams, rivers, and ponds. You may wonder how some water in our world is salty while some is not. The answer is found in the **rain cycle**. You see, God designed our world to basically water itself. The sun evaporates water from the earth. The evaporated water collects in the atmosphere and forms clouds. Eventually the clouds burst and rain falls down. The rain pours down over mountains and hills, filling the lakes and rivers. The reason these lakes and rivers are not salty is that the salt is not evaporated, only the water. The rain therefore is not salty. It is called, then, freshwater. This will be demonstrated in Lesson 34, "Hands-On Time." Now, don't allow this to confuse you. When we are talking about freshwater, we are not necessarily meaning that the water is fresh enough to drink. In fact, all bodies of water are full of living things and are often unclean. So, don't drink the water!

The Bible teaches us to be careful how we speak by using an example from nature.

"Thus no spring yields both salt water and fresh." (James 3:12)

As we progress through this unit, it will help you to remember where freshwater is found and where saltwater is found. The reason is that life in water is different depending on whether the water is fresh or salty. There are some plants and animals that can live in either freshwater or saltwater; however, most belong in one or the other. God created each animal to survive in specific conditions. He even created freshwater fish and saltwater fish differently. Most creatures would die if they were put in water other than the type they were created for.

We will begin our unit studying saltwater. Can you think of some animals that live in saltwater? Whales and porpoises live in the ocean, and you have already learned some things about them. Did you think of sharks? You're right if you did. Sharks live in the ocean. In this unit, you will study sharks, as well as other saltwater creatures.

 *Discovery Zone*

Did you list a narwhal? Male narwhals look like they have a very long tusk. It is actually a left incisor tooth!

ONE STEP FURTHER

Make a list of as many saltwater creatures as you can. After you've finished with all you can name, ask the members of your family to name as many as they can think of. Add these to your list. You can also use books, the Internet, or computer software if you want to make a longer list.

 HANDS-ON TIME: Mapping the Salt!

Objective: To locate bodies of saltwater and freshwater on a map of the world and of the United States.

Materials

- Copy of world map from Appendix A
- Copy of United States map from Appendix A
- Atlas or labeled world map

World Mapping Activity

1. Locate and label the following bodies of saltwater:
   - Atlantic Ocean
   - Pacific Ocean
   - Arctic Ocean
   - Indian Ocean
2. Label all the continents.

United States Mapping Activity

1. Locate and label the oceans. This should be easy since you just did this on your world map.

2. Also, locate and label the Gulf of Mexico. Is this saltwater or freshwater?

3. Label the following rivers and lakes, which are freshwater:

   - The Great Lakes—Superior, Huron, Erie, Michigan, Ontario
   - Mississippi River
   - Missouri River
   - Ohio River
   - Columbia River
   - Snake River
   - Rio Grande
   - Red River
   - Any lakes or rivers in your state

LESSON 31

MOLLUSKS

TEACHING TIME:
All Clammed Up

Do you know which mollusk makes pearls? The Bible tells us the gates we'll see one day will be made of pearls.

"The twelve gates were twelve pearls: each individual gate was of one pearl." (Revelation 21:21)

What do oysters, octopuses, clams, and squids have in common? They all live in the water, and they are all part of **Phylum Mollusca**. As a matter of fact, snails and slugs are mollusks, too, though they do not necessarily live in water. Let's learn more about what it means to be a mollusk.

Looking at the list above, you may wonder what actually ties them together. In other words, what makes a mollusk a mollusk? To begin with, let's look back to your first unit. You learned then that mollusks are soft-bodied animals. They usually have a hard shell surrounding them. There are species in freshwater, as well as saltwater, and some can live on land. Looking at the Latin root for mollusk, you will find the word *mollus*, which means soft. This will help you remember the definition. Mollusks are invertebrates and, as I'm sure you know, that means they have no backbone. In fact, they have no internal skeleton at all. This means they have no real way to protect themselves. Well, God knows that, so He created most mollusks with shells for protection. Some mollusks, such as octopuses, do not have shells, but God created them with other ways to protect themselves.

Types of Mollusks

Let's take a look at the five main classes in Phylum Mollusca. The first one we will look at is the **gastropods**. Gastropods make up the largest class of mollusks. Mollusks in this class have one-piece shells that are usually coiled. Whelks are part of this class. Whelks begin life in a chamberlike membrane and are so tiny you would have difficulty picking them up. As they grow, they add on to their shells. It is not uncommon to see whelk shells that are 6 to 8 inches in length and 3 inches in width.

The second largest class of mollusks is the **bivalves**. You may know that *bi* means two. Bivalves have two shells that are usually hinged on one side. Oysters and clams are both in this class.

Tooth shells, sometimes called tusk shells, are the third largest class of the five we will study. The reason they are sometimes called tusk shells is that they resemble tusks in appearance.

Chitons and **cephalopods** are the last two classes of mollusks we will look at. Chiton shells have eight movable parts and resemble a knight's armor. Cephalopods, on the other hand, can have shells, but don't always. The shells can be on the outside (as in the chambered nautilus) or on the inside (as in squid). Octopuses don't have any shells.

Two well-known members of the cephalopod class are the octopus and the squid. The giant squid is the largest of all invertebrates, weighing in at over 1,900 pounds! (This is really a big deal considering that the smallest mollusk is less than 1 inch in size.) Perhaps the most intriguing cephalopod is the **chambered nautilus**. Humans rarely see the chambered nautilus because it lives in very deep waters. God created this mysterious creature with the ability to rest on the ocean floor during the day and then rise at night for feeding. It is called *chambered* because the inside of the shell is sectioned off like the rooms of a house. A tube connects these "rooms" and forces water out of the shell, making it **buoyant** (able to float).

God's designs truly are remarkable. Even though oysters, clams, and the chambered nautilus may seem unimportant to us, God has taken care of them down to the smallest details.

 *Discovery Zone*

Most mollusks are able to bury themselves in the sand, which helps protect them from predators.

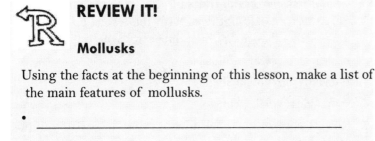 **REVIEW IT!**

Mollusks

Using the facts at the beginning of this lesson, make a list of the main features of mollusks.

- _____

- _____

- _____

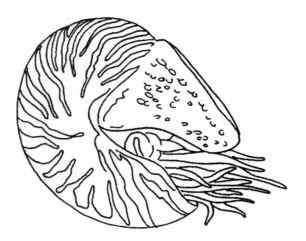

HANDS-ON TIME: Shell Identification Game

Objective: To memorize the main types of mollusks and their distinguishing features.

Materials

- Index cards
- Scissors
- Copy of accompanying Shell Identification page

Preparation

This game is for one or more players.

1. Using index cards, make two cards for each of the following terms:

   - gastropod
   - cephalopod
   - bivalve
   - tooth shell
   - chiton

2. For *each* of the above terms, create three cards; each card should list *one* of the traits of that type of mollusk. List only the traits; do not label with the terms. For example: for gastropods—make three different cards, one per trait.

   - largest class of mollusks
   - usually has coiled shells
   - includes whelks, conchs

3. Make a copy of the Shell Identification page. Cut out one of each type of mollusk and glue to an index card.

4. You should now have a total of 30 cards, as follows:
   - 10 cards with mollusk terms on them
   - 15 cards with mollusk traits on them
   - 5 cards with pictures on them

How to Play

1. To play this game, mix all the cards together, face down. Lay the cards out, still face down, in neat rows. Turn over two cards at a time, trying to make a match. Matches are made with any two cards that define, name, or picture the same type of mollusk. For instance, a card with the picture of a whelk and a card reading "gastropod" make a match. Two cards that say "gastropod" do not make a match. Play until all matches are made.

2. Have fun and learn your terms!

 *Discovery Zone*

Scallops can squeeze a stream of water out of the bottom of their shells that jettisons them off the ocean floor and away from predators.

SHELL IDENTIFICATION

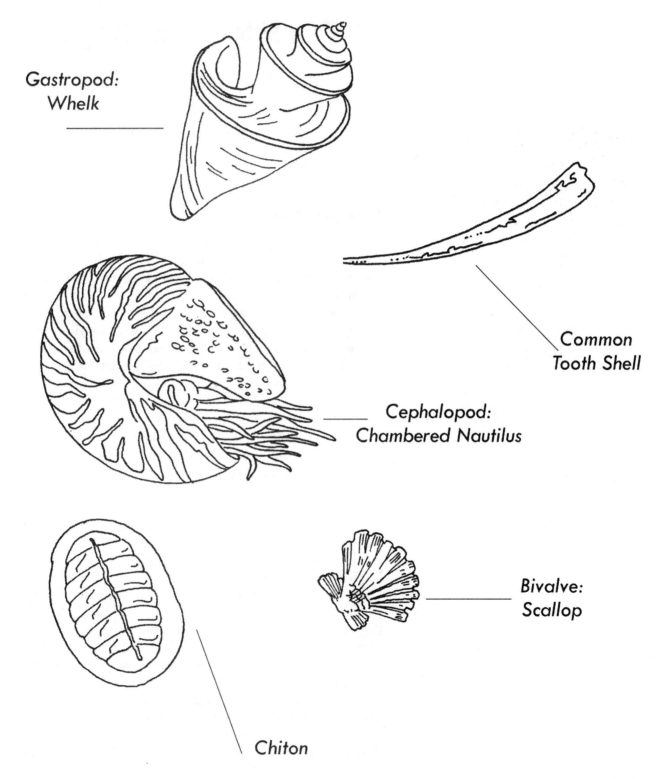

Gastropod:
Whelk

Common
Tooth Shell

Cephalopod:
Chambered Nautilus

Bivalve:
Scallop

Chiton

LESSON 32

SHARKS

TEACHING TIME:
The Skinny on Sharks

What do you know about sharks? Do you know where they live? Do you know what they eat? Most of us know some things about sharks. For instance, most of us know they live in the ocean. We also know that they are sometimes quite dangerous. Today we're going to look more closely at sharks. Hopefully, I will answer some questions you have and you will leave today's lesson knowing more than when we started.

Identifying Sharks

Let's begin with *what* sharks are. Sharks are a type of fish and though they resemble dolphins in appearance, they are not mammals. Instead, sharks are in the **Class Chondrichthyes**. There are approximately 375 species of sharks, which are grouped into eight different orders. They are probably most quickly identified by the **dorsal fin** located on their backs. Another identifying feature of sharks is their multiple rows of teeth. Sharks are cold-blooded, for the most part, and have flexible skeletons made of cartilage, not bone. Their outer covering, or "skin," is made up of scales that are like miniature versions of their teeth. These are called **placoid scales**, and they feel somewhat like sandpaper.

Have you ever seen a shark? Was it enormous? More than likely it was not. Some sharks are as small as eight inches in length. That's not very large, is it? These smallest sharks are the **dwarf dogfish**. Of course, the largest of sharks can grow up to 50 *feet* in length! I'd say that's large, wouldn't you? (We'll measure these out later in the lesson.) Sharks that get this large are the **whale sharks**. Though some sharks can grow to great lengths, the fact is that most sharks are less than 3 feet in length. Many people think all sharks are enormous because they've seen movies about sharks and the sharks were huge. Movies like this tend to portray **great white sharks**, which grow up to 20 feet in length. They are very large and are also known as vicious predators. It's good to know that all sharks are not like great whites.

God created sharks with features that make them great hunters. First of all, they have a very good sense of smell. As a matter of fact, over one-third of their brains are used for their sense of smell. They can detect even tiny amounts of

Can you figure out on which day God created sharks?
Read Genesis 1:21, 23.

"So God created great sea creatures and every living thing that moves, with which the waters abounded, . . . "
(Genesis 1:21)

food or blood in the water around them. God also created them with eyes that can see well even with little light. In addition to sight and smell, they can detect vibrations in the water caused by sound and movement. They can even detect some electrical currents in living animals.

Sharks most often dwell in **tropical waters**, which are usually warm. They are generally saltwater creatures, though there are some that live in freshwater. Depending on the species, they are found in either shallow waters near the coast or out in the open ocean. They are predators and are a vital link in food chains. As with any predator, without them we could have significant problems with other animal populations. Therefore, they are important to the ecosystem.

A Shark's Diet

As for shark food, the list is long. Though they will eat almost anything, each species tends to have its preferences. It may surprise you to know that the largest shark, the whale shark, eats tiny plankton and krill from the ocean. Other sharks are carnivorous and eat primarily fish. Most of these sharks also eat crustaceans and mollusks. Several of the larger species prefer mammals like seals and dolphins. The digestive system of sharks is quite sturdy, enabling them to digest whole fishes and mammals. Many people think sharks want to eat humans. The truth is most sharks do not intentionally seek out humans for food. In fact, worldwide, there are only about one hundred or so attacks per year on humans. Some years there may be a few more, some years a few less, but on average around one hundred. Out of these one hundred, there are very few deaths. In other words, you don't have to worry too much about being shark bait.

Measure a Shark

Using a yardstick or measuring tape:

1. Measure out the size of a dwarf dogfish. (8 inches)
2. Measure out the size of a whale shark. (50 feet)
3. Measure out the largest size of most sharks. (3 feet)

Other sharks you may want to measure:

- Nurse shark   13 feet
- Hammerhead   12 feet
- Great white   20 feet

Discovery Zone

Did you know there are only about 100 shark attacks on humans per year . . . worldwide!

Discovery Zone

*Visit **www.sheddnet.org** for an extensive, printable lesson on sharks.
This site is sponsored by the John G. Shedd Aquarium in Chicago.*

HANDS-ON TIME: Research a Shark

Objective: To learn about a specific type of shark.

Discover!

Today you get to research sharks. I recommend choosing one type of shark and learning all you can about it. If your parent agrees, you can use the Internet and find pictures of your shark, sometimes even live video.

- Try to discover what features make your shark special. In other words, how did God design this particular type of shark?
- Find out where it lives and what it eats.
- Is this shark known to attack humans? If so, where and under what conditions?
- Write a brief report showing your findings, and add it to your science notebook.
- For fun, complete the word search below containing the names of some of the different kinds of sharks.

Discovery Zone

Sharks have been known to smell a fragment (small piece) of tuna from over 75 feet away.

Now That's a Shark of Another Color

```
H T D M N L Y X S O I T G F S U P B
A A R U E B R I B U Z I R E Y B W E
J Y M G U T L S H Y R R E S O E E I
M X N M X V E X S O E E A R S Q T X
K A N L E M O N H T R X T U T V B S
R N P R J R J B T O F N W N V L N Q
V T T V S X H U W P L T H N U L P I
R I M L G T C E A M I F I E T I A M
P X V Z O E Z N A G D V T B X N B A
L W Q B I S L C Q D P R E F M D A K
H J L K R E H S E R H T A M B Z B O
N Q O W H A L E S H A R K P P N Q H
Y O Y I G V C O T G L B E M O K J T
C O H W D X W D N N U J Z W U E K V
O K U K Z V W H E C S G F L Q A L N
Y E R G X L Z N J U D V M P K E G B
D B N N X J A B M I J V D S M A D H
I X M P S D Y U K K K Y P D H J P S
```

ANGEL
BLUE
COOKIECUTTER
GREATWHITE
GREY
HAMMERHEAD
HORN

LEMON
LEOPARD
MAKO
NURSE
SILVERTIP
THRESHER
WHALESHARK

LESSON 33

CRUSTACEANS

TEACHING TIME:
Shrimp, Crabs, and Lobsters

When I go out to eat at a seafood restaurant I have a hard time choosing what to eat. Three of my favorite things are often on the menu . . . shrimp, crab, and lobster! When cooked just right and dipped in melted butter, they are hard to resist! These creatures are usually called shellfish, but they are actually **crustaceans**. Crustaceans are part of Phylum Arthropoda, the phylum with the most creatures, and are usually found in the water. There are, however, some species that live on land. They are often very tiny, but some lobsters can reach up to 2 feet in length. In all, there are over 26,000 known species of crustaceans.

As I mentioned before, arthropods make up the largest phylum on earth. (You may recall that insects are also in this phylum.) Shrimp, crabs, and lobsters, like other arthropods, have a hard external covering called an **exoskeleton**. Their bodies are divided into segments and the segments have limbs, usually in the form of legs, in pairs. They are also invertebrates, meaning they have no spines.

Crustaceans, specifically, have some traits that make them special. To begin with, two of their limbs are often pincers. In fact, when I eat crabs and lobsters, the best part is the claw meat found in their pincers! Also, crustaceans have **gills** instead of lungs. Gills allow them to stay **submerged** (underwater) all the time like fish. Would you believe that in many species the legs are also part of their respiratory (breathing) system?

The life cycle of crustaceans begins with an egg. The mother cares for the eggs until they hatch into the larva stage. The larva stage, as you learned studying insects, does not usually look like the adult stage. This is the clue that crustaceans go through metamorphosis. Sometimes there is more than one larva stage for crustaceans. Once these creatures reach the first larva stage, there is virtually no longer any parental care. In the adult stage, they may live for just a few days or up to 20 years or more, depending on the species.

Some other types of crustaceans include barnacles and krill. Barnacles are stationary. In other words, they cannot move from one place to another. They are often found on seaside rocks or on boats under the water. Krill are like very tiny shrimp. You probably remember that krill make up the diet of many large whales.

Not all crustaceans live in water. Scorpions, for example, live on land. Look at what Jesus said to His disciples.

" 'Behold, I give you the authority to trample on serpents and scorpions, and over all the power of the enemy, and nothing shall by any means hurt you.' " (Luke 10:19)

Crustaceans are quite important in the food chain. As mentioned in the beginning of this lesson, even humans like to eat them. They are a rich source of protein and many animals rely on them for food. Even though, we usually think of them as saltwater creatures, there are also many species that thrive in freshwater, providing food for the animals living there.

ONE STEP FURTHER

* Check with your local grocery stores to see if any sell live lobsters.

* If so, go to the store and observe them.

* Look for their exoskeleton, their sectioned bodies, their pincers, and their antennae.

* You might also ask if they have any fresh shrimp. Usually the heads have been removed, but sometimes they are still intact. Look for the features listed above.

HANDS-ON TIME: Shrimp Fest

Parental Guidance Required

Objective: To sample shrimp cooked two different ways and see an example of a crustacean.

Today we are going to have a shrimp fest. If you are allergic to shrimp or do not eat seafood for any reason, you will need to substitute another activity.

Materials

* 1–2 pounds of raw shrimp, preferably unpeeled
* Crab-boil spices (in your fish market)
* Oil for frying
* 2 eggs
* 1 cup of flour
* Salt and pepper
* Ketchup, cocktail sauce

Instructions

1. Peel half of the shrimp under parental supervision. I like to pinch off the legs first, and then tear away the remaining shell, beginning on the underside.

2. Using a table knife, devein the peeled shrimp on the back, by running the knife along the back, slightly splitting open the shrimp.

3. Discard the shells (exoskeletons).

4. Set aside the peeled shrimp. These will be used in another recipe.

 *Discovery Zone*

Krill, a main menu item for many whales, are miniature shrimp-like animals. A whale's stomach can contain up to 4 tons of krill!

5. Carefully wash your hands, using lots of soap and warm water.

Now for the unpeeled shrimp:

6. Put two quarts of water on to boil. Add in a bag of the crab-boil spices. (You can do this without the spices, if you prefer.)

7. When the water boils, add in the unpeeled shrimp. Return to a boil and continue boiling for 3 minutes or until the shrimp are opaque. (If the shrimp are very large, more cooking time will be needed.)

8. Strain the shrimp and let cool.

9. Peel as you eat. Serve with ketchup or cocktail sauce or eat plain!

Now for the peeled shrimp:

10. Prepare a pan for frying. You will need about 1 inch of cooking oil in the pan.

11. Beat 1–2 eggs in a bowl.

12. In another bowl, mix 1 cup of flour with salt and pepper to taste.

13. Dip the peeled shrimp, one at a time, into the beaten eggs, then lightly dredge them in the flour mixture.

14. Drop into the hot oil. Add in as many as your pan will hold, while allowing space between shrimp.

15. When the shrimp rise to the surface, turn and continue cooking until golden brown on both sides.

16. Remove from oil and drain on paper towel.

17. Serve with ketchup or cocktail sauce or eat plain!

 *Discovery Zone*

Safety Note

Always wash your hands with warm, soapy water after handling raw meat of any kind.

LESSON 34

FRESHWATER LIFE

TEACHING TIME:
No Salt, Please

Rivers are freshwater.

Jesus says in John 7:38, " 'He who believes in Me, as the Scripture has said, out of his heart will flow rivers of living water.' "

The past few lessons you've studied have been primarily about marine, or saltwater, animals. Today we will shift our focus to life in freshwater. As I told you before, freshwater is found in lakes, rivers, and streams. It is the water that comes from rain and snowmelt.

If you've ever hung around a pond or lake, you've probably noticed plants growing in and around the water. You may also have noticed plants, such as algae and lily pads, growing on top of the water. Since all plants need sunlight to grow, you will not find plants growing in deep water, only in shallow and relatively clear water. Plant life is a large and important part of life in freshwater. The oxygen produced by the plants is needed for the animals that live there.

Not only are plants important in freshwater life, but animals are, too. Do you know what types of animals live in freshwater? You've already learned about some of them in previous units. Snakes, alligators, and terrapins are some of the ones we have studied. Other freshwater creatures include amphibians, which we will discuss in an upcoming lesson; water-loving mammals, such as otters and beavers; and aquatic birds, such as ducks and geese. Sometimes, you can even find eagles living near freshwater, as they love to eat fish, which of course are abundant in any kind of water.

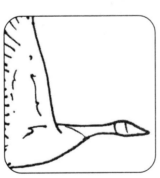

In healthy, clean bodies of water, life is abundant. Humans can hurt the wildlife in lakes and rivers, however, by not taking care of their trash properly and by destroying too much of the natural surroundings. God has placed humans in charge of this creation and as the Earth's managers, we have a responsibility to take care of it.

HANDS-ON TIME: Making Freshwater From Saltwater

Objective: To see how freshwater is made when *salt*water evaporates.

In *Exploring Creation With Physical Science*, Dr. Jay Wile gives the following step-by-step experiment for making freshwater from saltwater through the processes of evaporation, condensation, and precipitation.[1]

Note: Remember to record all of this in yor science notebook, using a "Checking It Out" form. You might even want to take a picture!

Discovery Zone

Much of the freshwater in our world is found in underground rivers and streams.

Supplies

- Water
- Salt
- Ice
- A tablespoon
- A small saucepan
- A saucepan lid or frying pan lid larger than the saucepan used
- A large bowl (It should not be plastic, as it will get hot.)
- Potholders
- A zippered plastic sandwich bag
- Stove

Introduction

In the hydrologic cycle,[2] water can be transferred from a saltwater source (the ocean) to a freshwater source through the process of evaporation, condensation, and precipitation. This experiment will show you how that works.

Procedure

A. Fill the saucepan about three-quarters full with water.

B. Add three tablespoons of salt to the water and stir to make as much salt dissolve as possible. Do not be concerned if you can't get it all to dissolve.

C. Taste the saltwater you have made. Please note that you should **NEVER** get into the habit of tasting things in an experiment unless someone who knows a lot more chemistry than you do (like me) says to do so. In this case, I know that you are not at risk of poisoning yourself by tasting the saltwater you have just made. However, there may be times when you make something in an experiment which *you* think will not hurt you, but is, in fact, quite toxic. So **DO NOT TASTE THINGS IN AN EXPERIMENT UNLESS I TELL YOU TO DO SO!**

D. Tastes bad, doesn't it? Now set the pan of saltwater on the stove and start heating it up. Your goal is to have vigorously boiling water, so turn up the heat!

E. While you are waiting for the saltwater to boil, take your zippered sandwich bag and fill it full of ice. Zipper it shut so that no water from the ice can leak out.

F. Once the saltwater has started boiling vigorously, place the bowl next to the saucepan. The bowl should not be on a burner. You do not want to heat the bowl. You just want it close to the boiling water.

G. Now use the potholder to hold the saucepan lid and put the zippered sandwich bag full of ice on top of the lid. You may have to use a finger or two from the hand holding the lid to make sure that the bag of ice stays on top of the saucepan lid.

H. Take the lid and hold it so that one end (the one with the most ice on it) is over the saucepan and the other end is over the bowl. Tilt the lid so that it tilts toward the bowl. In the end, your setup should look like this:

I. Hold the lid there for a little while and watch what happens on the underside of the lid. **BE CAREFUL! EVERYTHING HERE IS HOT!** Notice that water droplets are forming on the underside of the lid over the saucepan and they slowly drip down the lid towards the bowl.

J. If your arm gets tired, you can set the lid down so that part of it rests on the saucepan and the rest sits on the bowl. Make sure that the bowl is lower than the saucepan so that the lid still tilts toward the bowl.

K. Eventually, you will see water dripping off of the pan lid and into the bowl. Wait until there is enough water in the bowl to be able to take a drink. Once that happens, turn off the burner and wait a moment.

L. **Using potholders,** take the lid away and put it in the sink. Pour the half-melted ice out of the bag and throw the bag away (or recycle it). **Still using potholders,** take the bowl away from the stove and set it on the counter. Empty the saucepan and put it in the sink as well.

M. Allow the bowl to cool down completely, and then taste the water in the bowl. Once again, you can only do this because I am telling you to!

N. Does the water in the bowl taste like saltwater?

1. Reprinted from *Exploring Creation With Physical Science,* by Dr. Jay L. Wile. Published by Apologia Educational Ministries, Inc., Anderson, IN, 4th printing 2002; pp.110–111. Reprinted with permission.
2. As explained by Dr. Wile, the *hydrologic cycle* is the process by which water is continuously exchanged between earth's various water sources (*Exploring Creation With Physical Science,* p. 108). Look up the terms *evaporation, condensation,* and *precipitation* in your dictionary so you are familiar with them before proceeding further with this experiment.

LESSON 35

AMPHIBIANS

TEACHING TIME:
A Froggy Story

A type of animal we have not discussed yet is an **amphibian**. Amphibians are found in Kingdom Animalia, Phylum Chordata. They are unique because they live part of their lives in water and part on land. Frogs, toads, and salamanders are all amphibians.

A Dual Life

Let's first discover what living part of their lives in water and part on land means. This quality is sometimes referred to as a **dual life**. It will help you to know that amphibians go through metamorphosis. In other words, as you learned studying insects, there are several stages of development that don't really look like the adult stage. In the case of amphibians, most of them begin their lives as eggs that have been laid in water. Take a toad, for example. When toads hatch from their eggs, they have gills (like fish) for breathing. They have long tails and remain motionless for a time. At this stage, they are called **tadpoles**. Before long, front legs begin to form. Inside the body, lungs are beginning to develop. Eventually, the gills disappear, the body begins to look more like an adult toad (although there is still a tail), and the tadpole begins to spend more and more time on land and less in the water. Soon, it will spend virtually all of its time on land and will no longer have a tail. This process is basically the same for all amphibians. They begin life in water with gills and eventually develop lungs and adult bodies. Then they move from living in water to living on land. Most species still prefer living near water or in very damp environments.

Amphibians have some qualities that set them apart from other animals. You've just learned about the first; their dual life. Though they are sometimes mistaken for reptiles, they have no scales like reptiles do. Amphibians have four legs with webbed feet, and they have breathable skin. Last, they are cold-blooded.

Did you know that God used frogs as a curse against the pharaoh in Egypt? It was the second plague.

" 'But if you refuse to let them go, behold, I will smite all your territory with frogs.' " (Exodus 8:2)

Other Characteristics

Now that we know the traits they have in common, let's find out what makes them different. We'll begin with salamanders. Let me begin by stressing that they are *not* lizards. Lizards have rough skin with scales. Salamanders have smooth skin and no scales. Also, salamanders can spend much time underwater. Now you know why they have webbed feet. Lizards do not have webbed feet.

Although both are amphibians, frogs and toads are often mistaken for each other. Frogs are characterized by smooth, shiny skin. They need to stay wet, and therefore spend much time in the water. Toads, by contrast, have bumpy, dry skin. They spend nearly all of their time on land, returning to water only to breed.

Though amphibians do not always dwell in the water, they all begin life there. They are a unique type of animal and should not be confused with reptiles. They come in many different sizes and though we may think of them as green in color, one trip to an aquarium will show you that they come in many different and sometimes spectacular colors. Again, God is creative and careful in all that He does.

 *Discovery Zone*

Many amphibians have poison in their skin and are brightly colored to warn away potential predators.

HANDS-ON TIME: UNIT EIGHT WRAP-UP

Show What You Know!

Answer as many questions as you can without using your book or notes. You get **10,000** points for each correct response. After going through the review once with your book closed, open your book and try again. You get **5,000** points for each additional correct answer. So, **show what you know!**

1. Name two main types of water found on the earth. _____

    _____

2. Name the phylum containing oysters, clams, and squids. _____

    _____

3. Are mollusk bodies soft or hard? _____

4. Name as many of the five classes of mollusks as you can. _____

    _____

    _____

    _____

5. What does *buoyant* mean? _____

    _____

6. Name the fin located on a shark's back. _____

7. What type of scales cover a shark's body? _____

8. How long are most types of sharks? _____

9. Name at least two types of crustaceans. _____

    _____

10. What types of bodies of water contain freshwater? _____

    _____

11. Amphibians live a _____ , meaning part in water and part on land.

12. Name at least two types of amphibians. _____

    _____

FIRST ATTEMPT _____

(number of correct responses x 10,000)

SECOND ATTEMPT   + _____

(number of correct responses x 5,000)

TOTAL NUMBER OF POINTS _____

 **WRITING ASSIGNMENT**

In your science notebook, complete the creative writing assignment below. Have fun with it!

This is your chance to prove yourself as a top-notch travel agent. If you can successfully fill this next tour, you will have booked over $1 million dollars of travel and guaranteed a place for yourself on the Wall of Fame.

Your current tour assignment entails coordinating and promoting a rare cruise to an incredibly remote region of the Pacific Ocean. While visiting an uninhabited island, the passengers will have once-in-a-lifetime opportunities to explore the island's freshwaters and to snorkel and scuba-dive in its surrounding saltwater.

Create a list of the water life passengers may encounter. Put the details of the cruise into a written speech or a press release with special emphasis on the water life of the island. Decide who your target audience is and tailor your speech or press release to that group. Do you want to convince the readers of Biology Today? Emphasize the classifications and unique characteristics of each creature or the many kinds of life in one place. Are you targeting the scuba club? You may want to talk about where each animal lives and how to spot it once you're in the water.

With your expert knowledge and creative flair, you can do it!

APPENDIX A

REPRODUCIBLE FORMS AND MAPS

Checking It Out
Experiment Form

Name _____ Unit # _____ Date _____

Name of Experiment _____

Book(s) used _____

_____

Objective

Today I am trying to find out _____

_____

_____

Hypothesis

Based on what I have read and studied, I believe _____

_____

_____

The Experiment

To test out this theory, I plan t o _____

_____

_____

Desired Result _____

_____

Actual Result _____

_____

❑   I am pleased with the result I received

❑   I am not pleased with the result I received

I believe this experiment would have gone better if _____

_____

I learned _____

_____

Daily Reading Sheet

Name _____ **Unit #** _____ **Date** _____

Title, Author, Page #'s _____

_____

_____

Main Topic

_____

_____

_____

I learned _____

_____

_____

I enjoyed learning about _____

_____

_____

I never knew that _____

_____

_____

Facts

_____

_____

_____

I would like to know more about _____

_____

Vocabulary

_____

_____

_____   _____

_____   _____

_____   _____

Field Trip Journal

Name   Unit #   Date

Destination

Purpose

I saw

I also saw

I learned

The **most interesting** thing I saw (or learned) was

The **most unusual** thing I saw (or learned) was

I would like to have **learned more** about

I think I could learn more about this by

Plant Observation Form

Name   Unit #   Date

Type of Seed(s) Planted

Plant Container(s)

Type of Soil

Location of Plant

Record observations on chart below, for two weeks.

Here's an example:

Day	Sunny?	Clouds?	Soil?	Growth?	Observations
1	All day	No	Moist	None seen	Soil seems too wet

Day	Sunny?	Clouds?	Soil?	Growth?	Observations
1					
2					
3					
4					
5					
6					
7					
8					
9					
10					
11					
12					
13					
14					

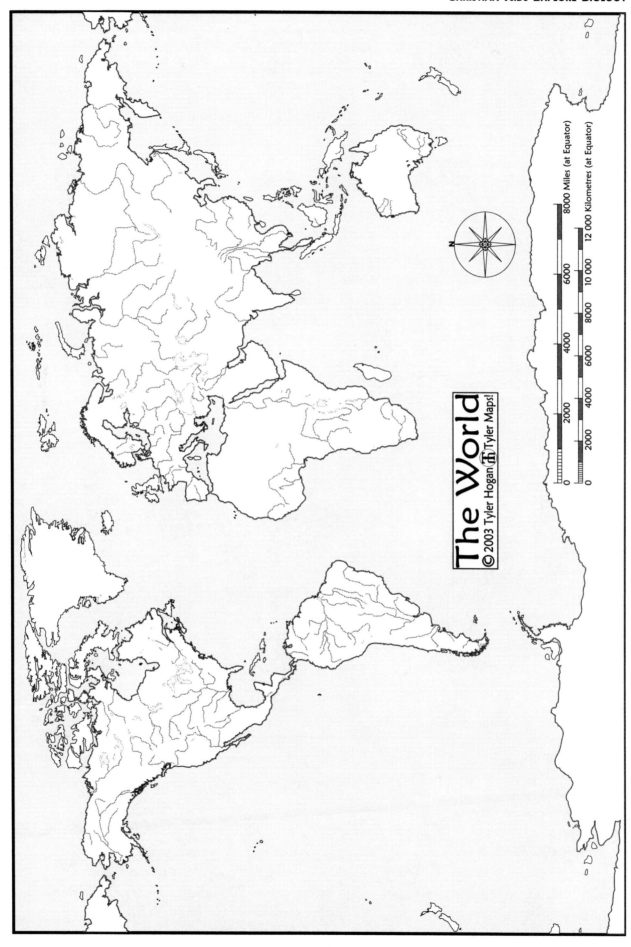

The World

© 2003 Tyler Hogan ⓣ Tyler Maps!

8000 Miles (at Equator)

12 000 Kilometres (at Equator)

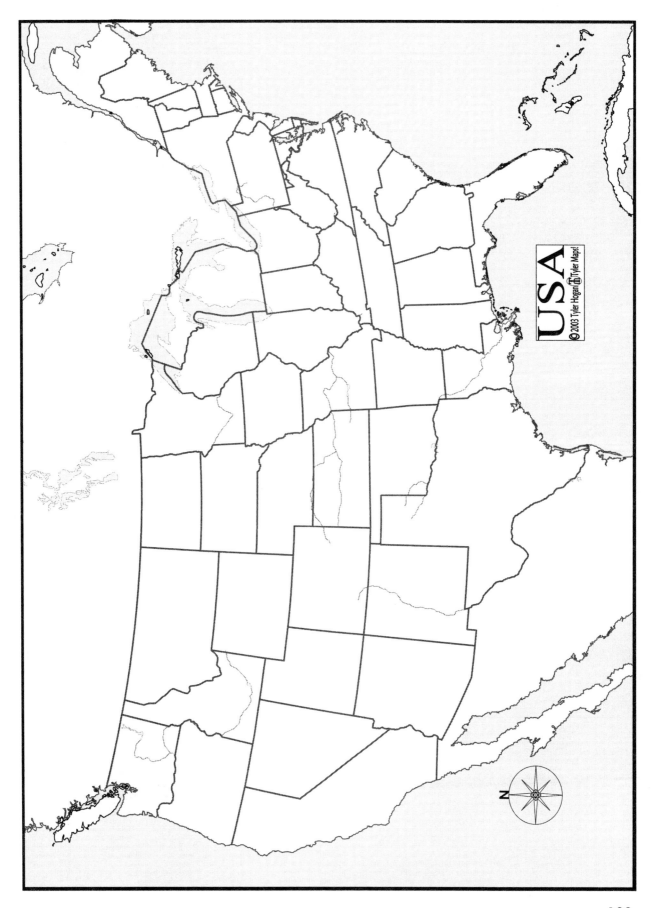

USA
© 2003 Tyler Hogan | Tyler Maps!

Appendix B

Memorization or Reference Lists

UNIT ONE MEMORY LISTS

Kingdoms
- Monera – Consists of bacteria and blue-green algae
- Protista – Consists of amoebas, diatoms, euglena, paramecia
- Animalia - Animals
- Plantae - Plants
- Fungi – Mildews, molds, mushrooms, yeasts

Organism Structure
- Organisms are made of systems
- Systems are made of organs
- Organs are made of tissues
- Tissues are made of cells
- Cells are made of protoplasm

Organism Characteristics
Organisms have the following characteristics:
1. Nutrition
2. Respiration
3. Excretion
4. Growth
5. Reproduction
6. Irritability
7. Movement

Biosphere Components
- Biosphere
- Biomes
- Ecosystems
- Habitats
- Species
- Flora
- Niche

Vertebrates
- Amphibians
- Birds
- Fishes
- Mammals
- Reptiles

UNIT TWO MEMORY LISTS

Photosynthesis Elements
- Light or sunlight
- Water (H_2O)
- Chlorophyll
- Carbon dioxide (CO_2)

Flower Anatomy
Female Anatomy (Carpels)
- Stigma
- Style
- Ovary
- Ovule

Male Anatomy (Stamens)
- Anther
- Filament

Other . . .
- Sepal
- Petal
- Pedicel (stem)
- Receptacle
- Corolla
- Calyx

Types of Fruit
- Dry fruits: Nuts, pods, grains
- Juicy fruits: Berries, tomatoes, cucumbers, oranges – contain many seeds
- Pomes: Apples, pears – have a core
- Drupes, or stone fruits: Peaches, avocados, olives – contain a pit that holds a seed

Tree Identification
Conifers
- Needle-like leaves
- Produce cones
- Evergreen
- Fragrant pine scent

Broadleaves
- Often deciduous
- Broad, flat leaves

Life Cycle of a Conifer
1. Pollen meets ovule
2. Ovule is fertilized
3. Ovule becomes seed
4. Seed develops into a cone
5. Adult tree

Life Cycle of a Flowering Plant

1. Pollen meets ovule
2. Ovule is fertilized
3. Ovule becomes seed
4. Adult plant

Tree Trunk Layers

(from inside to outside)

1. Heartwood
2. Sapwood
3. Annual rings
4. Cambium
5. Inner bark
6. Outer bark

Venus's Flytrap Digestion

1. Leaf lobes open.
2. Insect crawls across leaf and touches trigger hair.
3. Lobes shut, clamping down on insect.
4. Enzymes digest insect, taking 5 to10 days.
5. Lobes open again.

UNIT THREE MEMORY LISTS

Bird Traits

- Class Aves
- Warm-blooded
- Four-chambered heart
- Feathered
- Lightweight bones
- Lay eggs
- Beaks, not teeth
- Hooked beaks (birds of prey)
- Keen eyesight
- Cambered (curved) wings for lift

Common Taxonomy

- Birds that don't fly
- Birds of prey
- Game birds
- Aquatic birds: swimming, diving, wading
- Songbirds
- Hummingbirds

Bird "Plurals" List

- Bevy of quail
- Bevy of swans
- Brace of ducks

- Brood/clutch of chicks
- Cast of hawks
- Charm of finches
- Covey of partridge/quail
- Exaltation of larks
- Flight of birds
- Gaggle of geese
- Murder of crows
- Muster of peacocks
- Nest of pheasants
- Paddling of ducks
- Parliament of owls
- Peep of chickens
- Rafter of turkeys
- Siege of cranes/herons
- Skein of geese
- Spring of teals
- Team of ducks
- Volery of birds
- Watch of nightingales

UNIT FOUR MEMORY LISTS

Mammal Traits
- Class Mammalia
- Hair on their bodies
- Produce milk for their young
- Warm-blooded

Primary Types of Mammals (Orders)
- Monotremes
- Marsupials
- Canids
- Felines
- Bears
- Primates
- Aquatic mammals: Orders Sirenia and Cetacea

Mammal "Plurals" List
- Band of gorillas
- Cete of badgers
- Clowder/clutter of cats
- Crash of rhinos
- Cry of hounds
- Down of hares
- Drift of swine
- Drove of cattle/sheep
- Gam of whales

- Gang of elk
- Herd of elephants
- Husk of hares
- Kindle of kittens
- Labor of moles
- Leap of leopards
- Leash of greyhounds
- Litter of pigs
- Mob of kangaroos
- Mute of hounds
- Pack of hounds/wolves
- Pod of seals/whales
- Pride of lions
- Rag of colts
- Shrewdness of apes
- Skulk of foxes
- Sloth of bears
- Sounder of boars/swine
- Span of mules
- Tribe/trip of goats
- Troop of kangaroos/monkeys
- Yoke of oxen

Mammal Baby Names
- Antelope – calf, fawn, kid, yearling
- Bear – cub
- Beaver – kit, kitten
- Bobcat – kitten, cub
- Buffalo – calf, yearling, spike-bull
- Camel – calf, colt
- Caribou – calf, fawn
- Cat – kit, kitling, kitten
- Cattle – calf, yearling
- Chimpanzee – infant
- Cougar – kitten, cub
- Cow – calf
- Coyote – cub, pup, puppy
- Deer – fawn
- Dog – whelp, puppy
- Elephant – calf
- Giraffe – calf
- Horse – colt, foal, filly, yearling
- Kangaroo – joey
- Leopard – cub
- Mink – kit, cub
- Monkey – suckling, yearling, infant
- Muskrat – kit
- Rabbit – kitten, bunny
- Raccoon – kit, cub
- Sea lion – pup

- Seal – whelp, pup, cub, bachelor
- Sheep – lamb, lambkin, shearling, yearling
- Skunk – kitten
- Squirrel – dray
- Swine – shoat, trotter, pig, piglet
- Tiger – whelp, cub
- Walrus – cub
- Whale – calf
- Wolf – cub, pup
- Zebra – colt, foal

UNIT FIVE MEMORY LISTS

Human Classification
- Kingdom – Animalia
- Phylum – Chordata
- Class – Mammalia
- Order – Primates
- Family – Hominidae
- Genus – Homo
- Species – Sapiens

Human Body Systems
1. Cardiovascular system/circulatory system
2. Digestive system
3. Endocrine system
4. Integumentary system
5. Lymphatic system
6. Muscular system
7. Nervous system
8. Reproductive system
9. Respiratory system
10. Skeletal system
11. Urinary system

Sequence of Heart Pumping
1. Blood flows from vein into atrium.
2. Blood flows from atrium into ventricle.
3. Blood is forced into arteries.
4. Blood carries oxygen to body parts.
5. Blood is sent to lungs for more oxygen.
6. Blood is sent to veins.

Parts of the Skull
- Frontal bone
- Sphenoid bone
- Eye socket
- Nasal bone

- Zygomatic bone
- Maxilla
- Mandible
- Parietal bone
- Occipital bone
- Temporal bone
- Mastoid process
- Styloid process
- Zygomatic arc

Major Skeletal Parts

- Cranium – skull
- Vertebrae – backbone (spine)
- Sternum – breastbone
- Ribs
  Pelvic/hip region:
  - Ilium
  - Sacrum
  - Coccyx – tailbone
  - Pubis
  - Ischium
- Clavicle – collar bone
- Humerus – upper arm
- Radius – forearm
- Ulna – lower arm
- Carpus – wrist
- Metacarpus – hand bones
- Phalanges – fingers, toes
- Femur – thigh
- Patella – kneecap
- Tibia – shin
- Fibula – lower leg
- Tarsus – ankle
- Metatarsus – foot bones

UNIT SIX MEMORY LIST

Reptile Traits

- Class Reptilia
- Tough, dry scales
- Cold-blooded
- Three-chambered heart
- Lay eggs (some exceptions)
- Egg shell usually leathery
- Legs in pairs, if they have legs at all

Plurals
- Bale or dole of turtles
- Nest of vipers

UNIT SEVEN MEMORY LISTS

Characteristics of an Insect
- 3 pairs of jointed legs
- Wings in at least one stage of life
- Have antennae
- 3 body segments – head, thorax, abdomen
- No lungs
- Some type of metamorphosis

Stages of Complete Metamorphosis
1. Egg
2. Larva (wormlike)
3. Pupa (resting)
4. Adult

Stages of Incomplete Metamorphosis
1. Egg
2. Nymph
3. Adult

Butterfly Characteristics
- Symmetrical wing patterns
- Slender bodies
- Antennae have knobs
- Fold wings up when resting
- Active during daylight hours
- Colorful
- Prefer open areas

Moth Characteristics
- Symmetrical patterns
- Thick, hairy bodies
- Usually have little color
- Wings lie flat when resting
- Often feathery antennae with no knobs
- Nocturnal
- Prefer wooded areas

Honeybee Characteristics
- Make honey
- Live in large colonies
- Live in wax hives that are very strong and durable

Wasp Characteristics
- Slender bodies with constricted abdomens
- Long stingers that produce painful stings
- Weak nests made of a mixture of deadwood and their saliva

Hornet Characteristics
- A type of wasp
- Very large, papery nests
- Lay eggs in other wasps' nests
- Often no worker bees

Insect Plurals List
Ants – nest, army, colony, swarm
Bees – swarm, cluster, nest, hive
Caterpillars – army
Flies – business, hatch, grist, swarm, cloud
Gnats – swarm, cloud, horde
Hornets – nest
Lice – flock
Locusts – swarm, cloud, plague
Termites – colony, nest, swarm, brood
Wasps – nest, herd

UNIT EIGHT MEMORY LISTS

Five Main Classes of Mollusks
1. Gastropods – coiled like cones and whelks
2. Bivalves – hinged like oysters and clams
3. Cephalopods – inner or outer shell like squid and chambered nautilus
4. Chiton – movable "plates"
5. Tooth (tusk) shells – resemble tusks

Waterlife Plurals List
Eels – swarm, bed
Fish – school, shoal, haul, run, catch
Goldfish – troubling
Jellyfish – smuck, brood
Minnows – shoal, steam, swarm
Oysters/clams – bed
Sardines – family
Sharks – school, shoal
Turtles – bale, dole

Waterlife Baby Names
Clam – littleneck
Cod – codling, scrod, sprag
Duck – duckling, flapper
Eel – fry, elver

Fish – fry, fingerling, minnow, spawn
Frog – polliwog, tadpole
Goose – gosling
Oyster – spat, brood
Pelican – chick, nestling
Sea lion – pup
Seal – pup, whelp, cub, bachelor
Shark – cub
Toad – tadpole
Walrus – cub
Whale – calf

Shark Facts

1. 354 species of sharks
2. Range in size from 6 inches long to 49 feet long
3. 35 species have been known to attack humans
4. 12 species most commonly involved in attacks on humans
5. Largest great white measured was 20 feet, 4 inches long and weighed 5,000 pounds

Oceans of the World

Pacific Ocean
Atlantic Ocean
Indian Ocean
Arctic Ocean

*10 Largest Seas, Gulfs, and Bays

(beginning with the largest)

1. Coral Sea
2. Arabian Sea
3. South China Sea
4. Caribbean Sea
5. Mediterranean Sea
6. Bering Sea
7. Bay of Bengal
8. Sea of Okhotsk
9. Norwegian Sea
10. Gulf of Mexico

*Largest Rivers in the World

1.	Nile	Africa
2.	Amazon	South America
3.	Yangtze (Chang)	Asia
4.	Mississippi – Missouri	North America
5.	Huang (Yellow)	Asia
6.	Ob' – Irtysh	Asia
7.	Rio de la Plata–Parana'	South America
8.	Congo	Africa
9.	Parana'	South America
10.	Amur–Argun	Asia

*** 10 Largest Seas, Gulfs, and Bays and Largest Rivers in the World information taken from
Rand McNally *Answer Atlas*, copyright 2003**

APPENDIX C

SCRIPTURE MEMORY
SCRIPTURE TAKEN FROM NEW KING JAMES

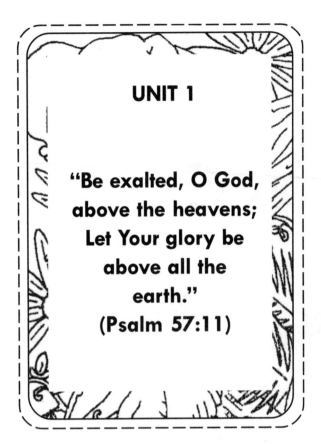

UNIT 1

"Be exalted, O God, above the heavens; Let Your glory be above all the earth."
(Psalm 57:11)

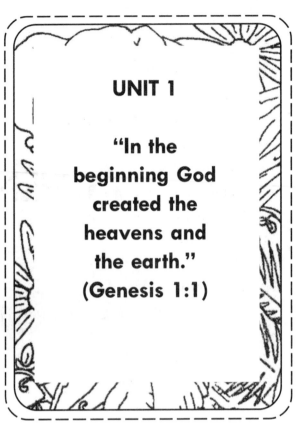

UNIT 1

"In the beginning God created the heavens and the earth."
(Genesis 1:1)

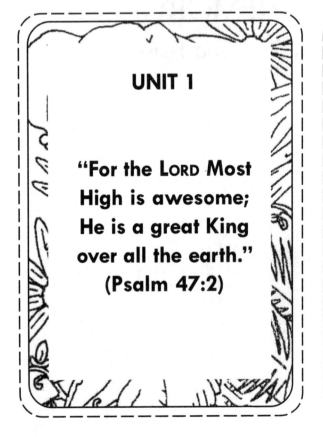

UNIT 1

"For the LORD Most High is awesome; He is a great King over all the earth."
(Psalm 47:2)

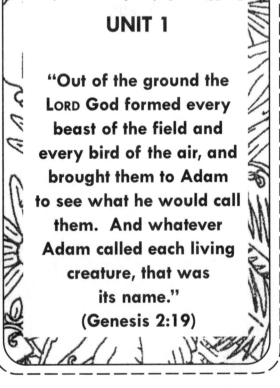

UNIT 1

"Out of the ground the LORD God formed every beast of the field and every bird of the air, and brought them to Adam to see what he would call them. And whatever Adam called each living creature, that was its name."
(Genesis 2:19)

UNIT 1

"Then God said, 'Let Us make man in Our image, according to Our likeness; let them have dominion over the fish of the sea, over the birds of the air, and over the cattle, over all the earth and over every creeping thing that creeps on the earth.'"
(Genesis 1:26)

UNIT 1

"Now John himself was clothed in camel's hair, with a leather belt around his waist; and his food was locusts and wild honey."
(Matthew 3:4)

UNIT 2

"Then God said, 'Let the earth bring forth grass, the herb that yields seed, and the fruit tree . . . ' "
(Genesis 1:11)

UNIT 2

" before any plant of the field was in the earth and before any herb of the field had grown. For the Lord God had not caused it to rain on the earth . . ."
(Genesis 2:5)

UNIT 2

"Then God said, 'Let the earth bring forth grass, the herb that yields seed, and the fruit tree that yields fruit according to its kind, whose seed is in itself . . .' "
(Genesis 1:11)

UNIT 2

"The fruit of the righteous is a tree of life, And he who wins souls is wise."
(Proverbs 11:30)

UNIT 3

"So God created . . . every winged bird according to its kind. And God saw that it was good."
(Genesis 1:21)

UNIT 3

"But those who wait on the Lord Shall renew their strength; They shall mount up with wings like eagles, They shall run and not be weary, They shall walk and not faint."
(Isaiah 40:31)

UNIT 3

"So I said, 'Oh, that I had wings like a dove! I would fly away and be at rest.' "
(Psalm 55:6)

UNIT 4

"But the very hairs of your head are all numbered."
(Matthew 10:30)

UNIT 4
"You shall take with you seven each of every clean animal, a male and his female; two each of animals that are unclean, a male and his female."
(Genesis 7:2)

UNIT 4

"For the king had merchant ships at sea with the fleet of Hiram. Once every three years the merchant ships came bringing gold, silver, ivory, apes, and monkeys."
(1 Kings 10:22)

UNIT 4

"So God created great sea creatures and every living thing that moves, with which the waters abounded . . ."
(Genesis 1:21)

UNIT 5

"So God created man in His own image; in the image of God He created him; male and female He created them."
(Genesis 1:27)

UNIT 5

"And the LORD God formed man of the dust of the ground, and breathed into his nostrils the breath of life; and man became a living being."
(Genesis 2:7)

UNIT 5

"My voice You shall hear in the morning, O Lord;
In the morning I will direct it to You,
And I will look up."
(Psalm 5:3)

UNIT 5

"For You formed my
inward parts;
You covered me in
my mother's womb."
(Psalm 139:13)

UNIT 6

"Behold, I send you
out as sheep in the
midst of wolves.
Therefore be wise as
serpents and
harmless as doves."
(Matthew 10:16)

UNIT 6

"And God made ...
everything that
creeps on the
earth according
to its kind.
And God saw that
it was good."
(Genesis 1:25)

UNIT 6

"So God created
great sea creatures
and every living
thing that moves,
with which the
waters abounded,
according to
their kind . . ."
(Genesis 1:21)

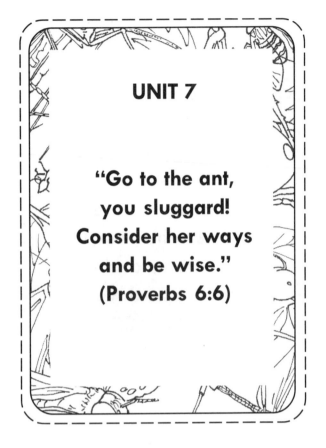

UNIT 7

"Go to the ant,
you sluggard!
Consider her ways
and be wise."
(Proverbs 6:6)

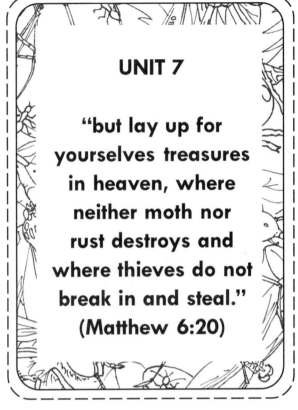

UNIT 7

"but lay up for
yourselves treasures
in heaven, where
neither moth nor
rust destroys and
where thieves do not
break in and steal."
(Matthew 6:20)

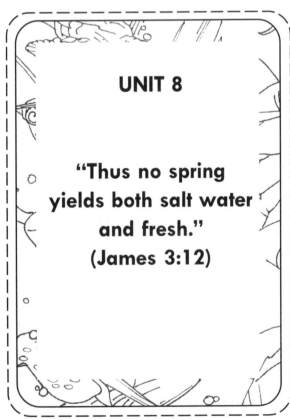

UNIT 8

"Thus no spring
yields both salt water
and fresh."
(James 3:12)

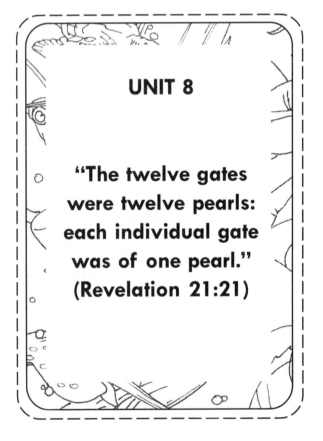

UNIT 8

"The twelve gates
were twelve pearls:
each individual gate
was of one pearl."
(Revelation 21:21)

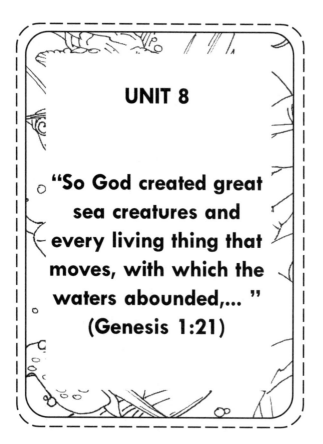

UNIT 8

"So God created great sea creatures and every living thing that moves, with which the waters abounded,... "
(Genesis 1:21)

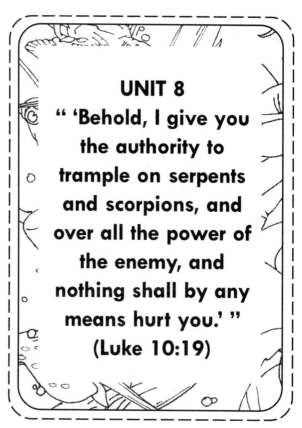

UNIT 8

" 'Behold, I give you the authority to trample on serpents and scorpions, and over all the power of the enemy, and nothing shall by any means hurt you.' "
(Luke 10:19)

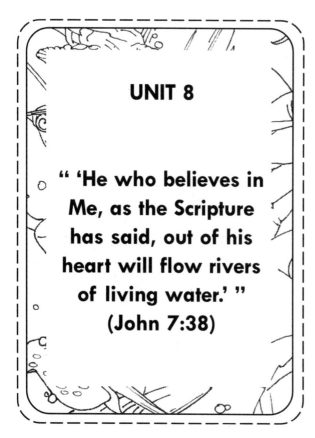

UNIT 8

" 'He who believes in Me, as the Scripture has said, out of his heart will flow rivers of living water.' "
(John 7:38)

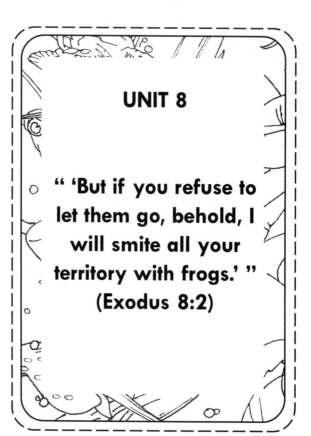

UNIT 8

" 'But if you refuse to let them go, behold, I will smite all your territory with frogs.' "
(Exodus 8:2)

APPENDIX D

INSTRUCTIONS AND ART
FOR ABC BOOK

ARTWORK BY DAVID W. TAYLOR

ANIMAL KINGDOM ABC BOOK

This is designed to be a year-long project. There are 26 letters in the alphabet, so plan accordingly.

1. Your objective is to find at least one animal for each letter of the alphabet.

2. Using your own artistic talent, stickers, stamps, photographs, or even your computer, design one page per letter. (An inexpensive scrapbook from the craft store would work well for this.)

3. For each animal listed, you are to name its phylum and order. Feel free to be more specific if you want. You can be as specific as species, if you so desire.

4. Try to find in what part of the world your animal is found.

5. In what type of climate is your animal found?

6. You can use the list and pictures in this appendix as an aid in getting started, but use other resources as well. Some science reference books have large animal classification charts in them.

7. Tip: Every time you study an animal, try and use it in your ABC book.

Variation 1: Do a Plant ABC Book.
Variation 2: Make a combination Plant and Animal ABC Book.

SUGGESTIONS FOR ANIMAL ABC BOOK

A – antelope, alligator, anteater, ant
B – bison, buffalo, butterfly, boa constrictor
C – crocodile, cat, crawfish, clams, camel, cobra, caterpillar, crab
D – dragonfly, dog, Doberman pinscher, deer, donkey, duck-billed platypus
E – elephant, eagle, egret, eel
F – fish, frog, flamingo, fly, falcon, fox
G – gorilla, grasshopper, goat, giraffe, goose, gecko, Gila monster
H – horse, hippo, hog, hummingbird, hawk, hyena, horsefly
I – iguana, Indian stick insect, insects
J – jackal, jaguar, jellyfish
K – kangaroo, koala, kookaburra, kitten, kingfisher, king snake
L – lion, lizard, lobster, leopard, longhorn beetle, locust, leech
M – mouse, mockingbird, macaw, moose, mongoose, Mexican true red-legged tarantula
N – narwhal, New World monkey, Nile crocodile, nighthawks
O – ostrich, octopus, opossum
P – polar bear, peacock, pony, Portuguese man-of-war, penguin, panda, porpoise, pelican
Q – quail, queen bee
R – rhinoceros, raccoon, rattlesnake, rat, ray, raft spider, ram, reindeer, rabbit
S – shrimp, shark, starfish, scorpion, snail, snake, squid, swan, squirrel, sheep
T – tree frog, tarantula, turtle, tortoise, terrapin, tiger, tiger shark, toucan
U – urchin, ungulates
V – vulture, Virginia opossum
W – wasp, whale, walrus, woodpecker, wolf, worm
X – Xenops (bird – Xenops minutus), X-rayed cat
Y – yellowjacket, yak, yellowfin tuna, Yorkshire terrier, yoke of oxen
Z – zebra, zebra shark, zorapterans (termite-like insects)

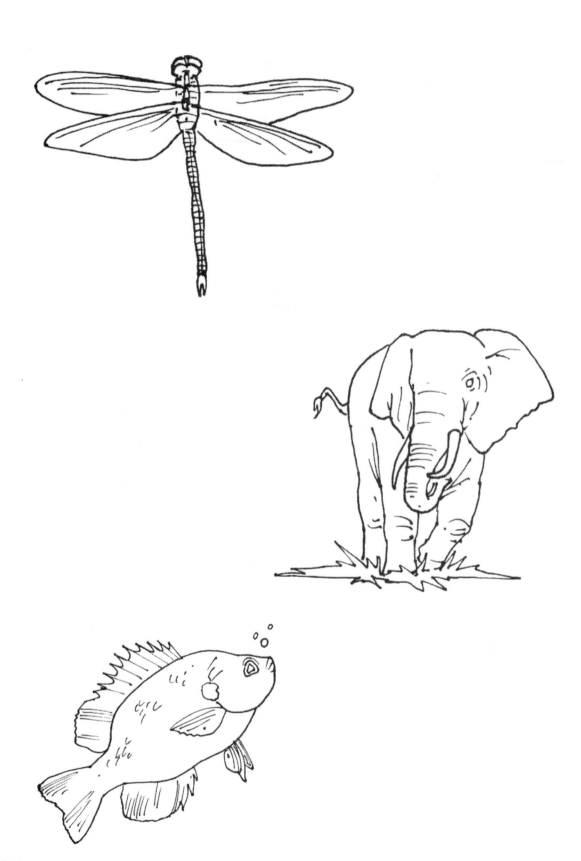

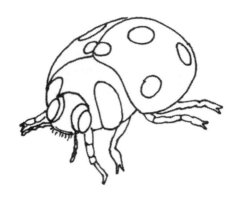

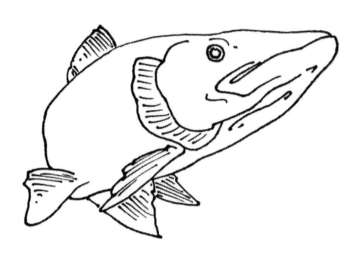

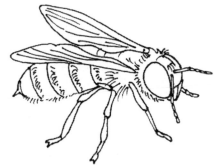

Appendix E

Additional Coloring Pages

Artwork by David W. Taylor

Creation Coloring Page

Flower Coloring Page

Songbirds Coloring Page

Birds of Prey Coloring Page

Aquatic Birds Coloring Page

Mammals Coloring Page

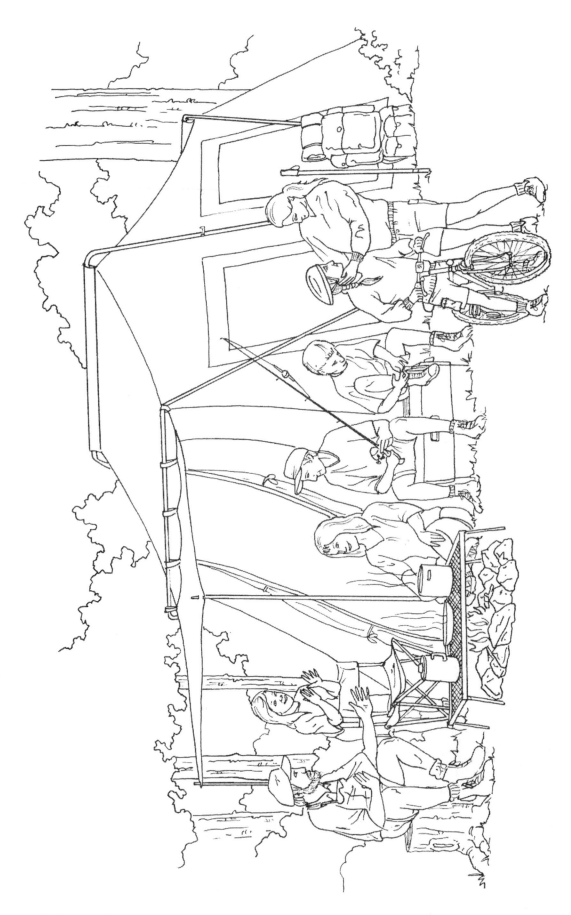

Human Coloring Page

Reptile Coloring Page

Insect Coloring Page

Arachnid Coloring Page

Saltwater Coloring Page

Freshwater Coloring Page

APPENDIX F

RECIPES AND SUPPLEMENTAL ACTIVITIES

Supplemental Activity 1

HANDS-ON TIME: The Food Chain

Objective: To learn more about the connections between plants and animals in the food chain.

Today you are going to work on food chains. Your assignment is to trace the food chain of your breakfast or lunch. You may even have time to do both.

Instructions

1. First of all, write down everything you ate today.
2. Next, figure out the ingredients of those items.
3. If you ate any meat or dairy products, you need to find out what animals they came from and what those animals eat.
4. Make a chart of your findings.

Example:

Let's take me, Mrs. Redmond, for example. For lunch today I had a cheeseburger with mayonnaise on a bun.

Secondary Consumer: Me

- The burger is beef, so it comes from a cow, which eats grass.
- The cheese is made from milk, which also comes from a cow.
- The bun is made from flour, which comes from wheat.
- The mayonnaise is made from eggs, which come from chickens, which eat grain.
- That makes the cow and the chicken the primary consumers.

Can you diagram this? You should put me, Mrs. Redmond, at the top. (Just draw me with a really pretty face!) You should have a line going to each thing I ate (cow, chicken, wheat). Then draw a line from each of those showing what they eat. Give it a try, and then do your own. Have fun!

Supplemental Activity 2

HANDS-ON TIME: Let's Make Dirt

Objective: To review the wonders of God's creation and enjoy a delicious treat!

Materials

- 1 large box instant chocolate pudding
- 1 package cream filled, chocolate wafer cookies, crushed
- Milk
- Gummy, chewy worms
- 1 new, clean flowerpot (bowl could be substituted)

Instructions

Line flowerpot with plastic wrap. (This keeps your pot clean and your pudding sanitary.) Mix pudding according to directions. Fill pot partially with cookie crumbs. Next add in all the pudding. Add a layer of gummy, chewy worms. Next cover the top with cookie crumbs. You may want to add in a small artificial flower or plant. (Make sure it is new and clean!) Have a few worms "crawling" out for added interest. Serve it up, remembering God's wonderful creation and review the important parts of plants that you studied today.

Supplemental Activity 3

HANDS-ON TIME: Leaf Search and Rubbings

Objective: To learn more about the different types of leaves and to examine them closely.

Field Trip Time

Today you are going to go on a leaf hunt. (Your yard may be the perfect spot!) You want to find as many *different types* of leaves as you can. Look for leaves that are not too crumbly or broken. Choose the best! Be sure to look for coniferous, as well as broad-leaved specimens. Complete a "Field Trip Journal" sheet.

Materials

• Tracing paper or computer paper
• Crayons, colored pencils, or chalk
• Your leaf collection

Instructions

1. Tape your leaf onto the back of your paper. Use as little tape as possible to make removal easy.
2. Turn the paper over and press down with one hand while you color over the leaf with the other. You should get an image of the leaf on the paper. Do not bear down too hard or you will not see the detail.
3. Now is a good time to examine the parts of the leaves. Notice the stem and the veins. These are important for delivering water and nutrients to the leaf.

ONE STEP FURTHER

Recommended for Older Students: Using a book on tree identification, try to determine what types of trees your leaves came from. Label them accordingly.

Supplemental Activity 4

HANDS-ON TIME: Researching Snakes

Objective: To learn more about the snakes that are native to your state.

Discover!

- Using the Internet, an encyclopedia or a field guide, determine what snakes are common in your state.
- Once you find out which snakes are found in your state, either write a paragraph or make a chart that shows your findings and tells more about each snake.

Optional: Field Trip

Plan a trip to a state park and speak with a park ranger. Ask the ranger to tell you about the snakes in your state. Perhaps there is also a Nature Center in the park that has an exhibit on snakes. Write a report or make a poster showing what you learned.

Supplemental Activity 5

HANDS-ON TIME: Make "Turtle Bread"

Objective: To review the body parts of turtles and have fun!

Note: This project will extend over about 3 hours.

Materials

- Flour
- Active yeast
- Salt
- Your favorite bread recipe
- Small box of raisins

Instructions

1. Using your favorite bread recipe, mix the dough
2. After the first rising, punch the dough down according to directions.
3. Use the dough to shape turtles for baking.

    a. Make the four legs. If you are making a marine turtle, make flippers for the legs.

    b. Make the shell. You will essentially need a ball of dough for this.

    c. Make the head.

    d. Make the tail.

4. On a baking sheet, place the legs, head, and tail in their proper positions. Lay the "shell" over these so that the parts are visible but "connected."
5. Use the raisins to make the eyes.
6. Bake according to your recipe.
7. Enjoy!

Supplemental Activity 6

BASIC PLANT TERMINOLOGY

```
N P U K P C W Q G O L A N S P
P X S V T G O G M E X N N X O
G O F L G V U N A Y K N L U R
N I S V O D W V I G O R V X C
S Y D B N B E L F F L P E J S
R P E L P S T S N R E G A G B
J Z E Q J P F F M T D R V D A
J C S V Y Z K G P E P H R H P
P L G T Y Z B S O K T V Z K A
K M V M C K F W L F F S K S W
Z S T O O R F E L C U O M J C
E Q Z E I J Q V E L S L Z V P
D F F G D M V K N Q H V L X U
O S B V M K V B D L W V M Q X
P H O T O S Y N T H E S I S W
```

CONIFER   ROOTS
LEAVES   SEEDS
PHOTOSYNTHESIS   STEMS
POLLEN

Supplemental Activity 7

ADVANCED PLANT TERMINOLOGY

```
W J F G Y E Y V D C D B C D I T P B E C
M S W P V Y T O D E H J L Z U A R D G O
H C M M Z J A E V E S L B N G K X U O N
P L D R A C C A O M I P O M H A V N M I
U V Z Y D I E Z B S S F E R Q E Z S W F
H O N W D L C V R X E T A R O P A V E E
J U E U D K H E A Z H Q S W Z P R Y T R
F K O A F K H D R Q T N U T W D H B S O
M U O O D T C R M L N S E M O P D Y Y U
S R L P N P F U Z C Y Y W E C O P D L S
B P E A O I I P I A S U C V R O R E A L
D V L H U V K E Q K O V N Y L G R E T L
Q V O O C C A S Z T T J E L I G R S A Q
H M M S X O T R Y Q O I E V S H N E C A
G L U C O S E M I Z H N S C O E E S V W
W L K R Z V C B T E P C W N C S C X J E
C R C E P S P T U K S W J J Y A Y T X C
B L W E F I H T E J L U V J V N Y H V W
P O L L I N A T I O N M L I T B I Z A Q
K M N L H C E G B P O R Z E V D L Y L M
```

ANTHERS
BROADLEAVED
CATALYST
CHLOROPHYLL
CONIFEROUS
DECIDUOUS
DRUPES
EVAPORATE
EVERGREEN

GLUCOSE
OVARIES
PHOTOSYNTHESIS
POLLEN
POLLINATION
POMES
ROOTS
SEED

Supplemental Activity 8

MAMMALIA VOCABULARY

```
M W N S M M Z J W X D D T L E N D X P M Z D Y E M
S E T A M I R P W E E I T E Z S L K L K G T F D T
P Y H P I L B L D L X K J H L T J H A O F Y Z P E
E C B P O K F O A Z D I S E S S F Q C H C C C Q Y
K A M X K S O H P E U C B E U R Z F E N O S X D A
X B T A O L W M S M A R S U P I A L N Z K S T Y O
M H X B B C Z H J J I F K J Y F E S T A P C A I L
P Q F M R M N A A D R H Y A T K P A A C O X Z V Q
F W R C K H I K D I R I D K A U K X N P Z S R L P
O A I E Q U S B E V R V D X L E P U K N D P T H O
W L F H S T G S K D T F V G P S P A U W H B W Q J
V N O V V T U Z K H T Q D X D Y O U F B U W W K X
E H K B A L E E N I I Q Q M E I J S Q T Y T K C E
M S F T W N A H G E F B A O L V Z Q H S S O L T J
M L R K F P B E U Q L N O N L C Q I I Q N F G M Q
K O L A E X R N N M D M D K I C F V K S R N B I H
Y D N U E S N I I I A D M E B L Z S B N O F U Q X
E G P O E B L P H K H N Y Y K W A H Q O I R J D R
I P C A T S O C P E Q L S J C Q J D Y I R E B D X
C S G Q A R E X L C L A B K U A R Y E L Q J A Y O
X N J T P F E H O L S U N Z D P E O T P D F N S U
T W F O A G U M D E C E Y E V A P C V A I S L V B
Q V I K O U P S E A Q W U J A Q W Z R B S B X N D
D S U Q W G S U R E T U F M D D O O W H J T R L F
E R U F K L A V U W J J V D M H I Z F U C A I Y I
```

APE
BALEEN
BEARS
BIPEDAL
CATS
DOLPHIN
DUCKBILLEDPLATYPUS
ECHIDNA
FUR
HAIR
HUMANS
LIONS

MARSUPIAL
MILK
MONKEY
MONOTREME
PLACENTA
PORPOISE
PRIMATES
TIGERS
UTERUS
WARMBLOODED
WHALE

Supplemental Activity 9

HANDS-ON TIME: How to Make Papier-Mâché

Materials

- Flour
- Water
- Newspaper strips – 6 inches by 1 inch, approximately
- Floral wire
- Balloons
- Acrylic craft paints

Instructions

1. Using equal parts of water and flour, combine to make a paste.
2. Adjust water and flour until desired consistency is achieved.
3. Using wire, create desired form. If you want a sphere, inflate a balloon and tie.
4. Dip newspaper in flour mixture and gently slide fingers along to remove excess paste.
5. Wrap paper around form, watching out for any large bulges.
6. Continue wrapping form until there are no gaps. Smooth over any bulges and wrinkles, using smaller strips of newspaper if necessary.
7. Set your object aside for drying time. I recommend allowing at least a full day for drying. Drying time will vary according to how many layers of paper are on the form as well as how much paste.
8. Object will dry into a hard hollow form. If using a balloon for your form, stick it with a straight pin to pop the balloon.
9. Paint object as desired.

Supplemental Activity 10

HANDS-ON TIME: Recipe for Play Dough

Adult supervision required.

Materials

- 2 cups of flour
- 1 cup of salt
- 4 teaspoons cream of tartar
- 2 tablespoons of vegetable oil
- 2 cups of water
- Wax paper
- Food coloring   (I recommend the type found in cake decorating sections of craft stores. It is concentrated and produces a true, rich color with very little product.)

Instructions

1. Mix flour, salt, and cream of tartar in a large pot.
2. Add oil and water. Mix until smooth.
3. Over medium heat, stir constantly until the mixture leaves the sides of the pot.
4. Put dough on wax paper. Allow mixture to cool until you can work it with your hands.
5. Divide dough into smaller sections, thinking how many colors you'd like to have. I recommend four sections: red, blue, green, and yellow.
6. Add appropriate food coloring a small amount at a time, until desired effect is achieved.
7. Store in zipper-style bags or airtight containers.

Supplemental Activity Word Search Solutions

BASIC PLANT TERMINOLOGY ANSWER KEY

```
N P U K P C W Q G O L A N S P
P X S V T G O G M E X N N X O
G O F L G V U N A Y K N L U R
N I S V O D W V I G O R V X C
S Y D B N B E L F F L P E J S
R P E L P S T S N R E G A G B
J Z E Q J P F F M T D R V D A
J C S V Y Z K G P E P H R H P
P L G T Y Z B S O K T V Z K A
K M V M C K F W L F F S K S W
Z S T O O R F E L C U O M J C
E Q Z E I J Q V E L S L Z V P
D F F G D M V K N Q H V L X U
O S B V M K V B D L W V M Q X
P H O T O S Y N T H E S I S W
```

ADVANCED PLANT TERMINOLOGY ANSWER KEY

```
W J F G Y E Y V D C D B C D I T P B E C
M S W P V Y T O D E H J L Z U A R D G O
H C M M Z J A E V E S L B N G K X U O N
P L D R A C C A O M I P O M H A V N M I
U V Z Y D I E Z B S S F E R Q E Z S W F
H O N W D L C V R X E T A R O P A V E E
J U E U D K H E A Z H Q S W Z P R Y T R
F K O A F K H D R Q T N U T W D H B S O
M U O O D T C R M L N S E M O P D Y Y U
S R L P N P F U Z C Y Y W E C O P D L S
B P E A O I I P I A S U C V R O R E A L
D V L H U V K E Q K O V N Y L G R E T L
Q V O O C C A S Z T T J E L I G R S A Q
H M M S X O T R Y Q O I E V S H N E C A
G L U C O S E M I Z H N S C O E E S V W
W L K R Z V C B T E P C W N C S C X J E
C R C E P S P T U K S W J J Y A Y T X C
B L W E F I H T E J L U V J V N Y H V W
P O L L I N A T I O N M L I T B I Z A Q
K M N L H C E G B P O R Z E V D L Y L M
```

244

MAMMALIA VOCABULARY ANSWER KEY

```
M W N S M M Z J W X D D T L E N D X P M Z D Y E M
S E T A M I R P W E E I T E Z S L K L K G T F D T
P Y H P I L B L D L X K J H L T J H A O F Y Z P E
E C B P O K F O A Z D I S E S S F Q C H C C C Q Y
K A M X K S O H P E U C B E U R Z F E N O S X D A
X B T A O L W M S M A R S U P I A L N Z K S T Y O
M H X B B C Z H J J I F K J Y F E S T A P C A I L
P Q F M R M N A A D R H Y A T K P A A C O X Z V Q
F W R C K H I K D I R I D K A U K X N P Z S R L P
O A I E Q U S B E V R V D X L E P U K N D P T H O
W L F H S T G S K D T F V G P S P A U W H B W Q J
V N O V V T U Z K H T Q D X D Y O U F B U W W K X
E H K B A L E E N I I Q Q M E I J S Q T Y T K C E
M S F T W N A H G E F B A O L V Z Q H S S O L T J
M L R K F P B E U Q L N O N L C Q I I Q N F G M Q
K O L A E X R N N M D M D K I C F V K S R N B I H
Y D N U E S N I I I A D M E B L Z S B N O F U Q X
E G P O E B L P H K H N Y Y K W A H Q O I R J D R
I P C A T S O C P E Q L S J C Q J D Y I R E B D X
C S G Q A R E X L C L A B K U A R Y E L Q J A Y O
X N J T P F E H O L S U N Z D P E O T P D F N S U
T W F O A G U M D E C E Y E V A P C V A I S L V B
Q V I K O U P S E A Q W U J A Q W Z R B S B X N D
D S U Q W G S U R E T U F M D D O O W H J T R L F
E R U F K L A V U W J J V D M H I Z F U C A I Y I
```

APPENDIX G

ANSWER KEY

ANSWER KEY

UNIT ONE
LESSON 1
Quick Quiz

1. life, living organisms

2. No

3. 6 (The seventh day was a day of rest.)

4. creationists

5. Evolutionists say the earth came into being accidentally and slowly evolved over millions of years. Creationists say the earth was created by design by God and was not accidental.

LESSON 4
Review It!

1. ecology

2. biosphere

3. biomes

4. to make it easier to study

5. climate, air, vegetation (plant life), water

LESSON 5
Review It!

1. herbivores, carnivores, omnivores

2. decomposers, producers, consumers

3. Answers will vary.

Unit One Wrap-Up

1. God created the world in six days and on the seventh day He rested. (Note: Student may list what was created each day.)

2. biology

3. any living thing

4. cells

5. organelles

6. eukaryotic

7. prokaryotic

8. a. Kingdom

   b. Phylum

   c. Class

   d. Order

   e. Family

   f. Genus

   g. Species

9. Birds — Chordata

    Starfish — Echinodermata

    Jellyfish — Cnidaria

    Earthworms — Annelida

    Insects — Arthropoda

    Clams — Mollusca

    Sponges — Porifera

    Roundworms — Nematoda

10. ecology

11. biosphere

12. smaller divisions of the biosphere visible from outer space

13. herbivores

14. carnivores

15. omnivores

16. decomposers

17. make their own food

18. consumers

UNIT TWO
LESSON 8
Did You Learn It?

1. ovaries, ovules

2. anthers

3. Answers may include: birds, bees, insects, wind, water, mammals

4. He made flowers brightly colored, which attracts the bees.

5. nectar

6. Answers will vary, but should generally follow this outline:

   • Flowers have nectar.

   • Bees fly to the flowers to get the nectar.

   • When bees go inside the flowers to get the nectar, pollen that is on the anthers sticks to the bees' knees.

   • When the bees fly to other flowers, pollen is deposited inside these new flowers.

   • In the new flowers, the pollen travels to the ovaries and fertilizes the ovules.

   • The ovules become seeds, which are scattered in many ways and become new plants.

LESSON 10
Review It!

Trees, Trees, Trees

1. broad-leaved, coniferous

2. gingkoes, cycads, tree ferns

Conifers

3. pine scent, needle-like leaves, produce cones, *ever*green

4. spruce, junipers   (Note: Student may list others. These are the ones in the lesson.)

Broad-leaved Trees

5. broad, thin leaves; sometimes produce flowers at certain times of the year; often deciduous, meaning they lose their leaves in autumn

Unit Two Wrap-Up

1. Plantae

2. roots, stems, leaves, flowers

3. the flower

4. the leaves

5. photosynthesis

6. green, catalyst

7. glucose, oxygen

8. light or sunlight, H_2O, CO_2, chlorophyll

9. ovule

10. anthers

11. Bees carry pollen from one flower to another. Answers might also include insects, birds, wind, mammals, and water.

12. the ovaries

13. female

14. dry fruits, juicy fruits, pomes, drupes

15. coniferous

16. deciduous

17. Answers will vary but should contain following basic information: Trees are designed to stop feeding their leaves and sending water to them in order for the tree to have enough nutrition to live through the winter. This lack of water and nutrients causes the leaves to stop producing chlorophyll, so the leaves are no longer green.

UNIT THREE

LESSON 11

Review It!

Student may list any of these: four-chambered heart, feathers, lightweight bones, lays eggs, warm-blooded

LESSON 13

Unit Three Wrap-Up

1. 5,000–10,000

2. camber

3. warm-blooded

4. songbirds, hummingbirds, wading birds, birds of prey, birds that don't fly, game birds, diving birds, swimming birds

5. hummingbird

6. The indigestible parts of prey formed into a ball and coughed up by the bird.

7. hooked beaks, long talons, silent wings

8. Kingdom Animalia, Phylum Chordata, Class Aves

9. four-chambered heart, feathers, lightweight bones, lays eggs, warm-blooded

UNIT FOUR

LESSON 14

Review It!

1. have hair somewhere on body, feed milk to their young, are warm-blooded

2. monotremes, marsupials

3. to nourish the growing baby until it is time to be born

LESSON 16

Review It!

1. Order Carnivora

2. jackals, foxes, coyotes, dogs, wolves

3. lions, tigers, housecats, cheetahs, jaguars, ocelots, and more

4. They can retract, or pull in, their claws.

5. warm-blooded. They are mammals, and all mammals are warm-blooded.

LESSON 17

Hands-On Time

• Kingdom Animalia

• Phylum Chordata

• Class Mammalia

• Order Primates

LESSON 18

Unit Four Wrap-Up

1. have hair on their bodies, produce milk for their young, are warm-blooded

2. monotremes, marsupials

3. in a part of the mother's body called the uterus

4. to nourish the baby before it is born

5. duck-billed platypus

6. marsupial

7. in the mother's pouch

8. Order Carnivora

9. meat eaters

10. cats, lions, tigers

11. claws

12. able to walk on two feet

13. primates

14. Answers will vary.

15. baleen whale

16. mammals

UNIT FIVE

LESSON 21

Review It!

1. bitter, salty, sour, sweet

2. olfactory receptors

3. nerve endings

4. optic nerve

5. outer ear, middle ear, inner ear

LESSON 22

Review It!

1. ovaries

2. ova

3. fertilize

4. uterus

5. placenta

6. umbilical cord

Unit Five Wrap-Up

1. Class Mammalia, Order Primates

2. the outer layer of the skin

3. ball-and-socket, hinge

4. 206

5. circulatory system

6. veins

7. arteries

8. respiratory system

9. sight, hearing, touch, smell, taste

10. bitter, salty, sour, sweet

11. over 10,000

12. olfactory receptors

13. nerve endings

UNIT SIX
LESSON 25
Review It!

Trait	Alligators	Crocodiles
Snout Shape	Broad, flat, and rounded in front	Long, narrow, and pointed in front
Lower Teeth Hidden or Visible?	Hidden	Visible
No. of Eggs in a Clutch	30–60	90
Life Span	Up to 50 years	Up to 65 years
Freshwater or Saltwater?	Freshwater	Both

LESSON 26
Review It!

1. tortoise
2. turtle
3. turtle
4. tortoise
5. tortoise
6. turtle
7. terrapin
8. turtle
9. terrapin
10. turtle
11. turtle
12. tortoise
13. turtle
14. tortoise

Unit Six Wrap-Up

1. Order Crocodilian
2. both
3. a snake
4. tails that break off easily
5. camouflage
6. an alligator
7. Cold-blooded animals must use their surroundings to warm themselves because their body temperature is not internally regulated like that of warm-blooded animals.
8. cold-blooded
9. a terrapin
10. flippers instead of true legs
11. a crocodile

12. Answers will vary. Possibilities include: Tortoises have longer life spans. Tortoises live on land; turtles live on land and in water. Tortoises have dome-shaped shells; turtles have somewhat flat, streamlined shells. Most tortoises are herbivores; turtles are usually omnivores.

13. hinged jaws that swing open very widely

14. poisonous

15. pits on the sides of their heads that can detect heat in their prey

UNIT SEVEN

LESSON 29

Unit Seven Wrap-Up

1. butterflies

2. Complete, because the animal that hatches from the cocoon looks totally different from the animal that formed the cocoon.

3. head, thorax, abdomen

4. on the outside of its body

5. an exoskeleton

6. queen bee, worker bee, drone

7. round dance, waggle dance

8. by carrying pollen from one flower to the next

UNIT EIGHT

LESSON 31

Review It!

1. Mollusks are soft-bodied animals.

2. Mollusks usually have a hard shell surrounding them.

3. Mollusks are invertebrates.

LESSON 32

Now That's a Shark of Another Color Word Search

```
H T D M N L Y X S O I T G F S U P B
A A R U E B R I B U Z I R E Y B W E
J Y M G U T L S H Y R R E S O E E I
M X N M X V E X S O E E A R S Q T X
K A N L E M O N H T R X T U T V B S
R N P R J R J B T O F N W N V L N Q
V T T V S X H U W P L T H N U L P I
R I M L G T C E A M I F I E T I A M
P X V Z O E Z N A G D V T B X N B A
L W Q B I S L C Q D P R E F M D A K
H J L K R E H S E R H T A M B Z B O
N Q O W H A L E S H A R K P P N Q H
Y O Y I G V C O T G L B E M O K J T
C O H W D X W D N N U J Z W U E K V
O K U K Z V W H E C S G F L Q A L N
Y E R G X L Z N J U D V M P K E G B
D B N N X J A B M I J V D S M A D H
I X M P S D Y U K K K Y P D H J P S
```

LESSON 35

Unit Eight Wrap-Up

1. saltwater, freshwater
2. Phylum Mollusca
3. soft
4. gastropods, bivalves, tooth shells, chitons, cephalopods
5. able to float
6. the dorsal fin
7. placoid scales
8. about 3 feet long
9. shrimp, crabs, lobsters
10. lakes, rivers, streams
11. dual life
12. frogs, toads, salamanders

Appendix H

Suggested Further Reading

by Rebecca Delvaux

CHRISTIAN KIDS EXPLORE BIOLOGY (CKEB) BOOK AND RESOURCE LIST

NOTE: Prices and web site URLs are as of early 2003.

This list includes far more resources than one could ever utilize. However, not all items will appeal to everyone nor be readily available in all locations. The majority of resources will likely be stocked in most public libraries or available through inter-library loan. Many are also available for purchase from major book retailers. For any items deemed somewhat difficult to locate, a retailer has been listed. Items labeled with a cross (✝) are explicitly from a Christian perspective.

With all resources, please USE YOUR OWN DISCRETION in their usage. Many do address topics such as evolution, may include illustrations not deemed appropriate, may interject thoughts contrary to Biblical thought, and so forth. You may be wondering why such books were even included in a young earth, Biblical curriculum book list. The answer is unfortunate, but quite simple. There simply aren't explicitly Christian resources for all CKEB topics. Thus, secular items, which were deemed useful in part or in full for one or more topics in CKEB, have been listed here for your consideration. You may find that the entire resource is perfectly fine. Others may just need a section or illustration to be skipped. Still others, may have only a small their portion that you will wish to utilize due to its content on a key topic that couldn't be found in another book with a better format.

It is my heartfelt prayer that you and your children will be richly blessed by this curriculum and the supplemental resources while we all seek to raise a generation of Biblical-thinking children in the realm of science. To this end, some resources for parents have also been included. One example is the free Homeschool Newsletter from Answers In Genesis. It will serve to better equip you in this respect. More details are under the Creation heading.

You may also wish to utilize some nature guides. There are many on the market and also available from public libraries. If looking for such books, you may wish to begin your quest with these: Peterson's, National Audubon Society, National Geographic, Sibley Guides (birds only), and Golden.

KEY:
✝ = explicitly Christian resource
LG = lower grammar READING level
UG = upper grammar READING level
LG/UG = resources which may be enjoyed by both levels
RA = read aloud for LG (& UG)
ISBN – often listed for the library edition (if purchasing, you may wish to check for other formats of lower cost)
ISSN – International Standard Serial Numbering for serial publications

PRIMARY RESOURCE VENDORS:
Most resources may be purchased from one or more of the following vendors. For some harder to locate items, a specific vendor is listed in the resource description.
- Answers in Genesis (AIG) www.answersingenesis.org
- Amazon.com www.amazon.com
- Barnes and Noble www.barnesandnoble.com
- Books-A-Million www.bamm.com
- Bright Ideas Press (CKEB & MOH publisher) www.brightideaspress.com; 877-492-8081
- Children's Books www.childsbooks.com; 864.968.0391.

- Christian Book Distributors (CBD) www.Christianbook.com
- Homeschool Source (lending library) www.thehomeschoolsource.com
- Home Training Tools www.hometrainingtools.com
- Moody Bible Institute videos www.moodyvideo.org
- Rainbow Resource Center www.rainbowresource.com
- ShowForth Videos www.bjup.com
- Tobins Lab www.TobinsLab.com (check here first for supplemental hands-on resources)
- The Timberdoodle Company www.timberdoodle.com
- Institute of Basic Life Principles (Bill Gothard) www.iblp.com
- The Book Peddler www.the-book-peddler.com; 440-284-6654

UNIT 1 – Introduction to Biology
CREATION

There are numerous creation resources available for all ages from Answers In Genesis (AIG) @ www.answersingenesis.org . Below are a few examples.

- ✝ AIG Homeschool Newsletter - Parents may appreciate this new homeschool newsletter. There is a suggested book to read, things to consider and discuss about the reading, links to audio files (from a source of 1000+ files; some over an hour in duration) related to the topic, and more. This is a means to continually educate yourself in science from a Biblical, young earth perspective so you will be armed with the truth while instructing your children in science. UG+/Parent   http://www.answersingenesis.org/cec/default.asp
- ✝ AIG Creation Club – This is a new feature for students 7th grade and up. To sign up, go to www.answersingenesis.org/home/area/Tools/clubs.asp
- ✝ The Amazing Story of Creation – From Science and the Bible, Dr. Duane Gish. (ICR; 1990) 122pp. $19 AIG   UG+/Parent
  Very readable book about creation and evolution with wonderful illustrations. Addresses topics such as dinosaurs, flowers, fish, birds, the stars, Earth, and mankind.
- ✝ The Caring Creator, Carine MacKenzie. These 37 pages will take your children through the Bible from creation to the coming King while also presenting a clear gospel message of the Creator of the universe. $7 AIG LG/UG
- ✝ The Creation Adventure Pack (VHS). (Gospel Communications, Answers Media, and Henderson Design and Productions)   Two 45 minute videos: 1) The Creation Adventure Team: A Jurassic Ark Mystery, and 2) The Creation Adventure Team: Six Short Days, One Big Adventure! $25 AIG LG/UG
- ✝ The Great Dinosaur Mystery AIG UG/LG
- ✝ Skeletons in Your Closet – Discovering Your Real Family Tree, Dr. Gary Parker. AIG LG+/UG
  Children from the Parker family are taught evolutionary ideas at school. At home, they learn the truth about their supposed human ancestors. Part of a series.   Other books include: Dry Bones and Other Fossils and Life Before Birth.
- ✝ Creation CD-ROM (Answers Media) AIG; $5; Parent resource.
  Quote from AIG web site: "A shattering critique of the PBS/NOVA Evolution series. Over 350 pages of powerful creation information, 40 minutes of video content, the complete book Refuting Evolution, and over 3 hours of audio messages."
- ✝ The X-Nilo Show, Answers in Genesis. (X-Nilo Productions; 1998). 28 minutes. $10 LG/UG
- ✝ Dinosaurs (Exploring God's World series), Michael and Caroline Carroll. (Cooke Publications; ISBN: 0781433665; 2000). 32pp.   LG/UG
  Written by an accomplished science journalist turned Christian who wishes to share the awesomeness of God's creation through word and photo.

- ✝ <u>Dinosaurs by Design</u>, Dr. Duane Gish. 88pp. AIG $16 LG/UG
Everything you ever wanted to know about dinosaurs. From a young earth, Biblical perspective.
- ✝ <u>Dinosaurs of Eden</u>, Ken Ham. (Master Books; 2001) 64pp. $14 LG/UG
Ken ham tells the story of the world from a young earth Biblical perspective from creation to the Tower of Babel. Includes animals and dinosaurs.
- ✝ <u>What Really Happened to the Dinosaurs?</u> Dr. John Morris and Ken Ham. (Master Books) 32pp. LG/UG
- ✝ <u>95 Animals of the Bible</u>, Nancy Pelander Johnson. 104pp. $13 AIG LG/UG
- ✝ <u>What's With the Mutant in the Microscope?</u> Stuff to Know When Science Says Your Uncle Is a Monkey Kevin Johnson and James White. (Bethany House Publishing, 1999). ISBN: 0-7642-2187-6 142pp. UG & Parent resource too
Creation science apologetics for kids! Solid information interwoven with plenty of humor.

SUPPLEMENTAL RESOURCES

- Animal Planet King T-Rex Radio Control Dinotronic This is no run-of-the-mill radio-controlled toy. T-Rex acts as if he were really alive. $29.99 @ www.toysrus.com (Video clip).

RELATED LITERATURE

- ✝ <u>Adam and His Kin</u> – The Lost History of Their Lives, Ruth Beechick. (Mott Media, Fenton, MI). ISBN: 0940319071. 176pp. LG/UG ✝
Historical fiction novel based upon author's research and Biblical accounts. Young earth viewpoint. Fascinating and thought-provoking. Brings the Biblical account to life. You'll never view Genesis the same after reading this book.
- <u>Oh Say Can You Say Di-No-Saur?</u> (Cat in the Hat's Learning Library), Bonnie Worth. (Random House (Merchandising); ISBN: 0679891145; 1999). 48pp. LG
One of several on this list that you'll see from this series. A fun content book for the beginning reader

CELLS

- ENJOY YOUR CELLS series of four (4) titles by Fran (may be listed as Frances) Balkwill. Updated series with lively text incorporating jokes and accurate illustrations. Written by working scientist, Fran Balkwill, Professor of Cancer Biology at St. Bartholomew's Hospital and the London Queen Mary School of Medicine plus winner of several awards including the COPUS Junior Science Book Prize. Content is also applicable to the human body unit. LG (UG may also enjoy)
- <u>Enjoy Your Cells</u> (Enjoy Your Cells, 1), Fran Balkwill. (Cold Spring Harbor Laboratory; ISBN: 0879695846; 2001). 32pp.
- <u>Germ Zappers</u> (Enjoy Your Cells, 2), Fran Balkwill. (Cold Spring Harbor Laboratory; ISBN: 0879695986; 2001). 32pp.
- <u>Have a Nice DNA</u> (Enjoy Your Cells, 3), Fran Balkwill. (Cold Spring Harbor Laboratory; ISBN: 0879696109; 2002). 29pp.
- <u>Gene Machines</u> (Enjoy Your Cells, 4), Fran Balkwill. Cold Spring Harbor Laboratory; ISBN: 0879696117; 2002). 31pp.

- MICROEXPLORER SERIES (4 book series) cartoon-style learning. Readers are shrunken and travel inside Professor Gene's MicroMachine from which they enter the body and begin adventurous journeys of fun and learning. Patrick A. Baeuerle is a renowned biochemist and molecular scientist teaming with Norbert Landa who is a children's nonfiction book author. Index. Content is also applicable to the human body unit. LG/UG
- <u>The Cell Works: Microexplorers</u>: An Expedition into the Fantastic World of Cells (Microexplorers Series), Patrick A. Baeuerle. (Barrons Juveniles; ISBN: 0764150529; 1998). 42pp.

- <u>Ingenious Genes</u>: Microexplorers: Learning About the Fantastic Skills of Genetic Engineers and Watching Them at Work (Microexplorers Series), Norbert Landa. (Barrons Juveniles; ISBN: 0764150634; 1998) 42pp.
- <u>How the Y Makes the Guy</u>: Microexplorers: A Guided Tour Through the Marvels of Inheritance and Growth (Microexplorers Series), Norbert Landa. (Barrons Juveniles; ISBN: 0764150642; 1998) 42pp.
- <u>Your Body's Heroes and Villains</u>: Microexplorers: Learning About Immune Cells: The Tiny Defenders That Safeguard Our Lives Against Nasty Bacteria and Viruses (Microexplorers Series), Norbert Landa and Patrick A. Baeuerle. (Barrons Juveniles; ASIN: 0764150510; 1998). 42pp.
- <u>Atoms and Cells</u> (Through the Microscope series) Lionel Bender. (Aladdin Books, Ltd.; ISBN: 0561172198; 1990). UG

- GREAT MINDS OF SCIENCE SERIES especially for kids 8 –12 years of age. A look into the life of famous scientists. Books include glossary, charts, further reading list, activities, and other helps. LG+/ UG
- <u>Antoni Van Leeuwenhoek: First to See Microscopic Life</u> (Great Minds of Science), Lisa Yount. (Enslow Publishers, Inc.; ISBN: 0766018660; 2001).
  Due to this scientist, we can know view microscopic objects and make great advancements in science.
- <u>Gregor Mendel: Father of Genetics</u> (Great Minds of Science), Roger Klare and Gregor Mendel. (Enslow Publishers, Inc.; ISBN: 0766018717; 1997). 128pp.
Father of genetic science which was initiated via his pea plant experiments. (plant unit also)

CLASSIFICATION SYSTEM

- ✝ <u>Newton's Workshop</u>: The Name Game (Animal Classification). (VHS); (Moody Institute of Science; ISBN: 1575672200; 1997). $14.95 CBD or www.moodyvideo.org .
- <u>The Science of Life</u>, Frank G. Bottone Jr. (Chicago Review Pr; ISBN: 1556523823; 2001). 144pp. UG
  Interesting book containing experiments to conduct for all five kingdoms of life. Includes a supply list and suppliers for those more difficult to obtain.
- <u>The Science of Classification</u>. Martin J. Gutnik, (Franklin Watts, A First Book, 1980). ISBN: 0531041603. 66pp. UG
  This book addresses classification of elements, nonliving objects, living vs. nonliving things, the biosphere, the food chain, evolution, and cells. Straightforward and fact-filled with black-and-white charts, diagrams, maps, and photographs. Glossary and index.
- CLASSIFICATION SERIES Approximately 64pp. UG
- <u>The Plant Kingdom</u>: A Guide to Plant Classification and Biodiversity (Classification series), Theresa Greenaway. (Raintree/Steck Vaughn; ISBN: 0817258868; 1999).
- <u>The Animal Kingdom</u>: A Guide to Vertebrate Classification and Biodiversity (Classification series), Kathryn Whyman. (Raintree/Steck Vaughn; ISBN: 081725885X; 1999).

- ANIMALS IN ORDER SERIES. Sara Swan Miller. (Franklin Watts, Inc.) Books about various animals. This series continues to have other additions to it. 48 pp. UG+/LG
- <u>Seahorses, Pipefishes, and Their Kin</u> (Animals in Order). ISBN: 0531121712; 2002).
- <u>Turtles: Life in a Shell</u> (Animals in Order), 1999.
- <u>Salamanders: Secret, Silent Lives</u> (Animals in Order). ISBN: ISBN: 0531115682; 1999.
- <u>Snakes and Lizards: What They Have in Common</u> (Animals in Order). ISBN: 0531115941; 2000
- <u>Frogs and Toads: The Leggy Leapers</u> (Animals in Order). ISBN: 0531116328; 2000).
- <u>Horses and Rhinos: What They Have in Common</u> (Animals in Order). ISBN: 0531115860; 1999.
- <u>Moles and Hedgehogs: What They Have in Common</u> (Animals in Order). ISBN: 0531116336; 2001.
- <u>Rodents: From Mice to Muskrats</u> (Animals in Order). ISBN: 0531159205; 1999.
- <u>Rabbits, Pikas, and Hares</u> (Animals in Order). ISBN: 0531116344; 2002.
- <u>Wading Birds: From Herons to Hammerkops</u> (Animals in Order). ISBN: 053113959X; 2000.

- Waterfowl: From Swans to Screamers (Animals in Order). ISBN: ISBN: 0531115844; 1999.
- Birds of Prey: From Falcons to Vultures (Animals in Order). ISBN: 053111631X; 2001.
- Perching Birds of North America (Animals in Order). ISBN: 0531115208; 1999.
- Woodpeckers, Toucans, and Their Kin (Animals in Order). ISBN: 0531122433; 2003.
- Shorebirds: From Stilts to Sanderlings (Animals in Order). ISBN: 0531164985; 2001.
- Owls: The Silent Hunters (Animals in Order) ISBN: 0531164969; 2000.
- Beetles: The Most Common Insects (Animals in Order). ISBN: 0531116298; 2001.
- Grasshoppers and Crickets of North America (Animals in Order). ISBN: 0531121704; 2002.
- Ants, Bees, and Wasps of North America (Animals in Order). ISBN: 0531122441; (to be published March 2003).
- Cicadas and Aphids: What They Have in Common (Animals in Order), ISBN: 0531115194; 1999.
- True Bugs: When Is a Bug Really a Bug? (Animals in Order). ISBN: 0531114791; 1998.
- Flies: From Flower Flies to Mosquitoes (Animals in Order). ISBN: 0531114864; 1998.

- GREAT MINDS OF SCIENCE SERIES especially for kids 8 –12 years of age. A look into the life of famous scientists. Books include glossary, charts, further reading list, activities, and other helps. LG+/ UG
- Carl Linnaeus: Father of Classification (Great Minds of Science), Margaret J. Anderson. (Enslow Publishers, Inc.; ISBN: 0894907867; 1997).
  His work in botany led to the system of classification. (also For human body unit)

ECOLOGY

- Ecology (The Study of Living Things), Terry J. Jennings. (G. Stevens; ISBN: 0836832302; 2002). 33pp. LG
- LET'S-READ-AND-FIND-OUT SCIENCE SERIES
- Oil Spill! (Let's Read-And-Find-Out Science), Melvin Berger. (HarperTrophy; ISBN: 0064451216; 1994). 32 pp. LG
  Ecological effects of the Valdez oil spill and what can be done to prevent future oil spills.
- Where Does the Garbage Go? (Let's-Read-And-Find-Out Science), Paul Showers. (Scott Foresman; ISBN: 0064451143; Revised 1994). 32pp. LG
  Ecological effects of waste products.
- Follow the Water from Brook to Ocean (Let's-Read-and-Find-Out Science), Arthur Dorrus. (HarperTrophy; ISBN: 0064451151; Reprint 1993). 32pp. LG
  Importance of clean water. Ecology of water.
- Be a Friend to Trees (Let's-Read-and-Find-Out Science), Patricia Lauber. (HarperTrophy; ISBN: 0064451208; 1994). 32 pp. LG (intro/ecology and tree unit)
- Recycle!: A Handbook for Kids, Gail Gibbons. (Little Brown & Co.; ISBN: 0316309435; Reprint 1996) 32pp. LG
- The Wump World, Bill Peet. (Houghton Mifflin Co; ISBN: 0395311292; 1981). LG
  Humorous animal story that also teaches the importance of ecology. (Bill Peet's style may appeal to UG too.)
- Farewell to Shady Glade, Bill Peet. (Houghton Mifflin Co; ISBN: 0395311284; 1981). LG
  Funny story about ecologically displaced animals and their adventure to find a new home. (Bill Peet's style may appeal to UG too)
- Sir Johnny's Recycling Adventure, Jackie Hutto. (Crestmont Pub.; ISBN: 0964229625; 1999). 48pp. UG
- Eyewitness: Ecology, (Eyewitness Books), Steve Pollock. (DK Publishing, Inc.; ISBN: 0789455811; 2000). 64pp. UG
- Ecoart! Earth-Friendly Art and Craft Experiences for 3-To 9-Year-Olds (Williamson Kids Can! Series), Laurie Carlson. (Williamson Publishing; ISBN: 0913589683; 1992). 160pp. LG

- <u>Worms Eat My Garbage</u>: How to Set Up & Maintain a Worm Composting System, Mary Appelhof. (Flowerfield Press; ISBN: 0942256107; Revised 1997). 162pp. UG
- <u>Fun With Recycling</u>: 50 Great Things for Kids to Make from Junk (Fun With), Marion Elliot. (Southwater Pub; ISBN: 1842154087; Spiral; 2001). UG

RELATED LITERATURE

- <u>The Lorax</u>, Dr. Seuss and Theodor Suess Geisel. (Random House; ISBN: 0394823370;1971). 61pp. LG
This Dr. Seuss book could be used to introduce the concept of ecology and conservation in a fun way.

BIOMES

- <u>What Is a Biome?</u> (Science of Living Things series), Bobbie Kalman. (Crabtree Pub; ISBN: 0865058873; 1998). 32pp. LG
- <u>Our Living World</u> (Our Living World), Jenny E. Tesar.. (Blackbirch Marketing; ASIN: 1567117104; 1993). 64pp. UG
- <u>First Reports</u> - Biomes: Coral Reefs, Deserts, Grasslands, Mountains, Oceans, Rain Forests, Tundra, Wetlands (First Reports Series - eight (8) book set). (Compass Point Books; ISBN: 0756500516; 2000). Approx. 32pp each. LG
- <u>UXL Encyclopedia of Biomes</u>, UXL. (UXL; Gale Group; ISBN: 0787637327; 1999). 620pp. UG
- <u>The Magic School Bus Explores the World of Animals</u> (Magic School Bus), Joanna Cole. (Scholastic; ISBN: 0439226783; 2001). 32pp. LG
Magic School bus explores six (6) different biomes while attempting to find the right home for an unusual animal that is found in Ms. Frizzles' classroom.

Estuary
- <u>Life in an Estuary</u>: The Chesapeake Bay (Ecoystems in Action), Sally M. Walker. (Lerner Publications Co.; ISBN: 0822521377; 2002). 72pp. UG

Desert
- <u>A Desert Scrapbook</u>, Virginia Wright-Frierson, (Simon & Schuster; ISBN: 0689806787; 1996) LG
Author/artist describes in words and soft watercolors the animals she has seen in the Sonoran Dessert. Has a science sketchbook feel to it.
- <u>Cactus Desert</u>, (One Small Square series) Donald M. Silver. (McGraw-Hill Trade; ISBN: 0070579342; 1997) LG
- <u>It Could Still Be a Desert</u> (Rookie Read-About Science), Allan Fowler. (Children's Press; ISBN: 0516261568; 1997). 32pp. LG
- <u>The Magic School Bus Gets All Dried Up</u>: A Book About Deserts, Joanna Cole, Bruce Degan, Suzanne Weyn. (Scholastic Trade; ISBN: 0590508318; 1996). LG
- <u>Eyewitness: Desert</u> (Eyewitness Books), Miranda MacQuitty. (DK Publishing; ISBN: 0789466007; 2000). 64pp. UG
- <u>Desert</u> (Biomes of the World), Edward R. Ricciuti. (Benchmark Books; ISBN: 0761401342; 1996). 64pp. UG

Tundra
- <u>Arctic Tundra</u>: Land With No Trees (Rookie Read-About Science), Allan Fowler. LG
- <u>Arctic Tundra</u>, (One Small Square series) Donald M. Silve. (McGraw-Hill Trade; ISBN: 007057927X; 1997) LG
- <u>The Tundra</u> (Biomes of the World series), Elizabeth Kaplan. (Benchmark Books; ISBN: 076140080X; 1995). 64pp. UG   Award-winning series.

Boreal Forest (Tiaga)
- <u>Taiga</u> (Biomes of the World), Elizabeth Kaplan. (Benchmark Books; ISBN: 0761401350; 1996). 64pp. UG

- <u>A Walk in the Boreal Forest</u>, (Biomes of North America), Rebecca L. Johnson. (Carolrhoda Books; ISBN: 1575051567; 2001. 48pp. LG/UG
  Beautiful series. Terrific photography, nature journal sidebars, sketches, and a very good biome map of North America. A pleasure for the eyes and mind. Glossary. Index. Further information including URLs.
- <u>Northern Refuge</u>: A Story of a Canadian Boreal Forest, Audrey Fraggalosch. (Soundprints; ISBN: 1568996780; 1999). 36pp. LG
  One learns of the Canadian boreal forest as a result of following the life of a moose cow from birth until it is self-sufficient.

Temperate Coniferous Forest:
- <u>Temperate Forest</u> (Biomes of the World), Elizabeth Kaplan. (Benchmark Books; ISBN: 0761400826; 1996). 64pp. UG Award-winning series.

Temperate Deciduous Forest
- <u>A Walk in the Deciduous Forest</u> (Biomes of North America series), Rebecca L. Johnson. (Carolrhoda Books; ISBN: 1575051559). 48pp. LG/UG
  Contains terrific photography, nature journal sidebars, and sketches. Includes a very good biome map of North America. A pleasure for the eyes and mind. Glossary. Index. Further information including URLs.

Rain Forest
- <u>A North American Rain Forest Scrapbook</u>, Virginia Wright-Frierson. (Walker and Co., 1999; ISBN: 0802786804). 36pp. LG/UG
  This beautiful book is overflowing with watercolors as if painted on-scene in a nature journal. Complete with descriptions. A true delight to the eyes and ears.
- <u>Nature's Green Umbrella</u> – Tropical Rain Forests, Gail Gibbons. (Morrow Junior Books, New York, 1994; ISBN: 0688123538). 32pp. LG/UG
  Lush watercolors and vivid rain forest floor descriptions comprise these pages.
- <u>In the Rain Forest</u> (Magic School Bus), Eva Moore. (Scholastic Trade; ISBN: 0439239605; 2001). 32pp. LG (also computer CD)
- <u>Eyewitness: Jungle</u> (Eyewitness Books), Theresa Greenaway. (ISBN: 0789466031; 2000). 64pp. UG
- <u>Rainforest</u> (Biomes of the World series), Edward R. Ricciuti. (Benchmark Books; ISBN: 0761400818; 1996). 64pp. UG Award-winning series.
- <u>Tropical Rain Forest</u> (One Small Square series), Donald M. Silver. (McGraw-Hill Trade; ISBN: 0070580510; 1998). LG (UG may also enjoy)
- <u>A Walk in the Rain Forest</u> (Biomes of North America series), Rebecca L. Johnson. (Carolrhoda Books). 48pp. LG/UG
- <u>Great Grizzly Wilderness</u>: A Story of a Pacific Rain Forest, Audrey Fraggalosch. (Soundprints; ISBN: 1568998392; 2000). 27pp. LG
  Story about a mother grizzly bear coming out of hibernation and teaching her two cubs how to find food for themselves before the next winter sets in. In the process, the reader will learn about the rain forest near the Pacific.

Grassland
- <u>Grassland</u> (Biomes of the World), Edward R. Ricciuti. (Benchmark Books; ISBN: 0761401369; 1996). 64pp. UG
- <u>Life in a Grassland</u> (Ecosystems in Action), Dorothy Hinshaw Patent. (Lerner Publications Co.; ISBN: 0822521393; 2002). 72pp. UG

Chaparral
- <u>Chaparral</u> (Biomes of the World series), Edward R. Ricciuti. (Benchmark Books; ISBN: 0761401377; 1996). 64pp. UG

264

Savanna
- African Savanna, (One Small Square series) Donald M. Silver. (McGraw-Hill Trade; ISBN: 0070579318; 1997) LG (UG)

FOOD CHAINS
- Who Eats What? Food Chains and Food Webs (Let's-Read-and-Find-Out Science), Patricia Lauber. (Scott Foresman; ISBN: 0064451305; 1995 reprint). LG
- The Magic School Bus Gets Eaten: A Book About Food Chains (Magic School Bus). Joanna Cole. Scholastic Trade; ISBN: 0590484141; 1996). LG
- What are Food Chains and Webs? Bobbie Kalman and Jacqueline Langille, (Crabtree Publishing Co., The Science of Living Things series, ISBN: 0865058881; 1998). 32pp. LG/UG
Vivid illustrations and photography combined with simple yet content-rich text. Glossary and index.
- Food Chains, Alvin and Virginia Silverstein and Laura Silverstein Nunn. (Twenty-First Century Books; ISBN: 076133002X; 1998). Index, glossary, further reading list. 63pp. UG

ABC BOOKS
- The Desert Alphabet Book, Jerry Pallotta. (Charlesbridge Publishing; ISBN: 0881064734; 1994).
- Arctic Alphabet: Exploring the North from A to Z, Wayne Lynch. (Firefly Books (J); ISBN: 1552093344;1999). 32pp. UG

BOOKS ADDRESSING MULTIPLE TOPICS OF THE UNIT
- ✝ Deserts and Jungles (Exploring God's World series), Michael Carroll. (Cooke Publishing; ISBN 0781432758). 32pp. LG/UG
Written by an accomplished science journalist turned Christian who wishes to share the awesome creation of the Creator through word and photo.
- The Magic School Bus Hops Home: A Book About Animal Habitats, Patricia Relf. (Scholastic Trade; ISBN: 0590484133; 1995). LG
- Field Trips: Bug Hunting, Animal Tracking, Bird-watching, Shore Walking, Jim Arnosky. (Harper Collins Juvenile Books; ISBN: 0688151728; 2002). 96pp UG CM
Like having your own personal guide complete with nature journal.
- Microorganisms: The Unseen World (Our Living World series). Edward R. Riccuiti. (Blackbirch Marketing; ASIN: 1567110401; 1994). 64pp. UG Award-winning series.
- JIM ARNOSKY BOOKS and his CRINKLEROOT SERIES. Mr. Arnosky utilizes an engaging, content-filled, nature-journal approach to his text and illustrations. Below are a few of his books related to this unit.
- Crinkleroot's Guide to Knowing Animal Habitats, Jim Arnosky. (Aladdin Paperbacks; ISBN: 0689835388; 2000). 32pp. LG
- Watching Desert Wildlife, Jim Arnosky. (National Geographic Society; ISBN: 0792267370; 2002). 32pp. UG
- Crinkleroot's Nature Almanac, Jim Arnosky. (Simon & Schuster (Juv); ISBN: 0689805349; 1999). 64pp. UG
- Crinkleroot's Visit to Crinkle Cove, Jim Arnosky. (Aladdin Paperbacks; ISBN: 0689816030; 1999). LG

RELATED LITERATURE
- ✝ Adam and His Kin – The Lost History of Their Lives, Ruth Beechick. (Mott Media, Fenton, MI). ISBN 0940319071. 176pp. LG/UG (Creation)

Historical fiction novel based upon author's research and Biblical accounts. Young earth viewpoint. Fascinating and thought-provoking. Brings the Biblical account to life. You'll never view Genesis the same after reading this book.

- The Jungle Books, Rudyard Kipling (full version). (Hugh Lauter Levin Associates; ISBN: 0883632012; 1992) 340pp. Also available in book-on-tape and abridgements. LG/UG/Read aloud
  Stories encompass a boy raised by wolves in the jungles of India. He encounters much wildlife in his adventures.
- Ali, Child of the Desert, Jonathon London. (Lothrop Lee & Shepard; ASIN: 0688125603; (April 1997). 32pp. LG/UG   (OOP/check your library)
  Survival tale of a Moroccan boy and his father in the Sahara Desert. Contains some Islamic references.

MISCELLANEOUS CORRELATED RESOURCES

- Bioviva. A board game in which players travel around the world to different habitats or biomes. Points are earned by answering T/F and multiple choice questions. Ages 8 and up. $24.99 www.toysrus.com
- Families In Nature Card Game by Bioviva. A card game about habitats and their inhabitants. Collect a complete set of cards for a habitat and you win. Ages 7 and up. $8 www.toysrus.com
- Magic School Bus Explores the Rainforest , Microsoft (CD-ROM). ASIN: B000059ZYO; $15.
- Into the Forest (game). Deck of 41 cards each with a beautiful color illustration and a list of what it eats and what it is eaten by. This is a game about the food chain in the forest. $11.50 www.timberdoodle.com
- Onto the Desert (game) Similar to Into the Forest but for the desert with desert forces as an element too. Includes a fact sheet and full-color poster of the desert habitat. $11.50 www.timberdoodle.com
- Triazle (CD-ROM multi-level puzzle). This computer puzzle has three (3) levels ranging from age 3-adult. The puzzle is inspired by the rain forest artwork of Dan Gilbert in addition to animations and sounds. $10   www.timberdoodle.com   (3–6 yrs, 6-8 yrs. & 8yrs–Adult)
- Instant Habitat Dioramas, Donald M. Silver. (Instructor Books; ISBN: 0439040884; 2001). 64pp. Parent Resource   (Simple steps to create a dozen 3-D habitats and the animals that live in them.)
- ✝ Creation CD-ROM (background and reference material for parents) AIG

NOTE: Look for items related to topics in this unit in the video, field trip, and magazine sections at the end of this list.

UNIT 2 – PLANTS

- What is a Plant? (The Science of Living Things), Bobbie Kalman. (Crabtree Publishing Co.; ISBN: 0865059594; 2000). 32pp. LG/UG
- How a Seed Grows (Let's-Read-And-Find-Out Books), Helene J. Jordan. (HarperTrophy; ISBN: 0064451070; 1992). 32pp. LG
- The Magic School Bus Plants Seeds: A Book About How Living Things Grow, Joanna Cole. (Scholastic Trade; ISBN: 0-59-022296-1; 1995). 32pp. LG
- A Handful of Dirt, Raymond Bial. (Walker & Co.). ISBN: 0-8027-8699-5. Index. 32pp. LG/UG
- The Plant Kingdom – A Guide to Plant Classification and Biodiversity (Classification series), Theresa Greenaway. (Raintree Steck-Vaughn Publisher; 2000). Index. 48pp. LG+/UG
- Eyewitness: Plant (Eyewitness Books) David Burnie. (DK Publishing; ISBN: 0-789465-63-9; 2000). 64pp. UG
- The Seasons of Arnold's Apple Tree, Gail Gibbons, (Voyager Books; ISBN: 0152712453; 1988). LG
- GREAT MINDS OF SCIENCE SERIES especially for kids 8 –12 years of age. A look into the life of famous scientists. Books include glossary, charts, further reading list, activities, and other helps. LG+/UG

- Gregor Mendel: Father of Genetics (Great Minds of Science), Roger Klare and Gregor Mendel. (Enslow Publishers, Inc.; ISBN: 0-76-601871-7; 1997). 128pp.
  Father of genetic science which was initiated via his pea plant experiments. (also listed for introductory/cells unit)
- Carl Linnaeus: Father of Classification (Great Minds of Science), Margaret J. Anderson. (Enslow Publishers, Inc.; ISBN: 0-89-490786-7; 1997).
  His work in botany led to the system of classification. (also for introductory/classification unit)

FLOWERS

- Oh Say Can You Seed: All About Flowering Plants (Cat in the Hat's Learning Library), Bonnie Worth, Aristides Ruiz. (Random House (Merchandising); ISBN: 0-37-581095-1; 2001) 48 pp. LG   One of several from this series included on the list. Great for a fun introduction to flowering plants or a possible LG reader.

TREES

- Tell Me Tree – All About Trees for Kids, Gail Gibbons. (Little, Brown, and Co., Boston, 2002; ISBN: 0-316-30903-6). 30pp. LG
  Watercolor illustrations flood the pages. A group of children ask the trees to tell them of tree parts, kinds, the growth process, environments, evergreen vs. broadleaf distinctions, uses, how to identify trees (less than 20), and interesting tidbits about trees. You may also wish to look for other titles by this prolific author/researcher/illustrator.
- The Magic School Bus Meets the Rot Squad: A Book of Decomposition (Magic School Bus), Joanna Cole. (Scholastic; ISBN: 0590400231; 1995). 32pp. LG
  How nature uses recycling via decomposition such as with a rotten log.
- Tree Book (Starting With Nature), Pamela Hickman. (Kids Can Press; ISBN: 1550746553; 1999). 32pp. UG
  Coniferous vs. deciduous trees addressed along with their leaves and cones in various regions and seasons of the year.
- Eyewitness: Tree (Eyewitness Books), David Burnie. (DK Publishing; ISBN: 0-789465-54-X; 2000). 64pp. UG
- Be a Friend to Trees (Let's-Read-and-Find-Out Science), Patricia Lauber. (HarperTrophy; ISBN: 0064451208; 1994). 32 pp. LG   (intro/ecology and tree unit)

FUNGI

- Slime, Molds, and Fungi (Nature Close-Up). (Blackbirch Press Inc.; ISBN: 1567111823; 1999). Index. 48pp. LG+/UG
- Fungi (Our Living World) Jenny Tesar. (Blackbirch Press Inc.; ISBN: 1567110444; 1994). Classification charts – plant, fungi, protista and monera. Glossary, index, and further reading list . LG+/UG
- Fungi (The Kingdoms of Life) Drs. Alvin, Virginia, and Robert Silverstein. (Twenty-First Century Books; ISBN: 0805035206; 1996). Latin helps, glossary, and index.   UG

ABC BOOKS

- ABC - Learn Your Trees With The Leaf Critters, Susan Y. Grewell. (Leaf Critters; UPC: 9780970324108; 1995).
- Flower Alphabet Book, Jerry Pallotta. (Charlesbridge Publishing; ISBN: 088106453X; 1990). 36pp.
- The Victory Garden Vegetable Alphabet Book by Jerry Pallotta and Bob Thomas. (Charlesbridge Publishing; ISBN: 0881064688; 1992).

RELATED LITERATURE

- The Potato: How the Humble Spud Rescued the Western World, Larry Zuckerman. Want to interject some fascinating history into your study of plants? This book will do it. Although written for adults, many children will find parts of it fascinating as a read aloud.
- Tree in the Trail, Holling C. Holling. (Houghton Mifflin Co; ISBN: 039554534X; Reprint 1990). UG The cottonwood tree's tale along the Sante Fe Trail for over 200 years. Indian medicine integrated into story. (Plant/tree unit)
- Apple Picking Time, Michelle Benoit Slawson. (Dragonfly; ISBN: 0517885751; 1998). 32pp. LG Story about a young girl's experience during apple picking season in her small town where everyone is involved in picking them. Nostalgic, community- and family-focused.
- The Secret Garden, Frances Hodgson Burnett. (Penguin; ISBN: 0141182180; 1999). 304pp. (also in audio format) UG/LG
- Berenstain Bears' Big Book of Science and Nature, Stan and Jan Berenstain. (Random House Trade; ISBN: 0679886524; 1997). 64pp. LG (animals, insects, plants, weather, and some experiments)

MISCELLANEOUS CORRELATED RESOURCES

- Scholastic Root-Vue Farm kit by Toys R Us, Dr. Toy Winner 100 Best Children's Products, Amazon.com SKN:361154, $20.
- Botany Adventures Kit, Scientific Explorer. $15 www.HomeTrainingTools.com If you have some budding botanists and wish to delve further into the study of plants, you might enjoy this kit which offers the opportunity to replicate some of Mendel's plant experiments - cross-pollination, the effects of light, dark, sound, differing environments on the growth of plants, and germination among other activities. LG/UG

NOTE: Look for other items related to various topics in this unit in the video, field trip, and magazine section at the end of this list.

UNIT 3—BIRDS

- ✝ Special Wonders of Our Feathered Friends, Buddy and Kay Davis. (Master Books, 2001). 80pp. $13 AIG LG/UG/Adult
  Written by staff members of Answers in Genesis. 30 beautiful photographs of animals from around the world supplement the educational text.
- ✝ 95 Animals of the Bible, Nancy Pelander Johnson. 104pp. $13 AIG LG/UG
- How Do Birds Find Their Way? Roma Gans. (HarperTrophy; ISBN: 006445150X; 1996) 32pp. LG
- A Nest Full of Eggs (Let's-Read-And-Find-Out Science), Priscilla Belz Jenkins. (HarperTrophy; ISBN: 0064451275; 1995). LG
- Watching Water Birds, Jim Arnosky. (National Geographic Society; ISBN: 0792270738; 1997). 32pp. LG CM
- All About Owls, Jim Arnosky. (Scholastic Trade; ISBN: 043905852X; 1999). 32pp. LG CM
- Fine Feathered Friends (Cat in the Hat's Learning Library), Tish Rabe. (Random House (Merchandising); ISBN: 0679883622; 1998) 48pp. LG One book of a series mentioned in this list for beginning readers or as read alouds for unit introduction.
- Eyewitness: Bird (Eyewitness Books), David Burnie. (DK Publishing; ISBN: 0789465507; 2000). 64pp. UG
- Birds (Our Living World series), Edward R. Ricciuti. (Blackbirch Marketing; ASIN: 1567110533; 1993). 64pp. UG Award-winning series.
- Check for other titles in the Animals in Order series listed under Classification in the first chapter.

ABC BOOKS
- The Bird Alphabet Book, Jerry Pallotta. (Charlesbridge Publishing; ISBN: 0881064513; 1990) 31pp.

RELATED LITERATURE
- Seabird, Holling C. Holling. (Houghton Mifflin Co; ISBN: 0395266815; 1978) UG (Salt water life or bird unit)
- Owl Moon, Jane Yolen. (Philomel Books; ISBN: 0399214577; 1987). 32pp. LG
  Owling in the moonlight on a cold winter eve – a girl and Pa listen, watch, and find delight. Caldecott Medal winner. (also in audio format)
- On the Wing: Bird Poems and Paintings, Douglas Florian. (Harcourt; ISBN: 0152004971; (March 1, 1996) 48pp. LG/UG This funny, prolific poet and artist created this truly unique collection of bird poetry and paintings. Sensational!

MISCELLANEOUS RESOURCES
- David Sibley's web site and on-line bird art collection. David Sibley began drawing birds at age 7 years and is still doing it. You may send questions to him @ david@sibleyart.com. Check-out his artwork @ www.sibleyart.com.
- Sibley on Birds weekly newspaper column – check your newspaper to see if they carry this new syndicated column distributed nationally by the New York Times Syndicate. Short, highly informative articles with full-color bird illustations.
- The Sibley Calendar 2003, David Allen Sibley. (Workman Pub Co.; ISBN: 0761126260; Wall edition 2002) 28pp. David Sibley is ranked in high regard by fellow birders for his written work and artwork on birds. This calendar contains a vast array of his paintings and a much information about birds. This might be appreciated by a bird-loving child especially of UG age.

NOTE: Look for other items related to various topics in this unit in the video, field trip, and magazine section at the end of this list. Check the list in Unit 1 under Classification System.

UNIT 4 –MAMMALS

- ✝ Special Wonders of the Wild World, Buddy and Kay Davis. (Master Books, 1999). 80pp. AIG LG/UG/Adult
  Written by staff members of Answers in Genesis. 30 beautiful photographs of animals from around the world supplement the educational text.
- ✝ 95 Animals of the Bible, Nancy Pelander Johnson. 104pp. $13 AIG LG/UG
- Eyewitness: Mammal (Eyewitness Books), Steve Parker. (DK Publishing; ISBN: 0789465604; 2000). 64pp. UG
- The Magic School Bus Explores the World of Animals, (Magic School Bus), Joanna Cole and Nancy White. (Scholastic Trade; ISBN: 0439226783; 2001). 32pp. LG
- Polar Mammals (True Book), Larry Dane Brimner. (Children's Press; ISBN: 0516261126; 1997). 48 pp. UG
- Is a Camel a Mammal? (Cat in the Hat's Learning Library), Tish Rabe. (Random House (Merchandising); ISBN: 0679873023; 1998) 48pp. LG
  Fun content-containing beginning reader or read aloud introduction to unit about mammals.
- The Biggest Animal on Land (Rookie Read-About Science), Allan Fowler. (Children's Press; ISBN: 0516200712; 1996). 32pp. LG
- Sorting Out Mammals -Everything You Want to Know about Marsupials, Carnivores, Herbivores, and More! Samuel G. Woods. (Blackbirch Press; ISBN: 1567113729; 1999). 32pp. UG
- Check for other titles in the Animals in Order series listed under Classification in the first chapter.

- LET'S-READ-AND-FIND-OUT SCIENCE SERIES.
- Zipping, Zapping, Zooming Bats (Let's-Read-and-Find-Out Science), Ann Earle. (HarperTrophy; ISBN: 006445133X; 1995). 32pp. LG (bats = flying mammals; dispels myths)
- Baby Whales Drink Milk (Let's Read and Find Out Science), Barbara Juster Esbensen. (HarperTrophy; ISBN: 0064451194; 1994). 32pp. LG Addresses what constitutes a mammal.

ABC BOOKS
- The Furry Animal Alphabet Book, Jerry Pallotta. (Charlesbridge Publishing; ISBN: 0881064645; 1990). 32pp.

RELATED LITERATURE
- Mammalabilia: Poems and Paintings, Douglas Florian. (Harcourt; ISBN: 0152021671; 2000) 48pp. Mammal poetry and art. LG/UG
- The Black Stallion, Walter Farley. (Random House; ISBN: 0679813438; 1991). 187pp. (numerous sequels plus an incredible rendition on video) UG/RA
- James Herriot's Treasury for Children. Illus. by Ruth Brown and Peter Barrett. (St. Martin's Press; ISBN: 0312085125; 1992). 256pp, hardcover. LG
  A complete anthology of his beloved children's stories.

MISCELLANEOUS CORRELATED RESOURCES
- LeapPad Leap 3 Science Book: Amazing Mammals! It will help your child learn about mammals while using a Leap Pad system. LG/UG

NOTE: Look for other items related to various topics in this unit in the video, field trip, and magazine section at the end of this list. Check the list in Unit 1 under Classification System.

UNIT 5 – THE HUMAN BODY

- ✝ Life Before Birth, Dr. Gary E. Parker. (Master Books; 1997) 87pp. LG/UG/Parent AIG $13
  A Christian book about human development beginning with DNA. Pro-life and pro-creation perspective. A book for the entire family.
- ✝ Human Body (VHS) Vol. 3 of The Wonders of God's Creation series by Moody Bible Institute. Absolutely awesome award-winning series with phenomenal photography and that glorifies God as the Creator. (This set: Planet Earth, Animal Kingdom, & Human Life.) Best price at www.timberdoodle.com $22.00 for set of three (3) VHS tapes. Retail is $39.95. There are around 20 incredible videos like this, produced by Moody and available from Moody and BJU Press. LG/UG/Adult
- ✝ My Listening Ears – Discovering the Wonders of God's World, Joanne E. De Jonge. (Eerdmans Publishing Co.; ISBN: 0802850669; 1992) 133pp.. LG/UG ✝
  What an absolute treat! I highly recommend this book. Funny narrative from a Biblical perspective that is overflowing with human body content which will leave you in awe of on one of God's creations – the human body.
- ✝ Fearfully & Wonderfully Made, Paul Brand (a surgeon). $12.99 @ www.childsbooks.com . The author is a surgeon who worked for 18 years in a leprosy colony in India. He imparts spiritual insights as each chapter addresses a different part of the physical body. Could also work as a family devotional book. 291pp. UG
- HUMAN BODY SERIES of four (4) titles by award-winning author Seymour Simon. Inspiring books which not only have incredible color, medical-quality photographs taken through the vehicles of MRIs (magnetic resonance induction) and SEMs (scanning electron microscope), but also simple language that explains complex concepts and terms. 1997-98. 32pp. LG+/UG

- Bones: Our Skeletal System
- The Brain: Our Nervous System
- The Heart: Our Circulatory System
- Muscles: Our Muscular System
- Genetics -The Study of Heredity. Ian Graham. (G. Stevens; ISBN: 0836832310; 2002). 33pp. LG
- Inside Your Outside, Tish Rabe. (The Cat in the Hat's Learning Library), (Random House; ISBN: 0375822763; 2003) LG

  Addresses the human body and is a continuation of the beginning reader series mentioned throughout this list.
- They Came From DNA, Billy Aronson - writer for PBS's Carmen San Diego show. (W.H. Freeman and Company, New York, Scientific American Mysteries of Science series; ISBN 0716765268; 1993). 80pp. LG+/UG.

  Lively book on DNA! It is full of puns and humor sure to tickle any listener's funny bone while also driving home key information about DNA. Told from the viewpoint of an alien (it is explained that some scientists think there is alien life but none has actually been found) on assignment here on Earth. Contains evolutionary portions which one may work around to utilize this engaging book.
- There's a Zoo On You! Kathy Darling. (Millbrook Press, Brookfield, CT, ISBN: 0761313575; 2000) 48pp. LG+/UG.

  You may disagree with the author's last name once you open this book! Addressed within its pages are a host of invisible microorganisms, bacteria, microbes, etc. which result in warts, armpit odor, dandruff, althlete's foot, eyelash mites, and more in the habitat of the various systems of human bodies. Spectacular TEMs (images made via a transmission electron microscope) fill this book setting off the "awe" factor.

- LET'S-READ-AND-FIND-OUT SCIENCE SERIES
- Me and My Family Tree (Let's-Read-and-Find-Out Science), Paul Showers. (Thomas C. Crowell; ISBN: 0690038860; 1978). You may be wondering why this book appears here. It is due to its coverage of heredity, traits, genealogy, and the cross-pollination experiments of Mendel. This would be a good book to start this unit. 33pp. LG
- My Five Senses (Let's-Read-and-Find-Out Science), Aliki. (HarperTrophy; ISBN: 006445083X; 1989). 32pp. LG
- The Skeleton Inside You (Let's-Read-and-Find-Out Science), Philip Balstrino. (HarperTrophy; ISBN: 0064450872; 1989). LG
- Hear Your Heart (Let's-Read-and-Find-Out Science), Paul Showers. (HarperTrophy; ISBN: 0064451399; 2001). 40pp. LG
- Your Skin and Mine (Let's-Read-and-Find-Out Science), Paul Showers. (Harper Collins Juvenile Books; ISBN: 006445102X; 1991). LG
- Germs Make Me Sick! (Let's-Read-and-Find-Out Science), Melvin Berger. (Scott Foresman (Pearson K-12); ISBN: 0064451542; 1995) 32pp. LG (also in audio format)
- What Happens to a Hamburger (Let's-Read-and-Find-Out Science), Paul Showers. (Harper Collins Juvenile Books; ISBN: 0064451836; 2001)
- Why I Sneeze, Shiver, Hiccup, and Yawn (Let's-Read-and-Find-Out Science), Melvin Berger. (Harper Collins Juvenille Books; ISBN: 0064451933; 2000). 40pp. LG
- How Many Teeth? (Let's-Read-and-Find-Out Science), Paul Showers. (HarperTrophy; ISBN: 0064450988; 1991). 32pp. LG (also includes information on dental hygiene)

- MAGIC SCHOOL BUS SERIES
- The Magic School Bus: Inside the Human Body, (Magic School Bus), Joanna Cole. (Scholastic Trade; ISBN: 0-59-041427-5; 1990). 40pp. LG

- Magic School Bus Explores the Senses (Magic School Bus), Joanna Cole. (Scholastic Trade; ISBN: 0590446983; 2001). 47pp. LG

- EYEWITNESS SERIES
- Eyewitness: Skeleton (Eyewitness Books), Steve Parker. (DK Publishing; ISBN: 0789465523; 2000). 64pp. UG
- Eyewitness: The Human Body (Eyewitness Books), Steve Parker. (DK Publishing; ISBN: 0789448831; 1999). 64pp UG

- FAMOUS SCIENTIST SERIES
- How Did We Find Out About Genes? Isaac Asimov. (Walker & Co.; ISBN: 0802764991; 1983). Index. 62pp. UG

BOOKS ADDRESSING MULTIPLE TOPICS OF THE UNIT

- ABC's of the Human Body: A Family Answer Book, Alma E. Guiness. (Reader's Digest; ASIN: 0895772205; 1987). 336pp. Parent resource
It is dubbed one of the most fascinating books about the human body. Acclaimed to set one in awe of the miracle of the body. Includes interesting historical facts related to the body such as what a woman's corset did to her body and internal organs in the 1800s. Written in Q & A style. Encompasses one unit for each of the major systems of the body.

RELATED LITERATURE

- The Story of My Life, Helen Keller. (Bantam Classic and Loveswept; ISBN: 0553213873; July 1991). The life of Helen Keller. This is her actual autobiography but many other books are available about her life in all reading levels. Audio books and videos have been produced as well. Other books by Helen include Light in My Darkness and To Love This Life, Quotations by Helen Keller. (Five senses). 120pp. UG/RA
- The World at His Fingertips: A Story About Louis Braille (Carolrhoda Creative Minds Book), Barbara O'Connor. (Carolrhoda Books; ISBN: 1575050528; 1997). 64pp. LG (UG)
Story format delineating the life of Louis Braille and his invention of Braille system for the blind. Explanation of the system and a glossary too. Books about Louis available for all reading levels.

MISCELLANEOUS SUPPLEMENTAL RESOURCES

- LeapPad Leap 3 Science Book: The Human Body – If you already own a LeapPad, you'll want to know about this 44 page book for it. All the major body systems, except the reproductive one are covered here. The book also includes clear overlays. Suggested age: 8-10yrs. $19.99 @ www.amazon.com
- SomeBody (game). Five human anatomy games. Two sets of cards – body parts and functions. No gender-specific details shown. Ages 6 – 10 years. $16.00 www.timberdoodle.com
- The Body Book Don M. Silver. (Scholastic; ISBN: 059049239X; 1995). 128pp. Recommended for 8-12 yrs of age but may be used with younger with help and with older. Teaches many of the major body parts and functions with tape, scissors, and a photocopier. $14.75 @ www.timberdoodle.com
- An Illustrated Adventure in Human Anatomy (set) www.HomeTrainingTools.com This tool has shiny, coated cardboard pages and a marking pen to use for the skeleton, nervous, muscular, digestive, vascular, and respiratory system activities. 44pp. LG/UG
- Miracle of Life (VHS) www.HomeTrainingTools.com Micro-photographic journey into the development of a baby in its mother's womb from conception to birth. Emmy Award Winner. 60 min. UG (suggested for grades 4 - 12)
- Senses Kit (kit) www.HomeTrainingTools.com If your kids are really into this unit, you may enjoy further exploration into the biology of their senses with this kit. LG/UG

- Stethoscope, Bowles www.HomeTrainingTools.com   LG/UG
- Blood Test Kit , individual kit www.HomeTrainingTools.com One complete kit to test for ABO and Rh. UG
- Tiny Tim Skeleton (set) www.HomeTrainingTools.com   16.5" skeleton with some movable parts, a stand, elementary chart and key card, unbreakable and washable plastic. LG/UG
- Visible Man Model, (set) 16" www.HomeTrainingTools.com anatomically correct model with removable organs, all major systems, and a 12-page guide.   UG

NOTE: Look for other items related to various topics in this unit in the video, field trip, and magazine section at the end of this list. See list for Unit 1 – cells.

UNIT 6 – REPTILES, SNAKES, CROCODILES AND ALLIGATORS, TURTLES, TORTOISES, and TERRAPINS

- ✝ Special Wonders of the Wild World, Buddy and Kay Davis. (Master Books, 1999). 80pp. AIG $13 LG/UG/Adult
  Written by staff members of Answers in Genesis. 30 beautiful photographs of animals from around the world supplement the educational text.
- ✝ 95 Animals of the Bible, Nancy Pelander Johnson. 104pp. $13 AIG LG/UG

REPTILES
- Reptiles (Our Living World series), Edward R. Ricciuti. (Blackbirch Marketing; ASIN: 1-567110-47-9; 1994). 64pp. UG   Award-winning series.
- The Amazing Book of Reptile and Amphibian Records Includes the Heaviest, Fastest, Most Poisonous, and Many More!, Samuel G. Woods. (Blackbirch Press; ISBN: 1567113680; 2000). 32pp. UG
- The Magic School Bus Gets Cold Feet: A Book About Warm-and Cold-Blooded Animals (Magic School Bus). Joanna Cole. (Scholastic Trade; ISBN: 0590397249; 1998) 32pp. LG
- Check for other titles in the Animals in Order series listed under Classification in the first unit.

SNAKES
- Snakes Are Hunters, Patricia Lauber. (HarperTrophy; ISBN: 0064450910; 1989) 32pp. LG
- All About Rattlesnakes, Jim Arnosky. (Scholastic Trade; ISBN: 0439376173; 2002) 32pp. LG
- Check for other titles in the Animals in Order series listed under Classification in the first unit.

CROCODILES AND ALLIGATORS
- The Alligator (Life Cycles), Sabarina Crewe. (Raintree/Steck Vaughn; ISBN: 0-81-724375-5; 1998). 32pp. LG/UG
- Gator or Croc? (Rookie Read-About Science), Allan Fowler. (Children's Press; ISBN: 0516260804; 1997). 32pp. LG
- Check for other titles in the Animals in Order series listed under Classification in the first unit.

TURTLES, TORTOISES, and TERRAPINS
- Frogs, Toads, and Turtles (Take-Along Guide series), Diane L. Burns. (NorthWord Press; ISBN: 1-559715-93-6; 1997). LG
- Look Out for Turtles! (Let's-Read-And-Find-Out Science), Melvin Berger. (HarperTrophy; ISBN: 0064451569; 1996). 32pp. LG
- Turtle in the Sea , Jim Arnosky. (Putnam, 2002). LG
  An exciting story of the battles faced in the life of turtles as they try to stay alive.
- Check for other titles in the Animals in Order series listed under Classification in the first unit.

ABC BOOKS

- The Yucky Reptile Alphabet Book, Jerry Pallotta. (Charlesbridge Publishing; ISBN: 0881064548; 1990). 32pp. Adventures of a snapping turtle going down the Mississippi. (Freshwater life or turtle unit)

RELATED LITERATURE

- Minn of the Mississippi, Holling C. Holling. (Houghton Mifflin Co; ISBN: 0-395273-99-4; 1978). UG
- Rikki-Tikki-Tavi, Rudyard Kipling. (William Morrow & Company; ISBN: 0688143202; 1997) 48pp. LG/UG/Read aloud
  While it is true that Rikki-Tikki-Tavi is not a reptile, his two stalkers, the cobras, are. Thrilling fictitious tale about a mongoose washed by a rainstorm into the garden of an English family residing in India. A tale excerpted from the Jungle Book.
- Lizards, Frogs, and Polliwogs: Poems and Paintings, Douglas Florian. (Harcourt; ISBN: 0-15-202591-X; 2001) 56pp. LG/UG Yes, it is a collection of poems and paintings about some reptiles and also amphibians. Creative!

NOTE: Look for other items related to various topics in this unit in the video, field trip, and magazine section at the end of this list. Check the list in Unit 1 under Classification System.

UNIT 7 – INSECTS
INSECTS IN GENERAL

- ✝ Bomby the Bombardier Beetle, Hazel M. Rue. (Master Books; ISBN: 0932766137; 1991). 40pp. $7 AIG & Amazon LG/UG
  The marvel of one's of God's creations.
- ✝ The Life and Adventures of Monica Monarch, Jules H. Poirier. 32pp. $12 AIG LG/UG
  Story about the 6,000-mile migration of a monarch butterfly infiltrated with information and many little-known facts.
- ✝ Hummy and the Wax Castle, Elizabeth Ernst & Dr. Richard B. Bliss. 57pp. AIG $7 LG/UG
  An illustrated story about bees that conveys the evidence for God's design in their nature.
- The Practical Entomologist, Rick Imes. (Fireside; ISBN: 0671746952; 1992). 160pp. UG
  As with any books not listed as specifically Christian, this does contain evolution as related to the author's view of entomology, but the rest of the book contains a wealth of information paired with vivid, clear photographs including scientific names without being at an overly adult level.
- Eyewitness: Insect (Eyewitness Books), Laurence Mound. (DK Publishing; ISBN: 0-789458-16-0, 2000). UG
- On Beyond Bugs! (The Cat in the Hat's Learning Library), Tish Rabe. (Random House (Merchandising); ISBN: 0-67-987303-1; 1999) 48pp. LG
  A sure delight for any beginning LG reader or as a read aloud to begin this unit. Part of a series mentioned throughout the list.
- Hard to See Animals (Rookie Read-About Science), Allan Fowler. (Children's Press; ISBN: 0516262599; 1998). 32pp. LG
- A Ladybug's Life (Nature Upclose), John Himmelman. (Children's Press; ISBN: 0-51-626353-6; 1998). 32pp. LG
- Sorting Out Worms and Other Invertebrates -Everything You Want to Know About Insects, Corals, Mollusks, Sponges, and More! Samuel G. Woods. (Blackbirch Press; ISBN: 1567113710; 1999). 32pp. UG

- Insect Invaders (Magic School Bus Chapter Book), Anne Capeci. (Scholastic; ISBN: 0439314313; 2002). 96pp. LG
- LET'S-READ-AND-FIND-OUT SCIENCE SERIES
- Ant Cities (Let's-Read-and-Find-Out Science), Arthur Dorros. (HarperTrophy; ISBN: 0064450791; 1998). 32pp. LG
- Chirping Crickets (Let's-Read-and-Find-Out Science), Melvin Berger. (HarperTrophy; ISBN: 0064451801; 1998). 32pp. LG
- Fireflies in the Night (Let's-Read-and-Find-Out Science), Judy Hawes. (HarperCollins; ISBN: 0064451011; 1991). 32pp. LG
- Spiders, Gail Gibbons. (Holiday House; ISBN: 0-82-341081-1; 1994). LG
- Flies (True Books: Animals), Larry Dane Brimner. (Children's Press; ISBN: 0-51-621161-7; 1999) UG

BEES AND WASPS

- ✝ Animal Kingdom (VHS) Vol. 2 of The Wonders of God's Creation series by Moody Bible Institute. Absolutely awesome award-winning series with phenomenal photography that glorifies God as the master Creator. (This set: planet Earth, Animal Kingdom, & Human Life.) Best price at www.timberdoodle.com $22.00 for set of three (3) VHS tapes. Retail is $39.95. There are around 20 videos like this produced by Moody available from Moody and BJU Press. LG/UG/Adult
- ✝ Hummy and the Wax Castle, Elizabeth Ernst & Dr. Richard B. Bliss. 57pp. AIG $7 LG/UG
- An illustrated story about bees that conveys the evidence for God's design in their nature.
- The Bee (Life Cycles), Sabrina Crewe. (Raintree/Steck-Vaughn; ISBN: 0-817-26225-3; 1997). 32pp. LG/UG
- The Magic School Bus Inside a Beehive (Magic School Bus) Joanna Cole. (Scholastic Trade; ISBN: 0590257218; 1998). LG

MOTHS AND BUTTERFLIES

- ✝ The Life and Adventures of Monica Monarch, Jules H. Poirier. 32pp. $12 AIG LG/UG Story about the 6000 miles migration of a monarch butterfly infiltrated with information and many little-known facts
- Crinkleroot's Guide to Knowing Butterflies & Moths, Jim Arnosky. (Simon & Schuster (Juv); ISBN: 0-68-980587-X; 1996). LG CM
- From Caterpillar to Butterfly (Let's-Read-And-Find-Out Science), Deborah Heiligman. (HarperTrophy; ISBN: 0064451291; 1996). LG
- A Luna Moth's Life (Nature Upclose), John Himmelman. (Children's Press; ISBN: 0-51-626354-4; 1998). 32pp. LG

ABC BOOKS

- The Icky Bug Alphabet Book, Jerry Pallotta. (Charlesbridge Publishing; ISBN: 0881064505; 1990). 31pp.

RELATED LITERATURE/POETRY

- Charlotte's Web, E.B. White and Garth Williams. (HarperTrophy; ISBN: 0-06-440055-7; 1999). 192pp. LG/UG (also in audio format)
- Insectlopedia: Poems and Paintings, Douglas Florian. (Harcourt; ISBN: 0-15-201306-7; 1998) 48pp. LG/UG Insect poetry and art.
- On Beyond Bugs! (The Cat in the Hat's Learning Library), Tish Rabe. (Random House (Merchandising); ISBN: 0-67-987303-1; 1999). 48pp. LG Not only written for the beginning reader, but full of content and traditional Cat In the Hat humor. He tells of different kinds of insects, their behavior and

characteristics. A great introduction to this unit, fun read-aloud, or a fun and informative reader for a LG child.

- <u>Berenstain Bears' Big Book of Science and Nature</u>, Stan and Jan Berenstain. (Random House Trade; ISBN: 0679886524; 1997). 64pp. LG   (animals, insects, plants, weather, and some experiments)

<u>Joyful Noise</u>:

- <u>Poems for Two Voices</u>, Paul Fleischman. Illus. by Eric Beddows. (HarperCollins Juv. Books; ISBN: 0064460932; 1992). 44pp. LG/UG
  Winner of 1989 Newbery Award. A children's book of poetry about insects. Written for two children to read together.

MISCELLANEOUS CORRELATED RESOURCES

- ♱ <u>95 Animals of the Bible</u>, Nancy Pelander Johnson. 104pp. $13   AIG LG/UG
- Bug Game. Three levels of matching and memory with 44 cards, a glossary, and bug fact page. $10 Timbrerdoodle.com
- <u>Butterfly Garden</u> (kit) by Insect Lore, Amazon.com, $20.
- <u>Ant Farm Village</u> (kit) by Uncle Milton, Amazon.com, $20.
- <u>Worm Acres Composting Kit</u> by Uncle Milton, Amazon.com, $35.
- <u>Beeswax Candles & Bee-havior Kit</u> by Creativity for Kids. LG/UG $16.99
  Parental supervision needed for wick cutting and for lighting of candles.

NOTE: Look for other items related to various topics in this unit in the video, field trip, and magazine section at the end of this list. Check the list in Unit 1 under Classification System.

UNIT 8 – WATER LIFE (FRESH/SALT) and AMPHIBIANS

FRESH WATER LIFE

- ♱ <u>Animal Kingdom</u> (VHS) Vol. 1 of The Wonders of God's Creation series by Moody Bible Institute. Absolutely awesome award-winning series with phenomenal photography that glorifies God as the Creator. A must-have for every homeschool! (This set: Planet Earth, Animal Kingdom, & Human Life.) Best price at www.timberdoodle.com $22.00 for set of three (3) VHS tapes. Retail is $39.95. There are around 20 incredible videos like this produced by Moody available from Moody and BJU Press. I plan to eventually purchase them all. LG/UG/Adult
- <u>What's It Like to Be a Fish?</u> (Let's-Read-And-Find-Out Science), Wendy Pfeffer. (HarperTrophy; ISBN: 0064451518; 1996). LG
- <u>The Salmon</u> (Life Cycles), Sabrina Crewe. (Raintree/Steck Vaughn; ISBN: 0817243712; 1996). 32pp. LG   (index, glossary, and map)
- <u>Wish for a Fish</u> (Cat in the Hat's Learning Library), Bonnie Worth, Aristedes Ruiz. (Random House (Merchandising); ISBN: 0679891161; 1999). 48pp. LG   Another in the series I've incorporated on this list. Potential use for introduction to unit or reader for LG child.
- <u>Eyewitness: Pond & River</u> (Eyewitness Books), Steve Parker. (DK Publishing; ISBN: 0789458381; 2000). 64pp. UG
- <u>Life in a River</u> (Ecosystems in Action), Valerie Rapp, (Lerner Publications Co.; ISBN: 0822521369; 2002). 72pp. UG
- <u>Pond</u> (One Small Square series), Donald M. Silver. (McGraw-Hill Trade; ISBN: 0070579326; Reprint 1997). 48pp. LG (UG may enjoy this too)
- <u>Life in a Pond</u> (Rookie Read-About Science), Allan Fowler. (Children's Press; ISBN: 0516202189; 1996) 32pp. LG

SALTWATER LIFE

- ♱ <u>Special Wonders of the Sea World</u>, Buddy and Kay Davis. (Master Books, 1999). 80pp. $13 AIG LG/UG/Adult
  Written by staff members of Answers in Genesis. 30 beautiful photographs of animals from around the world supplement the educational text.
- ♱ <u>A Trip to the Ocean</u>, Dr. John Morris. 40pp. $12 AIG LG
  A children's story with Tracker John and D.J. They go on a sea exploration introducing the reader to many of the sea creatures that God created.
- ONE SMALL SQUARE SERIES
- <u>Seashore</u> (One Small Square series) Donald M. Silver. (McGraw-Hill Trade; ISBN: 0070579326; 1997) LG
- <u>Coral Reef</u> (One Small Square series) Donald M. Silver. (McGraw-Hill Trade; ISBN: 0070579709; 1997). LG
- FIRST BOOKS SERIES - Great color photography. Glossary. Index. Resource list including URLs.
- <u>Tide Pools</u> (First Books Series), Carmen Bredeson. (Franklin Watts, Inc.; ISBN: 0531159582; 1999). UG
- <u>Life in the Deep Sea</u> (First Books Series), Elizabeth Tayntor Gowell. (Franklin Watts, Inc.; ISBN: 0531159574; 1999).
- EYEWITNESS SERIES.
- <u>Eyewitness: Seashore</u> Steve Parker. (DK Publishing; ISBN: 0789458268; 2000). 64pp. UG
- <u>Eyewitness: Ocean</u> (Eyewitness Books), Dr. Miranda MacQuitty. (DK Publishing; ISBN: 0789460343; 2000). 63pp. UG
- LET'S-READ-AND-FIND OUT SCIENCE SERIES
- <u>What's It Like to Be a Fish?</u> (Let's-Read-And-Find-Out Science), Wendy Pfeffer. (HarperTrophy; ISBN: 0064451518; 1996) 32pp. LG
- <u>What Lives in a Shell?</u> (Let's-Read-And-Find-Out Science), Kathleen Weidner Zoehfeld. (HarperTrophy; ISBN: 0064451240; 1994). 32pp LG
- <u>A Safe Home for Manatees</u> (Let's-Read-And-Find-Out Science), Priscilla Belz Jenkins. (HarperCollins Children's Books; ISBN: 006445164X; 1997). 32pp. LG
- <u>An Octopus is Amazing</u> (Let's-Read-And-Find-Out Science), Patricia Lauber. (HarphyTrophy; ISBN: 0064451577; 1996). 32pp. LG
- <u>What Color is Camouflage?</u> (Let's-Read-And-Find-Out Science), Carolyn Otto. (HarperTrophy; ISBN: 0064451607; 1996). 32pp LG (camouflage of hermit crab and fawn)
- MAGIC SCHOOL BUS SERIES
- <u>The Magic School Bus On the Ocean Floor</u> (Magic School Bus), Joanna Cole. (Scholastic Trade; ISBN: 0590414313; 1994). 48pp. LG (computer CD also)
- <u>The Magic School Bus Takes a Dive</u>: A Book About Coral Reefs (Magic School Bus), Joanna Cole. (Scholastic; ISBN: 0590187236; 1998). 32pp. LG
- <u>Exploring the Deep Dark Sea</u> Gail Gibbons. (Little Brown & Co; ISBN: 0316309451; 1999) 32pp. LG
  The tale of some kids who get to experience a submersible diving vessel in the ocean.
- <u>Ocean</u> (Biomes of the World), Edward R. Ricciuti. (Benchmark Books; ISBN: 0761400796; 1996). 64pp. UG
- <u>When the Tide is Low</u>, Sheila Cole. (HarperCollins; ISBN: 0688040667; 1985). 33pp. LG
  Story of a mother and her daughter going for a walk on the beach while the tide is low.
- ROOKIE READ-ABOUT SCIENCE SERIES
- <u>Life in a Tidepool</u> (Rookie Read-About Science), Allan Fowler. (Children's Press; ISBN: 0516260839; 1997). 32pp. LG
- <u>It Could Still Be Coral</u> (Rookie Read-About Science), Allan Fowler. (Children's Press; ISBN: 0516260820; 1997). 32pp. LG
- Check for other titles in the Animals in Order series listed under Classification in the first unit.

AMPHIBIANS

- <u>From Tadpole to Frog</u> (Let's-Read-And-Find-Out Science), Windy Pfeffer. (HarperTrophy; ISBN: 0064451232; 1994). LG
- <u>Frogs</u>, Gail Gibbons. (Holiday House; ISBN: 0823411346; 1994). LG
- <u>Eyewitness: Amphibian</u> (Eyewitness Books), Barry Clarke. (DK Publishing; ISBN: 078945906; 2000). 64pp. UG
- <u>Amphibians</u> (Our Living World series), Edward R. Ricciuti. (Blackbirch Marketing; ASIN: 0516093355; 1993). 64pp. UG

ABC BOOKS

- <u>The Ocean Alphabet Book</u>, Jerry Pallotta. (Charlesbridge Publishing; ISBN: 0881064521; 1990). 30pp. LG
- <u>The Underwater Alphabet Book</u>, Jerry Pallotta. (Charlesbridge Publishing; ISBN: 0881064556; 1991). LG
- <u>The Freshwater Alphabet Book</u>, Jerry Pallotta. (Charlesbridge Publishing; ISBN: 0881069000; 1996). LG

BOOKS ADDRESSING MULTIPLE TOPICS OF THE UNIT

- ✝ <u>95 Animals of the Bible</u>, Nancy Pelander Johnson. 104pp. $13 AIG LG/UG
- <u>Oceans and Rivers</u> (Exploring God's World series), Michael Carroll. (Cooke Publishing; ISBN: 078 1430682). 32pp. LG/UG
  Written by an accomplished science journalist turned Christian who wishes to share the awesome creation of the Creator through word and photo.
- EYEWITNESS SERIES
- <u>Eyewitness: Fish</u> (Eyewitness Books), Steve Parker. (DK Publishing; ISBN: 0789465698; 2000). 64 pp. UG
- <u>Eyewitness: Shell</u> (Eyewitness Books), Alex Arthur and Andreas Einsiedel. (DK Publishing; ISBN: 0789465582; 2000). 64pp. UG
- <u>Ocean</u> (Biomes of the World), Edward R. Ricciuti. (Benchmark Books; ISBN: 0761400796; 1996). Award-winning series. 64pp. UG

RELATED LITERATURE

- <u>The Cod's Tale</u>, Mark Kurlansky. (Putnam Publishing; ISBN: 0399234764; 2001). 48pp. LG/UG
  A story filled with the historical significance of codfish. Encompasses history from the times of Vikings, Basques, explorers from Europe to America in colonial times, the slave trade, American Revolution, and the 20th century's inventions of technology that have permanently altered fishing methods.
- <u>The Wind in the Willows</u>, Kenneth Grahame. (Aladdin Library; ISBN: 068971310X; 1989). 259pp. LG/UG/Read aloud
  Life is always an adventure for the animals living near the river – a mole, water rat, toad and badger.
- <u>Lizards, Frogs, and Polliwogs</u>: Poems and Paintings, Douglas Florian. (Harcourt; ISBN: 015202591X; 2001) 56pp. LG/UG
  Yes, it is a collection of poems and paintings about some reptiles and also amphibians. Creative means of incorporating content and humor.
- <u>In the Swim: Poems and Paintings</u>, Douglas Florian. (Harcourt; ISBN: 0152013075; 1997) 48pp. LG/UG Wow! Another book of poetry and art from Mr. Florian addressing freshwater and saltwater critters.
- Holling classic tales that integrate science, geography, and history.

- Pagoo, Holling C. Holling. (Houghton Mifflin Co.; ISBN: 039506826-6; 1957) UG
  A hermit crab in a tide pool. (Saltwater life unit)
- Seabird, Holling C. Holling. (Houghton Mifflin Co; ISBN: 0395266815; 1978) UG (Saltwater life or bird unit)
- Minn of the Mississippi, Holling C. Holling. (Houghton Mifflin Co; ISBN: 0395273994; 1978). UG
  Adventures of a snapping turtle going down the Mississippi. (Freshwater life or turtle unit)
- Paddle-to-the-Sea, Holling C. Holling. (Houghton Mifflin Co; ISBN: 0395292034; 1980). UG
  An Indian boy's carved figure and canoe sails through the Great Lakes and to the Atlantic Ocean. (Freshwater life)
- Tree in the Trail, Holling C. Holling. (Houghton Mifflin Co; ISBN: 039554534X; Reprint 1990). UG
  The 200- year tale of the cottonwood tree along the Sante Fe Trail. Some Indian medicine integrated into story. (Plant/tree unit)

MISCELLANEOUS CORRELATED RESOURCES
- MAGIC SCHOOL BUS SERIES
- The Magic School Bus On the Ocean Floor; (computer CD); ASIN: B000059ZYP; $15.
- Magic School Bus Whales And Dolphins, Microsoft (CD-ROM). ASIN: B000059ZYS.
- Fish (Our Living World series), Edward R. (Ricciuti. Blackbirch Marketing; ASIN: 1567110568; 1993) 64pp. UG Award-winning series.
- Crustaceans (Our Living World series), Edward R. Ricciuti. (Blackbirch Marketing; ASIN: 1567110460; 1994). 64pp. UG
  Part of the award-winning Our Living World series.

NOTE: Look for other items related to various topics in this unit in the video, field trip, and magazine section at the end of this list. Check the list in Unit 1 under Classification System.

ADDITIONAL RESOURCE IDEAS

WEBQUESTS
WebQuests (sometimes Webquests) are a fairly new means of teaching children in a multi-task method with depth of content yet in an engaging fashion. Since I first learned how to create them, hundreds of others have taken courses and developed them on a vast array of topics including many topics addressed in CKEB. You may enjoy utilizing some of these unique on-line learning tools for all ages of children. One list of WebQuests may be found @ www.edhelper.com/cat311.htm . Numerous others may be ascertained through a web search.

MULTI-UNIT BOOKS
- ✝ CHARACTER SKETCHES: FROM THE PAGES OF SCRIPTURE, ILLUSTRATED FROM THE WORLD OF NATURE SERIES.   (Institute in Basic Life Principles). Approx. 382pp. These books were originally designed for fathers to train their children's character through the mode of lessons from nature and the Bible. They could also be used for independent reading or to read aloud for homeschoolers. Illustrated. www.store.iblp.org Very large hardcover book with sturdy slipcover. $39 each UG/RA
- Character Sketches, Volume 1; ISBN 0-916888-01-0 (tons of stories/information about animals)
- Character Sketches, Volume 2; ISBN 0-916888-01-0
- Character Sketches, Volume 3; ISBN 0-916888-01-0
- Character Sketches, SET of all 3 volumes = $105
- Q Is for Quark: A Science Alphabet Book, David M. Schwartz. (Tricycle Pr; ISBN: 1582460213; 2001). 64 pp. UG Witty yet informative coverage of science topics from A to Z by the author of the popular math books of like style. Cartoon illustrations. Appeals to curious mind and the science-phobic.

- Beast Feast: Poems and Paintings, Douglas Florian. (Voyager Books; ISBN: 0152017372; 1998) 48pp. LG/UG
  Book of poems and paintings about animals, insects, and such. Humorous and serious poetry.
- The Kingfisher Young World Encyclopedia. (Kingfisher, 1995). ISBN 1856945193. 488 pp. LG
  This book can be a bit difficult to locate. It is suited for very young and early LG children. Its 488 pages address many aspects of science in simple language with supportive illustrations, diagrams, related poetry and literature, experiments, crafts, an index, sidebars, insets, photography in an uncluttered and visually appealing format.
- Mysteries & Marvels of Nature (Usborne), Barbara Cork, I. Wallace, and David Quinn. (EDC Publications; ISBN: 0746004214; 1984). 192pp. UG
  Compilation of six smaller books: Bird Life, Insect Life, Reptile Life, Ocean Life, and Plant Life. Illustrated and interesting facts shared. All CKEB units addressed but human body and mammals.
- The Usborne Complete First Book of Nature, (EDC Publishing, ISBN: 0746005636, 1990). 170pp. LG
  Seven individual titles compiled into one text. Topics include: birds, trees, flowers, butterflies and moths, wild animals, fishes, and creepy crawlies. Glossary. Titles may be purchased individually as well.
- DK Animal Encyclopedia, Barbara Taylor. (DK Publishing; ISBN: 0789464993; 2000). 376pp. LG/UG
  This book addresses topics from most CKEB units with the exception of the human body and plants. Nearly 2000 animal species addressed in ALPHABETICAL order. Index.
- DK Nature Encylcopedia, DK. (DK Publishing; ISBN: 0789434113; 1998). 304pp. LG+/UG
  Covers topics from most CKEB units except for the human body. Extensive photography including action sequences such as how a jellyfish propels itself. Organized by THEME. Glossary. Index.
- The Natural World (The Usborne Illustrated Encyclopedia), Lisa Watts. (EDC Publications; ISBN: 0746016891; 1995). 96pp. LG+/UG
  Open the pages of this book and you will notice it has a layout that has a simpler look and feel than the typical Usborne text. This one encompasses most of the CKEB units minus the human body. TOPICAL listings as opposed to alphabetical order. Glossary. Index.
- Handbook of Nature Study, Anna Botsford Comstock. (Cornell Univ. Pr; ISBN: 0801493846; Reissue 1986). 887pp. LG/UG/Adult
  This book is unique. It is quite comprehensive with the exception of its lack of coverage for oceans and marine life. Written in chapters with photographs, illustrations, and questions. Can be used with all ages.
- TAKE ALONG GUIDE SERIES. These are beautiful guides although not fully comprehensive in nature. The two books listed below are each a compilation of the eleven smaller guides which may also be purchased individually. Each guide contains illustrations, information about the subject being taught, and some scrapbook pages drawings or specimens. Simple, recognizable artwork makes these perfect for LG.
- Fun With Nature: Take-Along Guide (Take-Along Guide), Mel Boring, Diane L. Burns, Leslie A. Dendy, and Linda Garrow. (NorthWord Press; ISBN: 1559717025; 1999) 288pp. UG This book is a compilation of six titles: Caterpillars, Bugs and Butterflies; Frogs, Toads and Turtles; Rabbits, Squirrels and Chipmunks; Snakes, Salamanders and Lizards; Tracks, Scats and Signs; and Trees, and Leaves and Bark. (available from www.brightideaspress.com)
- More Fun with Nature: Take-Along Guide, Laura Evert, Mel Boring, Diane L. Burns, and Christiane Kump Tibbitts. (NorthWord Press; ISBN: 1559717955; 2002). 224pp. UG
  This compilation includes the following five (5) smaller guides: Wildflowers, Blooms, and Blossoms; Berries, Nuts, and Seeds; Birds, Nests, and Eggs; Seashells, Crabs and Sea Stars; and Rocks, Fossils, and Arrowheads.
- A Great Day for Pup: All About Wild Babies (Cat in the Hat's Learning Library), Bonnie Worth. (Random House (Merchandising); ISBN: 037581096X; 2002) 48pp. LG
  Beginning reader. Topic: animal babies from around the globe plus geography.

- Exploding Ants: Amazing Facts About How Animals Adapt, Joanne Settel, PhD. (Atheneum; ISBN: 0689817398; 1999). 40pp. LG/UG
  Amazing oddities about the manner in which animals, birds, insects, and parasites eat, lay their eggs, trick, defend, and protect themselves and their young. (animals, insects, birds, predators)
- It's Disgusting and We Ate It! True Food Facts from Around the World - And Throughout History! James Solheim. (Aladdin Paperbacks; ISBN: 0689843933; 2001). 37pp. LG
  Seaweed in your ice cream, earthworm soup, cooked spiders and grubs, bird nest soup, pigeon, chocolate-covered ants... All are foods eaten by humans in the past or present. Nutritional information, poems, illustrations, and history are included. Sure to spark lively discussions with all ages! (plants, animals, insects, habitats plus geography)
- Macmillan Animal Encyclopedia for Children, Roger Few. (Macmillan Publishing Co.; ISBN: 0027624250; 1991) Index and glossary. 120pp. LG/UG
- Natural History From A to Z – A Terrestrial Sampler, Tim Arnold. (Margaret K. McElderry Books; ISBN: 0689504675; 1991). A,B, C book with a mix of animals, plants, and insects. 58pp. UG
- Nature Treasures – Field Guide for Kids, Elizabeth Biesiot. (Denver Museum of Natural History and Robert Rinhehart Publishing; ISBN: 1570980829; 1996). Seasonal clues, descriptions, and lovely watercolor illustrations. LG
- ✝ Hands-On Nature: Bible Activities That Explore God's World, series of books for 2-3 yr olds, 3-4 yr olds, K-1 graders, 2-3 graders, 3-4 graders and 5-6 graders, Jeanne Grieser, Donna McKinney, Stephanie Richards, or Nancy Williamson. (ISBN: 1885358679 (3-4 grade edition), 1999). 96pp.. LG/UG Reproducible.
- World Book 2002 Premiere Edition CD-ROM set (4 disks – 2 are bonus Discovery School disks), version 6. (CounterTop Software, 2001). LG/UG/Adult
  You can print sections, diagrams, timelines, etc. Related topics have internal links. Vast numbers of illustrations, photographs, charts, diagrams, lists, definitions, animations, movie clips, related Internet links, and the like co-exist on these disks. They address all the topics of CKEB and then some. Also includes a research paper helper and timeline maker.
- ONE SMALL SQUARE SERIES
  You select and mark off a square in the type of area designated by the book, such as the woods, and observe every inch of that space. Suggestions are made in the book with further information as well. Truly wonderful and unique series. Includes information on plants, animals, insects, spiders, fish, and anything else that might be found in the square under observation. Written specifically for LG but UG may also like to do this.
- One Small Square: Woods, Donald M. Silver. (McGraw-Hill Trade; ISBN: 0070579334; 1997). 48pp. LG (UG may enjoy series too)
- Backyard, Donald M. Silver. (McGraw-Hill Trade; ISBN: 007057930X; Reprint 1997).
- Science Mini-Books and Manipulatives: 15 Reproducible Flap Books, Fold Outs, Pull Throughs, and Mini Books That Make Science Come Alive for Young Learners, Donald M. Silver. (Scholastic Professional Books; ISBN: 0590685678; 2000). 64pp. Parent Resource
- The Amazing Animal Activity Book – Dozens of Hands-On Projects That Teach Acorss the Curriculum (Scholastic Books; ISBN: 0590964046; 1997). 96pp. Parent resource for use w/ LG
- Berenstain Bears' Big Book of Science and Nature, Stan and Jan Berenstain. (Random House Trade; ISBN: 0679886524; 1997). 64pp. LG (animals, insects, plants, weather, and some experiments)

NATURE JOURNAL RESOURCES

- Keeping a Nature Journal: Discover a Whole New Way of Seeing the World Around You, Clare Walker Leslie. (Storey Books; ISBN: 1580173063; 2000). 192pp. Parent-Teacher
- Wild Days: Creating Discovery Journals, Karen Skidmore Rackliffe. (Karen Skidmore Rackliffe; ISBN: 1576360733; 1999). 134pp. Parent-Teacher

ADULT-LEVEL BOOKS

David Attenborough has produced numerous books on nature. While his books are not from a Christian viewpoint, they do contain incredible photography and there is a lot of it in each book along with many interesting facts about the book's topic. Be careful if reading sections aloud to children as there is information about evolution, reproduction, and other such topics which you may wish to avoid. Note that some books were produced in conjunction with a video series such as the ten videos done by the Discovery Channel that correlate to his book entitled <u>The Life of Mammals</u>. These may be available in your public library or shown again on the Discovery Channel. Other topics by this author include plants, birds, rain forests, whales, dolphins, and numerous others about nature in various habitats around the globe.

VIDEOS

As with all the resources on this list, only those with a cross ✞ beside them are specifically Christian in nature. Unfortunately, such videos are not available for all topics addressed in CKEB. When videos from a Christian perspective could not be located for a topic, other videos were listed. Thus, please use the following videos AT YOUR OWN DISCRETION. You may especially wish to preview those pertaining to the human body, evolution, ecology, or any other topics of concern to you before showing them to your children.

It would have been humanly impossible for the single compiler of this list to view and critique all the resources on this list. Doing so would have resulted in a miniscule list which wouldn't have served you very well. The goal of this list is to offer a smorgasbord of resources related to as many of the major topics in CKEB as possible. They are ones that should generally be available in public libraries, via inter-library loan, or that may be purchased.

As homeschoolers, it is assumed that you understand you will need to pick and choose materials to suit your personal beliefs, preferences, the spiritual, mental, and emotional maturity of your children, etc. This list can serve as a launching pad in that endeavor. It is hoped that it will broaden your awareness of materials you may wish to consider utilizing to educate your children in science. It is quite possible you may find one video of a series to be perfectly acceptable while another one may need a section to be fast-forwarded while yet another in that series has only a segment on a difficult topic that you find acceptable for any viewing.

- <u>The Homeschool Source</u> – homeschool lending library. This is relatively new and unique company created and run by a homeschool family. They offer homeschoolers an annual membership which allows them to borrow from their ever-expanding library of videos, books, and even homeschool curriculum for the cost of media mail shipping. Items may also be purchased after viewing. Many of their stocked items are explicitly Christian and not readily available in public libraries or video stores. For further information, visit their web site @ www.thehomeschoolsource.com or call toll-free 1-877-743-2401.

✞ VIDEOS FROM ANSWERS IN GENESIS
1-800-778-3390. www.answersingenesis.org;
- ✞ <u>Incredible Creatures That Defy Evolution</u>, Volume 1; Dr Jobe Martin. 47 minutes. Evidence from design in the animal kingdom that could only be attributed to a master Creator. UG
- ✞ <u>Incredible Creatures That Defy Evolution</u>, Volume 2; Dr. Jobe Martin; 47 minutes. Birds, insects, and sea creatures whose design could only be attributed to a master Creator.   UG
- ✞ Creation Adventure Team videos (available from Answers in Genesis; www.answersingenesis.com). Contain live-action , animitronics, cutting-edge special affects, 2D and 3D animation, songs, humor, and original music with Buddy and his friends.   LG & UG
- ✞ <u>Six Short Days</u>, One Big Adventure; 45 minutes. Buddy and his friends uncover the wonders of creation's six days with help from the "Bubble Gum Cam".

- ✝ <u>A Jurassic Ark Mystery</u>; 45minutes. Buddy and his friends travel the world while learning about dinosaurs – when they lived and died, about Noah's Ark and the Flood, if the dinosaurs were on the Ark, and more. LG & UG
- ✝ <u>The X-Nilo Show</u> – Dinosaurs and the Bible; 30 minutes. Humorous, fact-filled, and quick-paced science show for children. LG/UG

✝ MOODY SCIENCE VIDEOS. Award -winning videos. Many feature astonishing time-lapse photography or even microphotography. All are engaging, content-rich, and have Creator-magnifying narration. The very end of each video relates a spiritual concept to the science topic viewed throughout the video. The most incredible, awe-inspiring videos. Check for them in your church library, home school library, add them to your home video collection, or borrow from the lending library listed above in this section.. LG, UG & ADULT

✝ MOODY - SCIENCE CLASSICS SERIES.   Available from: BJU Press @ www.bjup.com , ShowForth Videos @ www.showforth.bjup.com or 1.800.845.5731, and Moody Video @ www.moodyvideo.org. Generally, 30 minutes and $9.95 each.
- ✝ <u>City of the Bees</u> – all about those busy bees and their special jobs but also relates how the human design by God is even more special.
- ✝ <u>Dust or Destiny</u> – interesting "oddities" of creation that indicate a Creator; fish, birds, bats, etc.
- ✝ <u>Experience with an Eel</u> – electric eel.
- ✝ <u>Facts of Faith</u> – what faith is and how to get it demonstrated via scientific experiments such as one million volts of electricity going through a man's body with no harm to him.
- ✝ <u>God of Creation</u> – the beauty and power of the universe from a flower to space.
- ✝ <u>God of the Atom</u> - man's need for salvation is demonstrated from the complex energy of a mere atom.
- ✝ <u>Hidden Treasures</u> - a view of nature through a microscope such as a drop of sea water, a snowflake and a microscopic flower.
- ✝ <u>Journey of Life</u> – incredible means that seeds take to reach their destination; compares the Word of God to living seed taking root in one's heart.
- ✝ <u>Mystery of the Three Clocks</u> – be reminded of God's ultimate control by learning of the clocks built-in to some of God's creations.
- ✝ <u>Of Books and Sloths</u> – the sloth is used to remind of God's Word and its accuracy.
- ✝ <u>Prior Claim</u> – shows some of man's inventions that were actually taken from ideas derived from God's creation such as the Venus flytrap, archer fish, and trap-door spider.
- ✝ <u>Professor and the Prophets</u> – insight will be gleaned into the authorship of Scripture via application of math probability to prophecies of the Bible.
- ✝ <u>Red River of Life</u> – reminds us how it was necessary for Christ's blood to be shed for our spiritual life; features the circulatory system via microphotography and stresses the importance of blood to the body.
- ✝ <u>Signposts Aloft</u> – demonstrates how the senses of an astronaut or pilot can be fooled in flight while explaining how they need their instruments and we need God's guidance.
- ✝ <u>Time and Eternity</u> – God is infinite. Time and space point us to Him. This videos shows how.
- ✝ <u>Voice of the Deep</u> – the depths of the ocean help to remind one they need a renewed mind.
- ✝ <u>Where the Waters Run</u> – spiritual life and death's dependence upon God's living water is stressed by learning the importance of physical water for life on Earth.
- ✝ <u>Ultimate Adventure</u> – "Dick Ewing was the first to cross the vast and scorching Sahara on motorcycle. Share his spine-tingly life and death struggle and the dramatic "encounter" with God that changed his life forever." Direct quote from www.moodyvideo.org. Could be used when studying deserts in the biome section of CKEB.
- ✝ <u>Distinctively Human</u> – this video is no longer available for purchase from Moody, but you may be able to locate a used one or find it in your church library.

✝ MOODY – <u>SCIENCE ADVENTURES SERIES</u> - Each features three (3) 10-minute segments; 30 minutes total. $14.95 each. Available from ShowForth Videos @ www.showforth.bjup.com ; 1-800-845-5731.

- ✝ The Clown-Faced Carpenter
  Part 1 – The Clown-Faced Carpenter - woodpeckers and the life cycle.
  Part 2 – The Journey to the Stars – the sun to outer reaches of space.
  Part 3 – Water, Water Everywhere – shows how crucial water is to life.
- ✝ The Wonder of You
  Part 1 – The Wonders of You – human body with NO graphic scenes!
  Part 2 – A Mystery Story – life cycle of a caterpillar.
  Part 3 – A Matter of Taste – eating habits of five animals and how God supplies their special dietary needs.
- ✝ The Power in Plants
  Part 1 – The Power in Plants – shows the immense power in a plant such as a sprout that cracks a home's foundation or a flower that cracks a sidewalk.
  Part 2 – Busy as a Bee – a day in the life of bees.
  Part 3 – It's a Small World – complexity of life in a single droplet of water.
- ✝ Treasure Hunt
  Part 1 – Treasure Hunt – crystals in caves and salt-shakers.
  Part 2 – Animals Move - illustrates the unique means animals have for moving about.
  Part 3 – Eight-Legged Engineer – the incredibly skillful spider.

✝ MOODY - Windows of the Soul – 50th Anniversary Special Release (limited time) about the five senses; available from Moody Video www.moodyvideo.org/sciclass.htm#windows or 1-800-842-1223.

✝ MOODY – <u>THE WONDERS OF GOD'S CREATION SERIES</u>; comes as a set of three (3) from Timberdoodle Co. www.timberdoodle.com or 1-360-426-0672. 60 minutes each. $22.00 for set of three ($39.95 value).

- ✝ Vol. 1 – Planet Earth – precision of life-sustaining qualities on Earth that exist nowhere else in the universe.
- ✝ Vol. 2 – Animal Kingdom – salmon migration, Monarch butterfly's 2000-mile yearly trip, and how honeybees communicate.
- ✝ Vol. 3 – Human Life - NO graphic scenes!

✝ <u>MOODY - THE NEWTON'S WORKSHOP SERIES</u> The description for this series is a direct quote from the Moody web site where they may be purchased. www.moodyvideo.org "Come on in to Grandpa Newton's workshop full of wonderful clutter—flashlights, toy soldiers, ultraviolet paint, homemade volcanos and solar systems, bugs of every shape and color, and interesting gadgets and watchamajiggers both large and small—all for weighing, watching, touching, trying, describing, but mostly for discovering. By incorporating family communication, problem solving and critical thinking into the learning process, Grandpa Newton introduces values and morals, the basic tools necessary to solve everyday problems. Your entire family will enjoy this wonderfully entertaining and educational series. Each video comes with a study guide packed with starter questions, facts, biblical references, devotional thoughts, and activity suggestions." Approx. 28 minutes each. 8 videos — $14.95 each

- ✝ Episode 1 – World Building – days of creation.
- ✝ Episode 2 – The Germinators – immune system.
- ✝ Episode 3 – The Name Game – animal classification.
- ✝ Episode 4 – As the World Spins – solar system.
- ✝ Episode 5 – The Bug Safari – entomology.
- ✝ Episode 6 – The Cell-a-bration – cytology.
- ✝ Episode 7 – The DNA Decoders – genetics.
- ✝ Episode 8 – The Pollution Solution – ecology.

✝ MOODY – THE CREATION DISCOVERY SERIES Here is a direct quote about this series from the Moody web site www.moodyvideo.org where these may be purchased: "Join zany Professor Walter Schnaegel and his young friends as they discover the fascinating world of plant life, geology and ecology... all from a biblical perspective. Three episodes jam-packed with fun, songs, science games, experiments and adventure." Approx. 30 minutes each. 3 videos — $14.95 each

- ✝ God's Powerful Plants – Energy That Grows On You
- ✝ God's Rockin' World – Foundations You Can Build Upon
- ✝ God's Earth Team – Protecting the Earth He's Given You

✝ EDGEMONT VIDEO
Available from ShowForth Videos @ www.bjup.com; 1.800.845.5731. These 35-minute videos present beautiful music with wondrous sites of God's creation LG, UG and ADULT

- ✝ Nature's Splendor II – orchestra.
- ✝ Nature's Melodies – harpist with orchestra.
- ✝ Reflections of Praise – violinist with orchestra.

- ✝ BIOLOGY DISSECTION LABS (ShowForth) - available from ShowForth Videos @ www.bjup.com; 1.800.845.5731. An earthworm, crayfish, perch, and a frog are dissected step-by-step with explanations and close-up shots. 72 minutes. $49.95 UG+/ADULT

- ✝ SCIENCE AND THE CHRISTIAN (BJU Press) – available from ShowForth Videos @ www.bjup.com; 1.800.845.5731. Help in understanding the limits, methods, and benefits of science which will enable one to better determine truth in the world of science. 48 minutes $19.95 UG+/ADULT

✝ ANSWERS IN GENESIS VIDEOS
- ✝ The Creation Adventure Pack (VHS). (Gospel Communications, Answers Media, and Henderson Design and Productions) Two 45 minute videos: 1) The Creation Adventure Team: A Jurassic Ark Mystery, and 2) The Creation Adventure Team: Six Short Days, One Big Adventure! $25 AIG LG/UG
- ✝ D is for Dinosaur (VHS, DVD, & book available), Ken and Mally Ham. (Answers in Genesis; 1992) 15 minutes $10 AIG LG/UG
  Conveys the history of dinosaurs from a Biblical perspective. Preview clip @ AIG web site.
- ✝ A is for Adam (VHS, DVD, ASL, & book available), Ken and Mally Ham. (Answers in Genesis) 21 minutes. $10 AIG LG/UG
  Teaches the real history of the world from creation to Christ and beyond.
- ✝ The X-Nilo Show, Answers in Genesis. (X-Nilo Productions; 1998). 28 minutes. $10 LG/UG
- Nature of the Holy Land (3 VHS set). (Vision Video; ISBN: 156364293X; 1999). Explore the ecosystems of the Mediterranean coast, the Jordan River, and the Dead Sea Valley to learn of Biblical times natural history up to the present. CBD 2.5 hrs. LG/UG

SCHLESSINGER MEDIA VIDEOS
Check your local library for these videos or purchase them at 1-800-843-3620 or www.LibraryVideo.com. The web site contains numerous preview clips.

While these videos are filled with engaging content, keep in mind they are secular in nature. Throughout each video is built-in review. Each one also includes a useful educator's guide with key terms, discussion questions, activities, and a list of related books and web sites. These guides may be printed for free directly from the web site www.LibraryVideo.com. Some series include such features as microphotography, computer graphics, science fair experiments to replicate, and much more.

<u>Animal Life for Children</u> (13 videos) K-4th; 23 minutes each.
- All About Amphibians
- All About Animal Adaptations
- All About Animal Behavior & Communication
- All About Animal Life Cycles
- All About Animal Needs
- All About Birds
- All About Bugs
- All About Dinosaurs
- All About Endangered & Extinct Animals
- All About Fish
- All About Food Chains
- All About Mammals
- All About Reptiles

<u>Animal Life in Action</u> (16 videos) 5th – 8th; 23 minutes each.
- Amphibians
- Animal Adaptations
- Animal Behavior & Communication
- Animal Classification
- Animal Interdependency
- Animal Life Cycles
- Animal Needs
- Birds
- Endangered & Extinct Animals
- Evolution
- Fish
- Food Chains
- Insects and Other Arthropods
- Mammals
- Marine & Other Invertebrates
- Reptiles

<u>Ecosystems for Children</u> (3 videos); K – 4th; 23 minutes each.
- All About Deserts & Grasslands
- All About Forest Ecosystems
- All About Water Ecosystems

<u>Biomes of the World in Action</u> (8 videos); 5th – 8th; 23 minutes each.
- Coniferous Forests
- Deciduous Forests
- Deserts
- Freshwater Ecosystems
- Grasslands
- Marine Ecosystems
- Rainforest Biomes
- Tundra

<u>Bill Nye the Science Guy</u> (3 of the 5 videos); 1st – 6th; 50 minutes each. (Not produced by Schlessinger Media but sold by them.)
- Dinosaurs: Those Big Boneheads!
- The Human Body: The Inside Scoop!
- Reptiles & Insects: Leapin' Lizards!

<u>Bug City</u> (3 videos); 3rd _ 6th; 23 minutes each.
- Amazing Insect Warriors
- Incredible Insects
- Really Gross Bug Stuff

<u>Bug City</u> (10 videos); 5th – 8th; 23 minutes each.
- Ants
- Aquatic Insects
- Bees
- Beetles
- Butterflies & Moths
- Crickets, Grasshoppers, & Friends
- Flies & Mosquitoes
- House & Backyard Insects
- Ladybugs & Fireflies
- Spiders & Scorpions

<u>Human Body for Children</u> (8 videos); K - 4th; 23 minutes.
- All About Bones & Muscles
- All About Blood & the Heart
- All About Health & Hygiene
- All About Nutrition & Exercise
- All About Cell & Body Systems
- All About the Brain
- All About the Human Life Cycle
- All About the Senses

<u>Human Body in Action</u> (10 videos); 5th – 8th; 23 minutes.
- The Brain & The Nervous System
- Cells
- Circulatory & Respiratory Systems
- Digestive & Excretory Systems
- Genes & Heredity
- Health & Nutrition
- Immune System
- Interrelationship of the Body Systems
- Reproductive & Endocrine Systems
- Skeletal & Muscular Systems

<u>National Geographic Amazing Planet Series</u> (2 of 6 videos); K - 6th; 30 minutes each. (Not produced by Schlessinger Media but sold by them.)
- Creatures of the Deep
- Shark-a-Thon

National Geographic Really Wild Animals Series (12 videos); PreK – 4th; 45 minutes each. (Not produced by Schlessinger Media but sold by them.)
- Amazing North America
- Awesome Animal Builders
- Deep Sea Dive
- Dinosaurs and Others
- Creature Features
- Farmyard Friends
- Hot Dogs & Cool Cats
- Monkey Business and Other Family Fun
- Polar Prowl
- Secret Weapons and Great Escapes
- Swinging Safari
- Totally Tropical Rain Forest
- Wonders Down Under

National Geographic Tales from the Wild Series (4 videos); PreK – 3rd; 30 minutes each. (Not produced by Schlessinger Media but sold by them.)
- Cain the Coyote
- Cara the Sea Turtle
- Gus the Alligator
- Tasha the Polar Bear

The Nature Connection Series (6 videos); 4th – 12th; 60 minutes each. Hosted by David Suzuki. Ecology focus. Previously aired on Discovery Channel. (Not produced by Schlessinger Media but sold by them.)
- Buying a Rainforest/Urban Ecology: Volume 1 – children buy tracts of tropical rainforest land and they discover urban nature.
- Fishing the Ocean/Where Our Food Comes From: Volume 2 – life of a fisherman and on a farm.
- Merv's Forest/Water Works: Volume 3 – selective logging and water's role in our biosphere.
- The Badlands/A Winter Walk: Volume 4 - Dinosaur National Provincial Park plus making of animal homes.
- Carmanah/Grasslands: Volume 5 – a rainforest in a valley plus Albertan foothill plants and animals.
- Tide Pools/Cattail Country: Volume 6 – island tide pools and marshland.

Marty Stouffer's Wild America: Wild Wings; K – 5th; 60 minutes. A look at wild American birds from a naturalist's viewpoint. (Not produced by Schlessinger Media but sold by them.)

My Underwater Journey: Reef City, Kona; K – 5th ; 28 minutes. Live action video about the reef, islands, and fish that live in this region of the Hawaiian Islands. (Not produced by Schlessinger Media but sold by them.)

Plant Life for Children (5 videos); K – 4th; 23 minutes.
- All About Caring for Plants
- All About Plant Adaptation
- All About Plant & Animal Interdependency
- All About Plant Pollination: Fruit, Flowers & Food
- All About Plant Structure & Growth

Plant Life in Action (6 videos); 5th – 8th'; 23 minutes.

- Photosynthesis
- Plant & Animal Interdependency
- Plant Biodiversity
- Plant Reproduction
- Plant Structure & Growth
- Plants & People: A Beneficial Relationship

Rainforest for Children (2 of 3 videos); 3rd – 6th; 25 minutes.
- Animals of the Rainforest
- (People of the Rainforest)
- Plants of the Rainforest

Simple Organisms in Action (1 of 4 videos); 5th – 8th grade; 25 minutes.
- Bacteria
- Fungi
- Protists
- Viruses

Tell Me Why Video Encyclopedia Series (10 of 26 videos); 3rd – 6th; 30 minutes. (Not produced by Schlessinger Media but sold by them.)
- Vol. 03 - Flowers, Plants and Trees
- Vol. 05 - Insects
- Vol. 07 - Life Forms, Animals and Animal Oddities
- Vol. 08 - Birds and Rodents
- Vol. 09 - Mammals
- Vol. 10 - Animals and Arachnids
- Vol. 11 - Fish, Shellfish and Other Underwater Life
- Vol. 12 - Pre-historic Animals, Reptiles and Amphibians
- Vol. 13 - A Healthy Body
- Vol. 14 - Anatomy and Genetics

A Video Visit With Jim Arnosky (3 videos); 2nd – 6th); 24 minutes. These award-winning videos contain footage shot while author and illustrator Mr. Arnosky was doing research for his wild animal books. (Not produced by Schlessinger Media but sold by them.)
- All About Alligators
- All About Deer
- Watching Water Birds

- What is a Savannah? Learning Geographical Terms; 3rd – 6th; 23 minutes. Delves into the physical features of the Earth including water sources, land forms, and climates. Addresses mountains, valleys, deserts, oceans, forests, and others. Teacher's guide plus worksheets. (Not produced by Schlessinger Media but sold by them.) BIOMES-RELATED.

FIELD TRIP/VACATION IDEAS
- ✟ Answers in Genesis (AIG) museum (once completed).
- Animal shelter
- Animal pest catcher – caution – could be too gruesome for some children
- Arboretum
- Art museum – look for works that integrate topics studied (i.e. mammals) and note the oldest such work of art; substitute library art books or on-line works if a museum is not readily available

- Aquarium
- Aquariums – freshwater and salt water in local pet shops, doctor's offices, restaurants, office buildings, homes, etc.
- Beehives – find a local honey producer and ask for a tour around his hives
- Bird watching
- Birders' club
- Bird sanctuary
- Boating/cruise – look for water life of all types
- Boreal forest (taiga) - walk/travel/virtual field trip (Internet)
- Botanical garden
- Butterfly garden
- Camping – enjoy God's creation
- Chaparral - walk/travel/virtual field trip (Internet)
- County/regional/university-based extension office – insects, plants, animals, etc.
- ✞ Creation Vacations; annually through AIG http://www.answersingenesis.org/docs2002/0115vacations.asp
- Desert - walk/travel/virtual field trip (Internet)
- Estuary - walk/travel/virtual field trip (Internet)
- Equestrian area
- Farm or petting zoo
- Fish hatchery
- Fishing boat/dock – watch the catch of the day get unloaded; buy some for dinner.
- Fishing – freshwater, saltwater or deep sea
- Fossil hunting in Rockford, IA, or other such locations
- Garden club meeting
- Grassland - walk/travel/virtual field trip (Internet)
- Grocery store or meat market – ask attendant at fish counter which fish are freshwater and which are saltwater fish; check for lobster, shrimp, crab, etc; perhaps buy some for dinner tonight.
- Horticulture club/garden
- ✞ ICR Museum of Creation & Earth History, 10946 Woodside Ave. North, Santee, CA 92071. Young earth creation museum. 619-596-6011
- Medical doctor's office
- Medical laboratory – hospital or doctor's office
- National Audubon Society club meeting or outing
- Natural science museums
- Nature preserve
- Nature walks – backyard, neighborhood, park, etc.
- Nearby college/university – visit various departments such as biology, botany, veterinary science, nursing/pre-med./etc.
- Orchards – visit and pick your own fruit from the trees; watch for bees and other insects crucial for pollination; ask for a tour
- Plant nursery
- Pet shop
- Rain forest - walk/travel/virtual field trip (Internet)
- Recycling center
- Reef – glass bottom boat or snorkeling
- Savannah - walk/travel/virtual field trip (Internet)
- Seafood restaurant
- Sea World
- Shelling at the beach

- Swimming with dolphins
- Taxidermist office
- Temperate coniferous forest - walk/travel/virtual field trip (Internet)
- Temperate deciduous forest - walk/travel/virtual field trip (Internet)
- Tree farm
- Tundra - walk/travel/virtual field trip (Internet)
- Veterinary office
- Woodworking shop – uses and differences of various types of wood
- Zoo

SCIENCE MAGAZINES

Ideas: subscribe, suggest as a gift idea, read at library, or order relevant back issues.

- ✝ Clubhouse Jr. by Focus on the Family sometimes will have a nature feature. ISSN: 0895-1136. Suggested donation of $15/year. Featured Resources section. No advertising. LG 1-800-232-6459
- ✝ Discovery – Scripture and Science for Kids. Apologetics Press, Inc. 1-800-234-8558 (orders only); www.DiscoveryMagazine.com . On-line sample issue. $12.00/year of monthly issues on high gloss full-color paper. 10% subscription discount for homeschoolers. 1-800-852-4482
- ✝.God's World News USPS #700-930; www.gwnews.com; (828)253-8063; $26.95/yr for 29 weekly issues/yr. September – May. Discount for multiple orders. Different magazine for each age group. Focus is on current events. They often involve science. No advertising. UG and LG 828-253-8063
- ✝ Nature Friend; ISSN: 0888-4862; $22/yr for 12 issues. The publisher states, "Nature Friend…upholds the principles of the Inspired Word of God, high Christian Family Standards, Divine Creation (no evolution), and practical Christian Stewardship of God's Creation." Full color with a 2 page nature poster in the center of each issue, plus puzzles, projects, reader mail, nature science articles, contests, arts and crafts. No advertising. 24 pp. LG & UG 1-800-852-4482

- ✝Creation Illustrated ISSN: 1086-1645; www.creationillustrated.com; E-mail: creation@foothill.net. $19.95/year w/ discounts for longer terms. Published quarterly. 64 full-color glossy pages. Includes a kids' story and an instructional guide with each issue. Non-denominational. (Adult w/ kid section).
- ✝ Creation (Answers in Genesis) 1-800-778-3390; $22/yr for quarterly full-color 56 page publications. Each issue contains a section for kids. (Adult w/ kid section) 1-800-778-3390

- Ask ISSN: 1535-4105; www.askmag.net; $23.95/ year of 6 issues. Very engaging with great illustrations, photos, maps, etc. Each issue has a theme. No advertising. LG (UG might too) 1-800-821-0115
- CLICK! ISSN: 1094-4273; www.clickmag.com; 1-800-821-0115; $32.97/year of 9 issues. Truly wonderful science magazine with a theme each month. No advertising. LG 1-800-821-0115
- Highlights for Children – Fun With a Purpose ISSN: 0018-165X; $29.64/yr; less with longer subscription. 12 issues/year. No advertising. LG+ & UG
- Kids Discover magazine; ISSN: 1054-2868; $26.95yr of 12 issues. Brilliant, glossy, full-color photography and illustrations with engaging text. No advertising. LG+/ UG 212-677-4457
- Kids Discover 2 magazine; a lower level of Kids Discover magazine. LG
- Muse www.musemag.com; ISSN: 1090-0381; $32.97/yr of 9 issues. A deeper look into science than CLICK and Ask. Themed. No advertising except one full-page ad on back cover. UG 1-800-821-0115
- National Geographic Kids magazine; ISSN: 03615-499 ; $17.95/yr for 10 issues; kids' related activities @ www.nationalgeogrphic.com/world changed monthly. No advertising. 36pp. LG & UG 1-800-647-5463
- Zoobooks www.zoobooks.com; $16/yr of 10 issues. Beautiful photography. Can be heavy on evolution in the text at times. No advertising. LG 1-800-992-5034

BRIGHT IDEAS PRESS
ORDER FORM

www.BrightIdeasPress.com

Returns Policy

Satisfaction guaranteed. If an item does not meet your needs, a refund minus postage will be given when the item is returned in re-saleable condition within 30 days.

www.brightideaspress.com

info@brightideaspress.com

Mail your check or money order to:

Bright Ideas Press
P.O. Box 333
Cheswold, DE 19936

Toll Free: 877.492.8081

VISA & MasterCard orders are accepted. See below for information.

SHIPPING TABLE

Prices Good Through December 31, 2004

Up to $50……...……….$5.00
$50 - $150………………10%
over $150……………..…free
Out of Country………....…call

Item #	Description	Qty.	Price	Amount
GC-100	The Ultimate Geography & Timeline Guide		34.95	
BIP-1	Hands-On Geography		14.95	
BIP-2	The Scientist's Apprentice		26.95	
BIP-3	Student History Notebook of America		12.95	
BIP-4	Over Our Heads In Wonder		9.95	
BIP-5	The Mystery of History - Volume I – Creation to the Resurrection		44.95	
BIP-6	Christian Kids Explore Biology		29.95	
BIP-7	The Mystery of History - Volume II – Rome, Early Church & Middle Ages		44.95	

SHIP TO ADDRESS: Please PRINT clearly

Name: _____

Address: _____

_____

Phone: ( ) _____

Email: _____

Special!
FREE SHIPPING
on *orders* over
$150.00

Sub Total	
⇐ Shipping Cost: See Shipping Table	
Total Amount Due	$

Credit Card Information

_____

VISA/MasterCard Number   Expiration Date

_____

Signature

Also Available from Bright Ideas Press...

  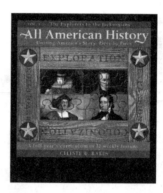 

The Mystery of History Volumes I & II by Linda Hobar

This award-winning series provides a historically accurate, Bible-centered approach to learning history. The completely chronological lessons shed new light on who walked the earth when, as well as on where important Bible figures fit into secular history. Grades 4 – 8, yet easily adaptable.

- Volume I: Creation to the Resurrection — ISBN: 1-892427-04-4
- Volume II: The Early Church & the Middle Ages — ISBN: 1-892427-06-0

All-American History by Celeste W. Rakes

Containing hundreds of images and dozens of maps, *All-American History* is a complete year's curriculum for students in grades 5 – 8 when combined with the *Student Activity Book* and *Teacher's Guide* (yet adaptable for younger and older students).

There are 32 weekly lessons, and each lesson contains three sections examining the atmosphere in which the event occurred, the event itself, and the impact this event had on the future of America.

- Student Reader — ISBN: 1-892427-12-5
- Student Activity Book — ISBN: 1-892427-11-7
- Teacher's Guide — ISBN: 1-892427-10-9

Christian Kids Explore Chemistry by Robert & Elizabeth Ridlon

One of Cathy Duffy's 100 Top Picks! Elementary chemistry that is both classical and hands-on. Conversational style and organized layout makes teaching a pleasure.

ISBN: 1-892427-18-4

Christian Kids Explore Earth & Space by Stephanie Redmond

Another exciting book in this award-winning series! Author Stephanie Redmond is back with more great lessons, activities, and ideas.

ISBN: 1-892427-19-2

For ordering information, call 877-492-8081 or visit www.BrightIdeasPress.com.

Bright Ideas Press books are available
online or through your favorite
Christian bookstore or homeschool supplier.

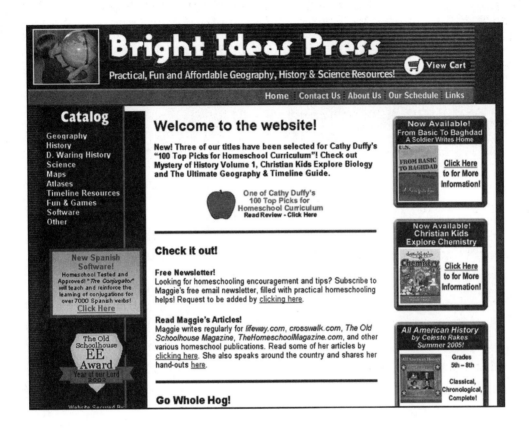

Hey Parents!

Here's a great place to:

Read curriculum reviews
See sample chapters of new books
Sign up for an exciting and useful e-zine
Join our Yahoo groups
Check our homeschool conference schedule
Explore Geography, History, and Science resources
Find great deals on our products!

Secure, online ordering available

www.BrightIdeasPress.com